# THE
# HEARTH
# *Witch's*
# EVERYDAY
# HERBAL

Anna Franklin is a third-degree witch and high priestess of the Hearth of Arianrhod, and she has been a practicing Pagan for more than forty years. She is the author of over thirty books and the creator of the *Sacred Circle Tarot*, *Fairy Ring Oracle*, and the *Pagan Ways Tarot* (Schiffer, 2015). Her books have been translated into nine languages.

Anna has contributed hundreds of articles to Pagan magazines and has appeared on radio and TV. She lives and works in a village in the English Midlands, where she grows her own herbs, fruit, and vegetables, and generally lives the Pagan life. Visit her online at www.Anna Franklin.co.uk.

# THE
# HEARTH
# *Witch's*
# EVERYDAY
# HERBAL

## A CONCISE GUIDE
## TO CORRESPONDENCES,
## MAGIC, AND LORE

## ANNA FRANKLIN

Llewellyn Publications
WOODBURY, MINNESOTA

FIRST EDITION
First Printing, 2024

Cover design by Shannon McKuhen
Interior floral background © Dover Publications
Interior floral woodcut © *1167 Decorative Cuts* (New York: Dover Publications, 2007)

Llewellyn is a registered trademark of Llewellyn Worldwide Ltd.

**Library of Congress Cataloging-in-Publication Data**
**(Pending)**
ISBN 978-0-7387-7535-7

Llewellyn Publications
A Division of Llewellyn Worldwide Ltd.
2143 Wooddale Drive
Woodbury MN 55125-2989

WWW.LLEWELLYN.COM

Printed in the United States of America

## Disclaimer

The information and medicinal suggestions in this book are not meant to replace the direction and guidance of a qualified health care professional. Please pay special care to the cautions included throughout this book's herbal profiles and take care to only use safely gathered and positively identified herbs.

# Contents

# CONTENTS

# CONTENTS

# CONTENTS

# Introduction

In this modern world, we have access to herbs from across the globe, whether we buy them from the occult shop or supermarket or grow non-native plants in our gardens.

There is a flourishing interest in how we might use herbs for healing, for self-care, and for magic. In this book, I provide an introduction to many of the herbs you may commonly come across with a brief look at their lore and how they might be used. Under each herb header, you will see its magical correspondences, magical uses, culinary uses (if there are any), healing uses, and how the herbs can be used for cosmetics and self-care, as well as any cautions you might need to take.

I hope this will be a useful resource for those on their journey into the incredible world of what Mother Nature offers us with herbs.

# The A-to-Z Herbal

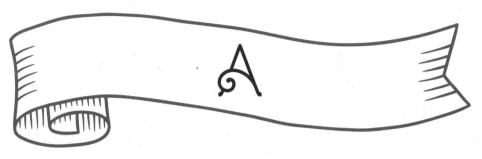

# Acacia

a.k.a Gum Arabic

*Acacia senegal*

. . . . . . . . . . . . . . . . . .

PLANETARY RULER: Sun

ELEMENT: Air/fire

ASSOCIATED DEITIES: Adonis, Apollo, Astarte, Christ,
Diana, Ishtar, Jehovah, Osiris, Ra, Vishnu

MAGICAL VIRTUES: Psychic abilities, clairvoyance,
protection, apotropaic, resurrection, immortality

## LORE

In Hebrew lore, acacia wood is venerated; the trees furnished the wood for both the Ark of
the Covenant and Noah's ark, and acacia trees were planted on graves. In Egyptian myth,
the goddess Isis searched for her lost husband, Osiris, travelling in an acacia-wood boat.
The Egyptians used acacia resin in medicine, to coat the bandages of mummies, and in
funeral rites. It is used as incense in India, Nepal, and China to honour the gods and keep
evil spirits away.

## MAGICAL USES

Carry a sprig of the wood or burn the incense to repel negativity and evil. Incenses made
with acacia wood, bark, or resin are useful for promoting meditational states, relaxation,

mental concentration, and psychic work. Use the incense during rites of death and resurrection. The gum is useful for making incense cones.

## CULINARY AND HOUSEHOLD USES

Gum arabic (also known as gum acacia) is a natural binding agent, consisting of sugars and glycoproteins, used to thicken and emulsify foods such as marshmallows, icing, various sweets, and chewing gum. In sugar-reduced foods, it compensates for the volume and creaminess that would otherwise be lost. It may be used to coat edible flowers.

## COSMETIC USES

Added to homemade creams, acacia resin has a lifting effect, smooths skin texture, and softens wrinkles. It can be utilised as a binder in homemade mascaras and lipsticks. Add the antibacterial powdered gum to homemade toothpaste to help prevent tooth decay.

## HOME REMEDIES

Gum arabic is a demulcent (soothes irritation); the resin beads can be sucked on for coughs, sore throat, catarrh/mucus, and mouth ulcers. The antibacterial action slows the growth of oral bacteria. Dissolve the resin beads in hot water and drink as a tea for diarrhoea and irritable bowel syndrome (IBS).

> *Caution: Gum arabic is generally considered safe, though some people are allergic to its dust. Do not take at the same time as prescription drugs. Avoid if you are on antibiotics. Do not confuse with other acacias (e.g., Acacia rigidula or Acacia farnesiana) or with the false acacias, the black locust, or any plants in the genus Robinia as some of these are toxic.*

# Agrimony

*Agrimonia eupatoria*

PLANETARY RULER: Jupiter

ELEMENT: Air

ASSOCIATED DEITIES: Aesculapius, Apollo

MAGICAL VIRTUES: Protection, warding, healing

## LORE

Agrimony was widely known as a healing herb in ancient times and remained a popular folk remedy until relatively recently. Its botanical name comes from the Greek *argemone*, signifying a plant that is healing to the eyes, while *eupetoria* is a reference to Mithradates Eupator, a man renowned for his herbal knowledge. In the Middle Ages, agrimony was believed to ward off witchcraft and hexes.

## MAGICAL USES

Use agrimony in protection magic, for warding off negative energies or spirits, and for blocking curses and magical attacks, returning them to their sender. Employ it as an incense, use some for saining/ritual fumigation, hang some in the home, or add it to herbal amulets. Pour an agrimony infusion into the bath and soak to cleanse your aura and rid it of unwanted intrusions. Agrimony also enhances the strength of healing spells.

## CULINARY AND HOUSEHOLD USES

A herbal tea can be made from leaves, flowers, and stems of agrimony, and these can also be added to China tea to create your own unique tea blend. The entire plant yields a yellow dye.

## COSMETIC USES

Dab a decoction of the root and leaves onto your skin to fight the bacteria that cause acne and blemishes. Agrimony can be added to lotions for skin irritations.

## Home Remedies

The aerial parts are used for medicine. The plant's astringent properties make agrimony tea useful for diarrhoea, upset stomachs, and cystitis. Use a standard infusion to cleanse wounds and as a mouthwash or gargle for sore throats. A weak infusion can be used as an eyewash to treat conjunctivitis.

> *Caution: Considered safe for most adults when used short-term, but do not take it for extended periods. It can increase skin photosensitivity or cause skin allergies in some people. Avoid when pregnant or breastfeeding, if you are diabetic (it lowers blood sugar), have liver or kidney problems, if you are constipated, or if you are taking drugs to lower blood pressure or blood-thinning agents (including aspirin).*

# Alder

*Alnus glutinosa* syn. *Betula alnus*

· · · · · · · · · · · · · ·

PLANETARY RULER: Venus

ELEMENT: Fire/water

ASSOCIATED DEITIES: Apollo, Arawn, Arthur, Bran, Branwen, Circe, Cronos, Guinevere, Gwern, Herakles, Marsyas, Orpheus, Phoroneus, Rinda

MAGICAL VIRTUES: Rebirth, resurrection, protection, divination, scrying, strength, endurance

## LORE

The common name *alder* is derived from the Old German *elawer*, meaning "reddish," because the cut wood seems to seep blood, which was a trait that made the tree unlucky to cut down. One of its old folk names is whistlewood as the branches seem to whistle in the wind and the wood was used to make flutes and whistles. The tree grows on the edge of water, but instead of decaying, alder timber becomes very hard when submerged, and it was used for bridge pilings and foundations. Alder burns incredibly hot and yields the best charcoal; it was much prized by blacksmiths for use in the forge.

## MAGICAL USES

A symbol of resurrection and the regeneration of the year in spring, alder bleeds the red blood of life and sacrifice. Use alder bark in Ostara and Beltane incense and as wood for the fire. Alder grows in the liminal space between land and water, bridging the entrance to the otherworld. Listen for the voices of the gods in its whistling branches; make an alder flute to call the spirits. Use alder bark and cones in incense when divining, and carry alder cones, catkins, and twigs when seeking the fairies. Alder endures in the water, where other wood would rot, and contains the power of the hottest fire; an alder talisman will help you when you need to draw on its strength.

## CULINARY AND HOUSEHOLD USES

Alder catkins can be eaten as a survival food. The alder yields several natural dyes: black or red (depending on the mordant) from the bark; yellow from the young shoots; fawn from the fresh wood; and green from the catkins. An alder cone (not a catkin) will keep water in an aquarium clear.

## COSMETIC USES

Alder is antimicrobial, and you can wash acne and boils with an alder bark decoction. An infusion of the leaves can be added to a footbath to soothe aching feet.

## HOME REMEDIES

The leaves, buds, and dried bark are used (the fresh bark may induce vomiting). Growing in damp conditions, alder treats conditions caused by the damp. A poultice made from the pulverised bark will help with arthritis and rheumatism. Make a macerated alder bud oil or salve for sore muscles. An alder bark decoction reduces fevers. A decoction of the bark is also astringent and may be used to staunch bleeding; to reduce inflammations of the throat, mouth, and gums; and as a mouthwash or gargle for tooth, gum, and throat problems.

> *Caution: Do not take medicinal amounts if you have liver or kidney conditions, and to be on the safe side, avoid if you are pregnant or breastfeeding. Use the bark dried, not fresh, as fresh bark may induce vomiting.*

# Alecost

a.k.a. Costmary

*Tanacetum balsamita* syn. *Chrysanthemum balsamita*

. . . . . . . . . . . . . . . . .

PLANETARY RULER: Moon/Jupiter

ELEMENT: Air

ASSOCIATED DEITIES: Aegir, mother goddesses

MAGICAL VIRTUES: Goddess rituals, women's rituals

## LORE

The name is derived from the Greek *kostos*, loosely meaning "a spicy herb," as alecost was used in the past to flavour and clear ale in place of hops. It was also called costmary and dedicated to the Virgin Mary or St. Mary Magdalene. Alecost was taken to North America by the Puritan settlers who would place a leaf in their Bibles as a bookmark—or maybe as something to chew on to allay hunger during the long sermons. Planting alecost next to other herbs is said to improve their flavour.

## MAGICAL USES

Alecost is very much a plant of women and the Goddess. Add an infusion to the final rinse when you are washing your robes to give them a pleasant fragrance and consecrate them to the Goddess. Add an infusion of the leaves and flowers to a ritual bath for the same purpose. To invite sacred dreams, stuff a pillow with dried alecost. Use it to make sacred beers and ales, and add it to incense or to ritual food. Use a leaf as a bookmark in your magical texts.

## CULINARY AND HOUSEHOLD USES

In the United States, alecost made a popular spring tonic, a minty herbal tea known as sweet Mary tea. Used sparingly, the young leaves can be added to salads, soups, stuffings, vegetables, rich meats, and cakes. The scented leaves can be used in potpourri, and an infusion of the leaves can be used to make a fragrant rinse for linen. Place some dried flowers and leaves in your wardrobe as a natural insect repellent and perfume.

. . . . .

## Cosmetic Uses

An infusion of the leaves can be used as a conditioning rinse for the hair and skin.

## Home Remedies

The fresh or dried leaves are used. Alecost tea may relieve the symptoms of colds, catarrh/mucus, and upset stomachs. The crushed leaves applied topically can soothe stings. An alecost hair rinse will treat headlice.

> *Caution:* Do not take large amounts or use over an extended period. Avoid if pregnant or breastfeeding.

# Almond, Sweet

*Prunus dulcis* syn. *Prunus amygdalus/Amygdalus communis* var. *dulcia*

· · · · · · · · · · · · · · ·

PLANETARY RULER: Sun/Mercury

ELEMENT: Air

ASSOCIATED DEITIES: Attis, Car, Carmenta, Carya, Metis, Phyllis

MAGICAL VIRTUES: Spring, regeneration, divination, fertility

## LORE

In the Near East, almond blossom is the herald of spring. Phyllis (Leafy) was a Thracian princess whose lover, Acamas, went to fight at the siege of Troy. When he failed to return with the other warriors, she died of grief. Taking pity, the goddess Athene turned her into an almond tree. Acamas's ship had only been delayed, but on his return, he could only embrace the bark of the almond tree. In response to his loving caresses, the tree burst into blossom. The story may be seen as symbolising the blooming of flowers in response to the embrace of the sun's warmth in the spring.

## MAGICAL USES

Almond blossoms may be used in chaplets and decorations at festivals to celebrate the spring. Almond wood or blossoms may be added to Ostara incense and employed in rituals of rebirth and regeneration—spiritual or physical. Almond nuts are a symbol of fertility; add them to spells, charm bags, and sachets for this purpose, or give them out as tokens of good fortune, especially at weddings and handfastings. Use an almond wand for fertility and regenerative magic. Almond oil is often used as a base for magical oils.

## CULINARY AND HOUSEHOLD USES

Sweet almonds are a popular delicacy when toasted, salted, and eaten whole; added to baked goods; or ground to make marzipan. In Denmark, Norway, and Sweden, Christmas dinners include a rice pudding, called *julgrot*, which has a lucky almond in it. When pounded in water, sweet almonds form almond milk, which can be used as a substitute for dairy products.

## Cosmetic Uses

Almond oil is often used as a carrier for essential oils, but it can be used alone as a treatment for dry skin as it is a light oil that is easily absorbed, emollient, and nourishing. Almond milk is rich in antioxidants and can also help moisturise your skin. Apply it, mixed with honey, as a face mask. Ground almonds mixed with honey can be used as a facial scrub. You can apply a hair mask of almond milk, leave it on for 10 minutes, and then rinse to reduce frizz.

## Home Remedies

Almonds are rich in fibre, plant sterols, and polyunsaturated fatty acids. They help lower LDL (bad) cholesterol and increase HDL (good) cholesterol. Eating a few almonds sometimes gives immediate relief to heartburn.

> Caution: *Since almonds are rich in arginine, they should be avoided by those who have a tendency toward cold sores or herpes infections; arginine tends to activate the virus.*

# Aloe Vera

*Aloe barbadensis syn. Aloe vera*

PLANETARY RULER: Moon

ELEMENT: Water

ASSOCIATED DEITIES: Aeacus, Amun Ra, Artemis, Chandra,
Indra, moon goddesses, Rhadamanthus, Venus, Vulcan, Yama

MAGICAL VIRTUES: Healing, protection, divination, spiritual development

## LORE

Native to North Africa and the Arabian Peninsula, aloe vera is a succulent with thick pale green leaves with lighter spots, which contain a viscous, clear gel. It has been used medicinally for thousands of years. In ancient Egypt, it was used for pain and inflammation, and Cleopatra and Nefertiti were reputed to have used aloe vera in their beauty care. In many parts of the world, aloe is used to ward off and expel evil spirits.

## MAGICAL USES

For protection, you may hang a leaf of aloe vera above your front door, keep a plant on your kitchen windowsill, add the dried leaves to protection incense, add aloe vera gel to protective salves, or smear the gel on protective talismans. The leaves may be dried and used in incenses dedicated to the moon goddess to bring understanding and insight and invoke her help during divination.

## COSMETIC USES

Its anti-inflammatory effect soothes irritation, while its emollient nature softens, moisturises, and reduces wrinkles, tightening the skin, and its antibacterial quality means it has an anti-acne effect. You can apply fresh aloe gel directly to your skin or add it to your homemade facial cleansers and moisturisers. To help with frizzy hair, smooth a little gel on dry and split ends before styling. Add to shampoo to treat an itchy scalp.

## HOME REMEDIES

Aloe gel is well-known and widely used as a topical remedy for skin irritation. Keep a plant in the kitchen as it is a handy first aid remedy for minor burns, fungal infections, ringworm, nappy rash, eczema, dermatitis, psoriasis, insect bites, sunburn, cuts, and skin abrasions. Just take a fresh leaf and open it to extract the clear gel within and apply this directly to the affected area. It reduces pain, speeds healing, and encourages cell repair.

> **Caution:** *For some sensitive people, aloe vera can cause contact dermatitis. Individuals who are allergic to other members of the lily family (which includes garlic, onions, crocus, hyacinth, lilies, and tulips) may also be sensitive to aloe.*

# Anemone

*Anemone* spp.

. . . . . . . . . . . . . .

PLANETARY RULER: Mars

ELEMENT: Fire

ASSOCIATED DEITIES: Adonis, Anemone,
Anemos, Aphrodite, Tammuz, Venus

MAGICAL VIRTUES: Spring, youth, protection,
apotropaic, death and mourning

## LORE

There are 150 species in the genus *Anemone*, but most of the lore belongs to the windflower/
pasqueflower (*Anemone pulsatilla*) and the wood anemone (*Anemone nemorosa*). Anemones
flower very early in the spring and are one of its first harbingers. They were used as decorations at Easter time, hence the folk names Osterblume (Easter flower) and pasqueflower
(Easter flower). In the ancient world, anemone was taken as a symbol of the vegetation god
who died and was reborn. In Greek myth, anemones were the tears of Aphrodite, shed for
the slain god Adonis, or his blood, while the red anemones that blossomed on the slopes of
Mount Lebanon were the blood of the slain vegetation god Tammuz. The windflower has
its own mythology, and in one story, it is the transformed nymph Anemone, who trembles
at the touch of her lover, the wind Zephyrus. The Roman writer Pliny affirmed that anemones only open when the wind blows. Anemones are generally toxic and contain an irritat-
ing juice, so they were often viewed as a devil's herb in folklore, while the Germans called
them Hexenblumen, or "witch's flowers." Wearing one in a buttonhole was bad luck. It was
even unluckier to take it into the house as it brought death with it.

## MAGICAL USES

Anemones are a herald of spring, and they may be used in rituals, incense, herbal talismans,
and spells connected with the spring equinox, new beginnings, and the resurrected vegetation god. Pick the first anemone found in spring while saying, "Anemone, I gather thee
for a remedy against all diseases," and keep it safe as a talisman against sickness. Anemones

may be used in the flower arrangements, decorations, and incense for rituals of death and mourning. Hang a bunch of anemones on outbuildings and stables to protect them and the animals within. Wear an anemone in a herbal amulet to ward off magic sent against you.

## CULINARY AND HOUSEHOLD USES

A bright green dye can be made from the pasqueflower for colouring Easter/Ostara decorative eggs (do not eat).

## HOME REMEDIES

*Anemone pulsatilla* does have a role in herbal medicine as a nervine, but it is toxic and not for home use.

> **Caution:** *Anemones are toxic and contain an irritating sap. Care should be taken when picking. They are not for internal consumption.*

# Angelica

*Angelica officinalis/Angelica archangelica*

· · · · · · · · · · · · · ·

PLANETARY RULER: Sun

ELEMENT: Fire

ASSOCIATED DEITIES: Sun gods, Venus

MAGICAL VIRTUES: Protection, anaphrodisiac, healing, cleansing, exorcism

## LORE

The name *angelica* comes from the Greek *angelos*, meaning "a messenger." In the Middle Ages, angelica was used against baneful magic and physical illnesses alike, and the herbalist Culpeper claimed that it was a remedy against all epidemics and infections. The root was carried as a charm to guard against the plague and was popularly believed to offer protection against evil spirits, apparitions, witches, and devils.

## MAGICAL USES

Angelica is a powerful herb of cleansing and protection. Use it in an incense/sain to purify a person or space. An angelica infusion may be used to cleanse places and objects, employed to seal doors and windows against negative influences, or added to a purification bath. Carry the dried root as a protective amulet. Use the dried root, flowers, and leaves in healing incense and oils and for rites and spells of healing.

## CULINARY AND HOUSEHOLD USES

The stalks, leaves, and flowers are edible and naturally sweet (diabetics should avoid them). The green stems are candied for cake decoration, cut and prepared like asparagus, chopped and stewed with rhubarb and apples, or added to jams and marmalade. The leaves may be added to cooked fruit dishes, salads, soups, and stews. Angelica is also used as a flavouring for liqueurs. The aromatic root makes a good addition to potpourri blends.

## COSMETIC USES

Use an angelica infusion as face wash for acne.

· · · · ·

## HOME REMEDIES

The dried root is used by herbalists but is not recommended for home use; the leaves are gentler in action. A leaf infusion can be used as an eyewash; added to a bath to calm the nerves and soothe arthritic pain; used as a mouthwash for mouth sores and sore throats; or drunk as a digestive aid. A compress soaked in a strong infusion may be applied to the affected parts to treat gout or rheumatism.

> *Caution:* *Care should be taken when collecting as angelica can be confused with several poisonous species. Angelica is generally considered safe to be used in food quantities, but the root should only be used under medical supervision. Medicinal quantities of angelica should not be taken over an extended period of time. Avoid if you are pregnant or breastfeeding; have heart problems or high blood pressure; are diabetic; or are taking any blood-thinning medications, including aspirin.*

# Apple

*Malus* spp.

. . . . . . . . . . . . . . .

PLANETARY RULER: Venus

ELEMENT: Water

ASSOCIATED DEITIES: Aphrodite, Apollo, Arthur, Athene, Bel, Ceridwen, Demeter, Diana, Dionysus, Dumuzi, Eve, Flora, Grannos, Hera, Herakles, Hermes, Hesperides, Iduna, Inanna, Juno, Mabon, Manannan, Maponus, Mêliae, Modron, Morgana, Nehallenia, Nemesis, Olwen, Pomona, solar heroes, sun gods, Tellus Mater, Titaea, Venus, Vertumnus, Vishnu, Zeus

MAGICAL VIRTUES: Love, fertility, abundance, otherworld travel, divination

## LORE

Surrounded by an abundance of myth and folklore and associated with many gods, the apple was one of the most sacred trees of ancient Europe to the extent that, under Celtic law, to chop one down was punishable by death. Its associations with the otherworld, love, eroticism, marriage, fertility, and choice have been echoed in art down the ages.

## MAGICAL USES

If you cut an apple in half across the middle, the centre reveals a five-pointed star, the pentacle, showing its magical nature. Use apples or an apple wand for spells, incenses, and charm bags for love, fertility, and abundance. Add dried apple bark, blossoms, peel, and pips to incenses of love and plenty. At Samhain, make an offering of apples to the spirits, drink cider instead of wine, and add apple pieces to your cakes. Don't forget to wassail your apple trees at Yule.

## CULINARY AND HOUSEHOLD USES

There are so many ways to use apples in the kitchen; to list them would need its own book! It is worth mentioning that they are rich in pectin, so a few pieces of apple can be added to pectin-poor fruits, such as strawberries, to set jams and jellies. The antimicrobial properties destroy a variety of harmful organisms, making cider vinegar one of the best natural home cleaning agents out there.

## COSMETIC USES

Apple cider vinegar has a number of cosmetic uses. It is a natural deodorant that kills odour-causing bacteria when dabbed under the arms. It will strengthen fingernails when they are bathed in it. If you have dandruff, add it to your final hair rinse. Combine it 50/50 with malt vinegar and add it to hair rinses to impart a golden colour.

## HOME REMEDIES

Apples help neutralise the acid products of gout and indigestion. As mentioned, they contain pectin, which helps bulk up the stool to treat diarrhoea and constipation. Stewed apples can be eaten for fevers and arthritic and rheumatic conditions. Add cider vinegar to footbaths for athlete's foot. Gargle with a mixture of apple cider vinegar and warm water for sore throats. Apple cider vinegar detoxifies, and it is helpful for arthritis, gout, rheumatism, and skin conditions.

*Caution:* *None known.*

# Ash

*Fraxinus* spp.

· · · · · · · · · · · · · · · · · · · ·

**PLANETARY RULER:** Sun

**ELEMENT:** Water/fire

**ASSOCIATED DEITIES:** Athene, Cernunnos, Gwydion, Herne, Llyr, Mars,
Neptune, Odin, Poseidon, Saturn, Thor, Uranus, Woden, Ymir, Zeus

**MAGICAL VIRTUES:** Connecting the realms,
prophetic dreams, healing, apotropaic

## LORE

In Scandinavian myth, the first man, Ask, was made from ash, while the first woman,
Embla, was made from alder (or elm). The god Odin created Yggdrasil, a massive ash tree
that linked all the worlds of creation, stretching from the underworld, through earth, and
to heaven. Odin hung from the world tree for nine days and nights to gain the secrets of
the runes, giving one of his eyes in sacrifice.

## MAGICAL USES

The ash tree has the power to connect the realms of above, below, and middle-earth. Meditate with an ash tree to travel the realms. An ash wand conducts energy through all three
realms. Carry an ash staff when seeking connection. The smoke of burning ash wood
drives away evil and bad luck. Place a pouch of ash leaves beneath your pillow for prophetic
dreams or add ash bark to divination incense. An old spell used ash to cure warts by taking
them from the sufferer. An individual would chant, "Ashen tree, ashen tree, pray buy these
warts of me," and a pin was then used to prick the wart before being inserted into the tree.

## CULINARY AND HOUSEHOLD USES

The keys (winged seeds) can be pickled. The young leaves may be added to salads or used to
make a refreshing tea. A green dye may be obtained from the leaves.

## COSMETIC USES

An ash infusion wash (or ash infusion used as the liquid component of homemade creams) may help reduce skin puffiness.

## HOME REMEDIES

The bark and leaves of *Fraxinus excelsior* and other species have been used in traditional medicine, though ash is little used in modern herbalism. An infusion of the leaves is a laxative and diuretic with anti-inflammatory properties that may be useful in cases of arthritis, gout, and rheumatism. The infusion is also astringent and may be used as a wash for small wounds, skin sores, itchy skin, bruising, and swelling.

> *Caution:* Do not take internally if you have stomach or intestinal complaints and, to be on the safe side, if you are pregnant or breastfeeding. Large amounts may cause vomiting.

# Basil

*Ocimum* spp.

· · · · · · · · · · · · · ·

PLANETARY RULER: Mars

ELEMENT: Fire

ASSOCIATED DEITIES: Aphrodite, Christ, Erzulie, Krishna, Lakshmi, Vishnu

MAGICAL VIRTUES: Blessing, peace, harmony, protection, dispelling
negativity, exorcism, healing, love, luck, wealth, abundance

## LORE

In Hinduism, holy basil, also called tulsi, is the holiest of all plants and a manifestation of
Lakshmi, the goddess of wealth. All forms of ghosts and demons run away from any place
where it is planted. In Tudor England, basil was considered lucky and protective; it was
often gifted to a couple setting up house or given to departing guests.

## MAGICAL USES

Basil is a protective spirit, deflecting negative energy from its surroundings; warding off
evil spirits, baneful magic, and psychic attacks; and bringing peace, prosperity, and blessing
into the home. Keep a basil plant in the kitchen to foster domestic harmony. Make a basil
infusion and sprinkle it with a fresh sprig of basil in all the corners of each room to cleanse
your house or sacred space. Dab a spot of basil oil on your forehead for personal protection.
Basil resonates with the flow of abundance. Carry a basil leaf in your purse or wallet to

attract wealth, and sprinkle a basil infusion over the threshold of your business premises to attract customers. It is a herb of love, so use it in love spells, incenses, and charm bags. Wear basil oil to attract a lover.

## CULINARY AND HOUSEHOLD USES

When cooking with basil, use it fresh and add it towards the end of the cooking process to retain the scent and flavour of its volatile oils. There is something about the pairing of basil and tomatoes that makes food magic, and basil can be added to pizza, all tomato-based pasta sauces, tomato soup, and lasagne. Basil leaves add a fresh, peppery zing to salads and sandwiches, and they work particularly well with mozzarella or feta cheese and tomatoes.

## COSMETIC USES

Basil helps protect from free radical damage. It tightens the skin, improve its tone, and boosts the growth of new skin cells. Massage basil tea into your skin and rinse it off. A basil face pack can be made by blitzing a handful of basil leaves with honey.

## HOME REMEDIES

Basil tea or a hot basil compress can help arthritic pain. Basil tea has a mildly sedative action. A basil infusion can be employed as a wash for ulcers, cuts, wounds, and eczema (it contains anti-itching compounds). Use as an antifungal mouthwash for oral thrush.

> *Caution:* *Basil is generally considered safe in food amounts. Do not take medicinal amounts of basil for more than four weeks, and avoid it if you are diabetic, have high blood pressure, are on anticlotting medications, or are pregnant or breastfeeding.*

# Bean

*Leguminosae spp.*

PLANETARY RULER: Mercury

ELEMENT: Air

ASSOCIATED DEITIES: Blodeuwedd, Carnea, Cardea, Demeter

MAGICAL VIRTUES: Apotropaic, death, funerals

## LORE

There are many types of beans, and they have been cultivated since ancient times for food. Because the seeds resemble testicles, the bean was a sacred plant in some cultures. In them, eating beans was completely forbidden or only allowed at certain times. The Jewish high priest was forbidden to eat beans on the day of atonement, for instance, while the Greek philosopher Pythagoras so strongly believed that beans contained the souls of the departed that he refused to consume them. Beans were widely associated with death and constituted a traditional part of the funeral supper. To this day in Italy, beans are distributed among the poor and bean dishes are eaten on the anniversaries of the deaths of famous people. Perhaps because they were associated with the spirits of the underworld, beans had the power to dispel them. In ancient Rome, the head of the household would go out to the threshold of his home on three days of the year, spitting beans from his mouth to rid the home of evil spirits. In the Middle Ages, spitting beans into a witch's face was said to deprive her of her powers and spitting beans at apparitions would force them to disappear. Today in Asia, bean flowers are scattered about the house to placate demons.

## MAGICAL USES

Dried beans are used to dispel negativity and evil, and you can put them in your rattles to clear a sacred space or an aura of negative energies. Spit beans into spaces to disperse negative energy. Use bean flowers in funeral incense and bean dishes at funeral suppers. Bean flowers can be added to incense to invoke Blodeuwedd, Carnea, and Cardea. Bake a bean in a twelfth-night cake. Whoever finds it will be ruler of the feast.

## Culinary and Household Uses

Beans are full of protein and contain many vitamins and minerals. They can be used as a meat replacement in soups, chillies, curries, casseroles, and pasta dishes or added cold to salads.

## Home Remedies

There is some evidence that people who regularly consume legumes are at a lower risk of heart disease and certain cancers. Beans improve gut health and good gut bacteria colonies.

> *Caution:* *Some types of beans require soaking and boiling for 10 minutes to remove the lectin toxins. Gas and intestinal discomfort can be experienced by people who are unused to eating beans. Beans may not be suitable if you have IBS, have inflammatory bowel disease (IBD), or need to reduce carbohydrates.*

# Beech

*Fagus* spp.

. . . . . . . . . . . . . . .

PLANETARY RULER: Saturn/Mercury

ELEMENT: Air/earth

ASSOCIATED DEITIES: Apollo, Athene, Bacchus, Ceridwen,
Cronos, Diana, Dionysus, Donar, Freya, Frigg, Hel, Hermes,
Holle, Loki, Mercury, Odin, Ogma, Thor, Zeus

MAGICAL VIRTUES: Protection, prophecy, rune
work, wisdom passed on, fertility

## LORE

Throughout the ages, lovers have carved their initials in beech trees, runes have been inscribed on beech staves, and mediaeval books were bound in beech wood. Indeed, the word *book* is derived from *beech*. For the Romans, it was an oracular tree, and in Greece, it was present at the grove of Dodona, where the god Zeus spoke through the rustling of the leaves. In the Northern tradition, it was sacred to the thunder god Thor/Donar (lightning is supposed never to strike a beech tree), who also spoke in the whispering beeches. Because it produces many nuts, the beech tree is a symbol of fertility; in popular superstition, a good year of beechnuts meant many children would be born, though it also signified a harsh winter to follow.

## MAGICAL USES

The beech tree is a symbol of knowledge passed on and guidance through the written words of the ancestors. It is said that the whisperings of the gods are in its branches. Listen to the words that try to reach you. The wood is excellent for carving and making rune staves. Carve your magic into a piece of beech bark and carry it with you. A forked divining rod made from beech is an excellent tool. Beech is called the Mother of the Woods and is a feminine tree of protective and nurturing magic, giving shade and nourishment to all who shelter beneath it. Meditate beneath a beech to connect to the Mother Goddess. Use beech bark in protective charms and amulets to place yourself under the shield of the Goddess. Use beechnuts in fertility magic, charms, and spells.

## CULINARY AND HOUSEHOLD USES

The very young leaves taste a bit like lettuce and can be added to salads. Beechnuts (mast) can be eaten as a famine food, and the Roman historian Pliny the Elder noted that beech-mast saved the people of Chios from starvation during a siege, though the nuts are slightly toxic in large amounts. During World War II, the French roasted beechnuts as a coffee substitute. They can be pressed to make an oil for cooking.

## COSMETIC USES

A beech bark decoction may be used as an astringent skin wash.

## HOME REMEDIES

A beech bark decoction or beech bark tar (obtained from a distillation of the wood) is an antiseptic and can be used to treat skin problems such as psoriasis and eczema.

> **Caution:** *Eating large quantities of the raw nuts is toxic. Avoid internal use when pregnant or breastfeeding.*

# Begonia

*Begonia* spp.

. . . . . . . . . . . . . . .

PLANETARY RULER: Mars

ELEMENT: Fire

ASSOCIATED DEITIES: Gods and goddesses
of justice and harmony

MAGICAL VIRTUES: Balance, harmony,
peace, justice

## LORE
Originating in the subtropical and tropical moist climates of South and Central America, Africa, and southern Asia, begonias are categorized according to root types into fibrous-rooted, tuberous, and rhizomatous varieties. In modern folklore, the different coloured flowers contain their own symbolism. White begonias mean innocence, red begonias symbolise romance and passion, and pink begonias represent friendship.

## MAGICAL USES
For harmony and balance, keep a begonia plant in your home, in your garden, or by the door; carry dried begonia flowers in herbal talismans and sachets; or hang the dried flowers in your house. The dried flowers can be used in spells and incenses that call for and promote justice.

## CULINARY AND HOUSEHOLD USES
Tuberous begonias have edible leaves and flowers with a sour, citrus-like taste. They can be eaten raw or cooked, used for flower garnishes, and added to spreads, dips, and salads.

## COSMETIC USES

Dry begonia petals to use in crafts and natural beauty recipes. Add them to soothing bath salts to give them a delicate floral scent.

> *Caution:* Begonias contain oxalic acid, so they should be consumed in moderation and avoided by people with kidney disease, rheumatism, or gout. In some sensitive people, the sap of begonias can cause irritation and contact dermatitis.

# Benzoin

*Styrax benzoin*

. . . . . . . . . . . . . . .

PLANETARY RULER: Sun

ELEMENT: Air

ASSOCIATED DEITIES: Aphrodite, Ares, Freya,
Hathor, Khephera, Mut, Nike, Typhon, Venus

MAGICAL VIRTUES: Cleansing, purifying, calming,
balance, harmony, concentration

## LORE

Benzoin (also called gum benzoin) is a balsamic resin obtained from trees in the genus *Styrax*, which are native to Sumatra, Thailand, Vietnam, Java, and China. The beautiful fragrance of the gum has made it a popular ritual incense and cosmetic ingredient since ancient times, and it was traded across the seas in early history, appearing in ancient Egyptian records.

## MAGICAL USES

Benzoin resin is employed in incense making where, as well as adding a sweet scent, it acts as a preservative. When used during meditation, the incense clears and concentrates the mind, cleanses and purifies the space, and calms, soothes, and balances the emotions. It can also be added to sun and air incenses and to the incenses of any of the listed deities.

## CULINARY AND HOUSEHOLD USES

In small quantities, gum benzoin can be added to baked goods as a flavouring and vanilla scent. Use it as a preservative in potpourri.

## COSMETIC USES

Benzoin is antibacterial. Mix benzoin powder with a little rose water and use as a skin exfoliant. Dissolve it in hot water, then massage into your scalp to treat irritation, itching, and

. . . . .

dandruff. Add it to your homemade beauty products as a natural preservative, perfume anchor, and antioxidant.

## HOME REMEDIES

Available as a resinous powder and essential oil, benzoin is included in commercial cough drops. For home use, create a steam by dissolving benzoin in boiling water and inhale the steam for chest complaints, asthma, and bronchitis. Dab the infusion on ulcers, bed sores, wounds, eczema, psoriasis, and rashes.

> *Caution:* Food amounts of benzoin are considered generally safe, but taking medicinal amounts internally is not recommended. Benzoin applied to the skin can cause rashes for some sensitive individuals.

# Bergamot

a.k.a. Bee Balm
*Monarda didyma*

· · · · · · · · · · · · · · · · ·

PLANETARY RULER: Mercury

ELEMENT: Air

MAGICAL VIRTUES: Wealth, meditation, clairvoyance, vision

## LORE

Three distinct plants are called bergamot: the bee balm herb (*Monarda didyma*); the bergamot orange (*Mentha citrata*); and the citrus plant (*Citrus bergamia*), which all bergamot oil
is extracted from. Bee balm is native to North America. The pretty, fragrant flowers of bee
balm are very attractive to bees, hence the common name.

## MAGICAL USES

Carry some bee balm in your wallet or purse to attract money. Bergamot is used as an
incense or tea to relax and clear the mind for meditation and to open the channels for clairvoyance and vision. Make a dream pillow stuffed with dried bee balm.

## CULINARY AND HOUSEHOLD USES

After the Boston Tea Party in 1773, when imported tea was thrown in the harbour by pro-
testors, bergamot tea, known as Oswego tea, became a popular drink in New England. It
is an infusion of the young leaves. Bergamot flowers may be crystallised and used as cake
decoration, and you can add the fresh flower petals to salads. The flowers and young leaves
add a spicy flavour to cakes and scones.

## COSMETIC USES

A heated macerated oil of the flowers can be used to smooth and condition your hair.

## HOME REMEDIES

The young leaves and flower petals can be used fresh or dried. Sleeping on a bee balm pillow, or drinking bee balm tea before bed, may help induce restful sleep. The tea is a nervine

· · · · ·

and may help reduce anxiety and stress. Taken before meals, the tea is a digestive that may help to stimulate appetite, relieve nausea, and prevent bloating and flatulence. It may also relieve a headache. A decongestant steam of the leaves will aid chest complaints, coughs, flu, and catarrh/mucus, or you can take bee balm syrup or electuary for coughs, colds, and flu. A hot compress dipped in a strong infusion can be applied to shingles, chicken pox, cold sores, insect bites, and, because it is antiseptic, to wounds and sores. The antimicrobial and anti-inflammatory effect of bee balm in a strong infusion is valuable when used as a mouthwash or gargle for toothaches, mouth ulcers, gingivitis, or sore throats. Add a strong infusion to the bath to soothe aching muscles.

**Caution:** *Do not use if pregnant or breastfeeding.*

# Bindweed

*Convolvulus* spp.

. . . . . . . . . . . . . .

PLANETARY RULER: Saturn

ELEMENT: Water

ASSOCIATED DEITIES: Harvest gods

MAGICAL VIRTUES: Binding spells, cursing

## LORE

Bindweed's botanical name comes from the Latin *convolvere* (to entwine), telling us it grows voraciously and strangles everything it grows up—no wonder it is a symbol of dangerous obstinacy. Its folk name bearbind comes from the Old English *beow* (barley), as the stems were once used to bind grain during the harvest. In England it was known as thunder flower, as picking bindweed was believed to result in a storm before the day was out. A more sinister folk name is young man's death, which comes from the superstition that if a girl were to pick bindweed, her lover would die.

## MAGICAL USES

While most climbing plants twine sunwise, bindweed twines widdershins. It is therefore used in binding and cursing magic. The roots can be wrapped around an image of a person to bind them from doing harm.

## CULINARY AND HOUSEHOLD USES

The young leaves may be cooked like spinach, though this is not recommended, as they have a laxative effect! The roots may be used as an emergency natural string, but know they will degrade quickly. A green dye can be obtained from the whole plant.

## HOME REMEDIES

Bindweed root is a purgative, though its action is unpredictable and not suitable for self-medication. All the *Convolvulus* genus have purgative properties in a greater or less degree. A tea of the leaves or flowers is a laxative, but its use is not recommended as the results can be volatile.

> **Caution:** *Do not confuse with the unrelated morning glory (Ipomoea spp.) or bindweed (ragwort), which was used in a spell by German and Irish parents to protect children from being stolen by fairies.*

# Birch, Silver

*Betula alba*

. . . . . . . . . . . .

PLANETARY RULER: Venus

ELEMENT: Water

ASSOCIATED DEITIES: Bride, Brigantia, Brighid, Earth Mother,
Kupala, Kupalo, Lady of the Woods, Rusalki, summer goddesses, Thor

MAGICAL VIRTUES: Purification, new beginnings, protection, fertility

## LORE

The name comes from the Indo-European root word *bharg*, meaning "white" or "shining."
In myth and lore, birch is a tree of purification. Criminals were flogged with birch twigs to
drive the evil spirits from them, and birch twigs are still used in some saunas to purify the
body by stimulating circulation. The tree also has the power of fertility and growth as in
the rune *Beorc/Berkana* and the white wand of the Celtic goddess Brighid, which she used
to bring life back to the land after the winter. In Britain the association of birch with sex
and fertility survived into the nineteenth century, when navvies (canal diggers) and their
women considered themselves properly married if they jumped across a birch broom.

## MAGICAL USES

Birch has the power of new beginnings, cleansing and purification, and banishing winter
and negativity. Add it to purification incense. Use a birch besom to sweep a circle or temple
clear of negative energies. Protective amulets can be made by binding a four-armed cross of
birch twigs with red thread. Hang it at the highest point of the house. Handfasting couples
may jump the birch besom as a symbol of fertility.

## CULINARY AND HOUSEHOLD USES

Birch beer and wine are made from the sap. Birch sap may also be used as a natural sweet-
ener. Birch bark can be used for tinder and tanning leather.

## Cosmetic Uses

To treat cellulite, use a birch infusion or macerated oil on the affected area. The sap may be diluted to wash the skin to remove blemishes and blotches, tone, and improve elasticity; it can also be used in hair treatments to strengthen the hair.

## Home Remedies

Birch promotes the removal of toxins from the body, and an infusion of birch leaves can be used to help dissolve kidney and bladder stones. It helps remove toxins and waste products, so it may be beneficial in the treatment of urinary complaints, cystitis, rheumatism, arthritis, and gout. Externally, use a compress steeped in a birch bark decoction for chronic skin conditions, such as eczema and psoriasis. A macerated oil of the bark may be applied to the skin for dermal conditions, arthritis and rheumatism, cellulite, and muscular aches and pains.

> **Caution:** *Some sensitive individuals report diarrhoea, nausea, itching, rashes, and a stuffy and runny nose after taking birch.*

# Black Pepper

*Piper nigrum*

PLANETARY RULER: Mars

ELEMENT: Fire

ASSOCIATED DEITIES: Balabhadra, Hanuman, Jagannath,
Lakshmi, Pana Narasimha, Shakti, Subhadra, Surya

MAGICAL VIRTUES: Banishing, protection, courage

## LORE

In Hindi, black pepper is *marich*, one of the names for the sun, as it is believed to be filled
with hot solar energy. It is offered to the sun god Surya at the end of the winter solstice
month. In some traditions, black pepper is used to combat spirit possession. Islamic exor-
cists use ingredients such as lime, vinegar, black pepper, and ginger, which are thought to
burn *jinni* (spirits), in connection with prayers to drive jinni from a victim's body.

## MAGICAL USES

Assigned to the planet Mars and the element of fire, black pepper resonates with warrior
energy, courage, and fortitude. Put it to use in spells and rituals to remove emotional block-
ages, fear, and apathy. Add it to herbal talismans, sachets, and charm bags. You can also add
black pepper to incense used for exorcism and banishing.

## CULINARY AND HOUSEHOLD USES

Black pepper is an incredibly versatile cooking spice, and it is used in soups, stews, marinades, pickles, and more. For the best flavour, grind pepper just before use.

## COSMETIC USES

Use crushed black peppercorns in an exfoliating facial scrub that will invigorate your skin
and remove dead cells from the surface. This scrub is especially useful for acne sufferers as
it has antibacterial and anti-inflammatory qualities.

## Home Remedies

Added to food, black pepper is a carminative—it stimulates digestion and eases gas and bloating. It is also a natural painkiller; a black pepper compress can treat neuralgia. Black pepper, as a tea or compress, reduces the inflammatory compounds that make arthritic pain worse. It is a decongestant and useful in the treatment of colds, coughs, and flu.

> **Caution:** *Since it is used medicinally in very small amounts, black pepper is considered safe for most people. However, you should avoid larger amounts if you are pregnant or breastfeeding or taking lithium or medicines changed by the liver. Excessive consumption can lead to gastrointestinal irritation. Avoid if you have acid-peptic disease, stomach ulcers, ulcerative colitis, or diverticulitis.*

# Blackberry

a.k.a. Bramble

*Rubrus frucicosus*

. . . . . . . . . . . . . .

PLANETARY RULER: Venus

ELEMENT: Water

ASSOCIATED DEITIES: Brigantia, Brighid,
fairies, harvest deities, chthonic gods

MAGICAL VIRTUES: Death, the underworld, healing

## LORE

Throughout Europe the blackberry is considered an unlucky plant associated with death and the underworld. In all Celtic countries a taboo exists on eating blackberries after Old Michaelmas Day (October 11) when it is said that the devil enters blackberry thickets and spits on them. In Brittany and Cornwall, the reason given for the taboo is that blackberries belong to the fairy folk. However, bramble also has a reputation as a powerful healing plant. To cure whooping cough, a child was passed under a bramble nine times whilst reciting the following:

*In bramble, out cough, here I leave my whooping cough.*

## MAGICAL USES

Blackberries provide the wine at the autumn equinox, which marks the completion of the vegetation cycle and the departure of the God to the underworld. Eat some at the feast, decorate the altar with them, or use the plant's wood in the sacred fire. Blackberry wine or tea can be taken prior to underworld journeys and vision quests. A wand of blackberry wood summons fairies and chthonic deities but should be used with caution. The dried leaves and berries can be added to incenses or teas used at healing ceremonies that are designed to leave the diseases behind and should be carried out at the dark moon.

### CULINARY AND HOUSEHOLD USES

The berries can be made into wine, jam, sorbets; baked in pies and cakes; or eaten fresh. The leaves can be added to herbal tea blends. A black dye is made from the leaves, the young shoots produce a light grey dye, the root produces an orange dye, and the berries give a bluish-grey dye.

### COSMETIC USES

An infusion of the leaves can be added to a bath to freshen the skin in summer. The leaves are astringent, and an infusion can be used as a skin toner.

### HOME REMEDIES

Use blackberries to make a tea or gargle to treat sore throats, loss of voice, and sore mouths. Blackberry vinegar is good for colds and sore throats. A decoction of the leaves is used to bathe haemorrhoids and treat skin complaints and acne. It can also be used for cleaning and stanching wounds.

> *Caution:* In food and moderate amounts, blackberry leaf is considered safe for most people, but do not drink blackberry leaf tea at mealtimes. In larger, long-term amounts, the tannins in blackberry leaf tea can have toxic effects on the liver. Avoid completely if you have liver disease.

# Blackthorn

*Prunus spinosa*

. . . . . . . . . . . . .

PLANETARY RULER: Saturn

ELEMENT: Earth

ASSOCIATED DEITIES: Ceridwen

MAGICAL VIRTUES: Cursing, protection, death, fertility

## LORE

The common name *blackthorn* is self-explanatory—the shrub has sharp thorns and dark bark. It is also called Sloe, either from the Old High German *slêha*, meaning "bluish," the colour of the fruit, or perhaps related to the words *slay* and *strike*, as its dense wood was used to make fighting clubs. The plant has a dark and magical reputation. Witches were reputed to carry black wands of blackthorn, and the sorcerer Major Weir was burned at the stake in 1670 with his blackthorn rod. The vicious thorns of the shrub were used for pricking wax images intended to cause harm. In some myths, Christ's crown of thorns was made of blackthorn. The plant's lovely white flowers appear in early spring, before the leaves, but in folklore, they are said to invite death when taken into the house. It was bad luck to wear the flowers in your buttonhole. In Germany, blackthorn was burned on Walpurgis Night (May Eve) to ward off evil spirits.

## MAGICAL USES

Blackthorn is a tree of cursing and death, and the thorns can be used to prick wax images. Any staff or wand made from blackthorn must be used with great care for strength and power without compassion and wisdom can just as easily destroy the wielder as the target. The berries are ripe around the time of Samhain and are used to make a potent wine or liqueur for the festival, echoing the plant's paradoxical themes of strife, death, and fertility.

## CULINARY AND HOUSEHOLD USES

The tart berries can be made into wine or liqueur, including sloe gin, as well as syrups, jellies, and jams. The leaves and dried fruits can be made into tea. The flowers may be crystallised for cake decoration. The berries yield a red dye.

## COSMETIC USES

The pulp of ripe sloes can be used as an astringent face mask. The pulped berries can also be used to clean the teeth, and blackthorn leaf tea can be used as a mouthwash. Sloes can also be made into an antibacterial paste for whitening teeth and removing tartar.

## HOME REMEDIES

A blackthorn flower or berry infusion can be used as a gargle for mild inflammation of the mouth and throat or tonsillitis. The infusion can also be drunk as an expectorant for coughs. Sloe syrup is a laxative and diuretic in cases of constipation.

> **Caution:** *Sloes can be toxic in very large quantities. Avoid during pregnancy and lactation.*

# Bluebell

*Hyacinthoides non-scripta* syn.,
*Scilla nonscriptus*, or *Agraphis nutans*

. . . . . . . . . . . . . . .

PLANETARY RULER: Saturn/Moon

ELEMENT: Air

ASSOCIATED DEITIES: Fairies, Apollo

MAGICAL VIRTUES: Fairy magic, love, lust, truth, protection

## LORE

In Greek myth, Hyacinthus was a handsome youth, loved by both the sun god Apollo and Zephyrus, the god of the West Wind. One day Apollo was playing quoits with Hyacinthus and threw a quoit, which the jealous Zephyrus blew off course so that it struck and killed Hyacinthus. The grieving Apollo raised a flower from his fallen blood, and on it was written the Greek letter a, which indicated the sound of wailing. As the English variety of the flower has no trace of this letter, botanists called it *Hyacinthus nonscriptus*, or "not written on." Bluebell woods are places of fairy spells and enchantments. In Somerset, it is believed that you should never go into the woods to pick bluebells, as it will anger the fairies.

## MAGICAL USES

Grow some in your garden to attract nature spirits but know that fairies do not like bluebells to be picked from the wild—it will anger them. Bluebells are the most potent plant for fairy magic. Add to herbal charm bags or incense to attract fairies. Bluebells usher in Beltane and embody the lusty currents of the season. Use them in love and lust spells and charms. As a plant of protection, bluebells in the bedroom will keep away nightmares. They may also be used in truth spells.

## CULINARY AND HOUSEHOLD USES

The plant is toxic and cannot be eaten, though the viscid juice, which exists in every part of the plant, has been used as a substitute for starch. It was also used as a glue for fixing

. . . . .

feathers on arrows and as bookbinders' gum for the covers of books. The Elizabethans used it to stick paper.

## HOME REMEDIES

Bluebells are very toxic, though they produce a wide spectrum of interesting alkaloids and are coming under the close scrutiny of scientists who are screening a range of plants to discover if they contain substances of use in modern pharmaceutical drugs.

Caution: *Toxic—do not ingest! The sap can cause contact dermatitis.*

# Borage

*Borago officinalis*

PLANETARY RULER: Jupiter

ELEMENT: Air

ASSOCIATED DEITIES: Euphrosyne, warrior gods

MAGICAL VIRTUES: Courage, strength, warrior
magic, joy, gladness, expansion

## LORE

The common name *borage* may come from the Latin *corago* (*cor* meaning "heart" and *ago* meaning "I bring"). Borage has been a valuable medicinal herb since ancient times, and as a remedy for depression, it has been commended by herbalists through the ages.

## MAGICAL USES

Borage stimulates courage and strength when used in charms, spells, rituals, and potions. Carry borage flowers near your heart when you need to feel brave. Use dried borage flowers and leaves in Jupiter incense and rituals for expansive energies, wonder, and excitement.

## CULINARY AND HOUSEHOLD USES

The whole plant has a delicate flavour reminiscent of cucumber. The pretty blue flowers may be added fresh to salads, used for garnishing summer drinks, frozen in ice cubes and added to cocktails, or candied for cake decoration. The young leaves may be included in salads, added to pickles and salad dressings, or used in poultry, fish, and cheese dishes. Steeped in water, the leaves and flowers add a cool cucumber flavour—just add a slice of lemon.

## COSMETIC USES

Borage has anti-inflammatory properties with a cooling, cleansing, and skin-softening effect. Use steam-wilted borage leaves in a face mask for dry skin.

## HOME REMEDIES

Borage tea is a mild antidepressant. In stressful times, infuse the flowers and leaves in wine and drink to stimulate the adrenal glands and boost your ability to manage. It can also be used for fevers and during convalescence. A poultice of the leaves can be used to soothe bruises and inflammations, insect bites, and rashes.

*Caution: Borage should not be taken by people with liver conditions. Pregnant individuals and epileptics should not take borage seed oil (starflower oil). Do not use internally if you are on blood-thinning medication (including aspirin) or ingesting blood-thinning herbs.*

# Broom

a.k.a. Scotch

*Cytisus scoparius*

. . . . . . . . . . . . . . . .

PLANETARY RULER: Mars

ELEMENT: Air

ASSOCIATED DEITIES: Blodeuwedd

MAGICAL VIRTUES: Love, sex, marriage, purification, protection

## LORE

The botanical name *scoparius* is from the Latin word for besom since the twiggy branches were used as the original broom. It was unlucky to bring the flowers indoors as the plant will "sweep someone out of the house," though the flowering tops were used for Whitsuntide decorations. A plentiful bloom of flowers presaged a good harvest. Broom was widely connected with love, sex, and marriage; the Breton matchmaker carried a broom rod as a sign of office, while in many places, jumping the broom constituted an irregular wedding. In Welsh lore, the flower maiden Blodeuwedd was created from the flowers of broom, oak, and meadowsweet. In Italy it was regarded as a charm against witches.

## MAGICAL USES

Use a bunch of broom twigs to sweep and purify your sacred space. Add broom flowers to love and lust incenses, charm bags, and spells. Use the flowers for wedding/handfasting bouquets and decorations, as well as incense and rituals of Blodeuwedd and Ostara. An incense or sain/ritual fumigation of broom repels negativity.

## CULINARY AND HOUSEHOLD USES

The flowers and flower buds are edible and have a slightly nutty flavour. Add them fresh to salads or pickle or salt them. The seeds are toxic eaten fresh, but when roasted and ground, they provide a caffeine-free coffee substitute. The young green shoots impart a bitter flavour to beer and were used for that purpose before the introduction of hops. The twigs may

. . . . .

be used for besoms or basket weaving. A green dye may be obtained from the young green tops, and it was sometimes used for dying decorative Easter eggs in Europe.

## COSMETIC USES

Add a macerated oil or infusion of the flowers to homemade face creams and sunscreens to prevent UV damage. Use a rinse of broom flower infusion to lighten and brighten blond hair.

## HOME REMEDIES

Traditionally, broom has been used as a diuretic, cathartic, and cardiac tonic but owing to concerns over its toxicity, it should not be taken internally in medicinal amounts. A salve can be made from the flowers for the topical treatment of gout.

> *Caution:* Medicinal amounts of broom taken internally can be toxic. Symptoms include blurred vision, dysrhythmias, nausea, and twitching. Do not take if you are pregnant (it acts on the uterus), suffer from heart problems, or have high blood pressure. Do not take with antidepressants or lithium.

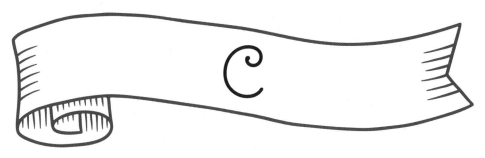

# Calendula

a.k.a. Pot Marigold

*Calendula officinalis*

. . . . . . . . . . . . . . . . .

PLANETARY RULER: Sun

ELEMENT: Fire

ASSOCIATED DEITIES: Aphrodite, Apollo, Ganesh, Lakshmi, Rama, Vishnu

MAGICAL VIRTUES: Solar rituals, protection,
love, marriage, mourning, divination

## LORE

The botanical name comes from the Latin *calends*, meaning "the first day of each month," as calendula was said to be in bloom on each calend of the year. Its rayed petals and light-sensitive opening and closing associated it with sun gods. In Greek myth, the sun god Apollo turned his ex-lovers Clytia and Caltha into calendula flowers. Marigolds are part of every Hindu celebration, representing the sun, brightness, and auspicious energy. The name *officinalis* shows that calendula was included on the official list of herbal medicines.

## MAGICAL USES

Since it's sacred to the sun, use marigold at the solstices and equinoxes in incense or as a bathing herb; it can also be thrown onto the bonfire. The petals can be added to water, macerated in oil, and added to incense used in rituals of divination or to consecrate divinatory tools. Place marigold flowers beneath your pillow to induce clairvoyant dreams. Marigold is a powerful herb of protection, and it may be added to incenses, charm bags, protection oils and powders or simply grown in pots around the home. Calendula petals may be used in love spells and added to love sachets and incenses.

## CULINARY AND HOUSEHOLD USES

Marigold petals add colour and flavour to rice, chowder, custard, soups, cream cheese or yoghurt dips, and potato salad. Add them to baked goods and egg dishes, or use them as a garnish for salads and vegetables. They can be candied, added to cordials, and made into wine, vinegar, or marigold buns.

## COSMETIC USES

Calendula is restorative and soothing, and it is especially good for dry and aging skin when added to homemade creams and oils. A calendula infusion may be used as a skin wash or toner for oily and acne-prone skin. It can also be used as a colour-enhancing rinse for red hair.

## HOME REMEDIES

Used as a wash, a calendula infusion takes the prickle out of burns, scalds, and insect bites and stings; it may also be used to bathe sore eyes. In a tea, the bitter taste of the flower petals activates the liver and aids in the digestion of fats. Use a calendula infusion as a healing mouthwash after a tooth extraction and for mouth ulcers and gum disease.

> *Caution:* Make sure you correctly identify your plant as Calendula officinalis, *the pot marigold, as other types of plants called marigold can be toxic.*

# Caraway

*Carum carvi*

. . . . . . . . . . . . . .

PLANETARY RULER: Sun/Mercury

ELEMENT: Air

ASSOCIATED DEITIES: Sun goddesses

MAGICAL VIRTUES: Fidelity, love, memory, protection, retention

## LORE

Caraway seeds were widely believed to confer the gift of retention—any object that contained them could not be stolen or lost. Caraway dough was fed to chickens, doves, and pigeons to keep them from straying. However, it is unlucky to give it away, and there is an old saying that goes:

> *You baked for me caraway bread but prepared yourself for tears.*

## MAGICAL USES

For protection, use caraway tea to cleanse the ritual working area or home, seal doors and windows with caraway oil, or add the herb to protection incenses. Use caraway to anoint any objects or tools to prevent their loss and bind them to you. Feed your lover caraway cake to prevent them from straying. As a mercurial herb, caraway is associated with thought, memory, and communication. Use it in Mercury incense or spells and rituals connected with communication, messages, and study.

## CULINARY AND HOUSEHOLD USES

Caraway seeds are aromatic and used in rye breads, biscuits and cakes, sauerkraut, pâtés, cheeses, soups, curries, and sweets. The leaves may be added to soups and stews, and the roots can be boiled as a vegetable like carrots.

## COSMETIC USES

Caraway seeds contain antioxidants that will protect your skin and hair. Grind some caraway seeds, mix them with honey, and apply as a face pack. Leave the pack on for ten minutes and rinse with warm water. You can also use this as a treat for your hair; leave it on for 30 minutes, then shampoo as usual.

## HOME REMEDIES

Drink caraway tea or chew the seeds to treat gas, bloating, and indigestion. Caraway tea is a remedy for infant colic, colds, and chest congestion; it contains mild antihistamines that help to relax the muscles that cause coughing spasms. Skin irritations, boils, and rashes can be washed gently with caraway tea.

> **Caution:** Do not take medicinal amounts for more than eight weeks. To be on the safe side, medicinal amounts should be avoided if pregnant or breastfeeding. It slightly lowers blood sugar, so if you are diabetic, monitor your levels carefully. Caraway should be avoided by those with hemochromatosis, as it increases iron absorption.

# Cardamom

*Elettaria* spp. and *Amomum* spp.

· · · · · · · · · · · · · ·

PLANETARY RULER: Venus

ELEMENT: Water

ASSOCIATED DEITIES: Erzulie, Hecate, Medea,
Venus, Aphrodite, Three Graces

MAGICAL VIRTUES: Lust, love, harmony, balance, grace, attractiveness

## LORE

Cardamom is a perennial plant native to parts of Asia, including India and Malaysia, from the same botanical family as ginger and turmeric. It was known in ancient Egypt, Rome, and Greece, and it is mentioned in *The Arabian Nights* as an aphrodisiac. It was introduced into Scandinavia by the Vikings and remains very popular there, especially on St. Lucy's Day (December 13), when it is baked with saffron into sun- and wheel-shaped cakes called *lussikatter* (Lucy Cats).

## MAGICAL USES

Include the seeds in sachets and charm bags carried to attract love and make you more desirable. Include the crushed seeds in love incenses, spells, and rituals. You can also add the ground seeds to mulled wine or mead to incite desire. Perfume your sheets with cardamom for a romantic night; put the crushed seeds in sachets and store them with your linen.

## CULINARY AND HOUSEHOLD USES

Green cardamom (*Elettaria cardamomum*) is used as a flavouring agent in Indian cuisine, and the herb is added to meat and vegetable dishes, breads, pickles, chutneys, desserts, sweets, and beverages. Black cardamom (*Amomum subulatum*) is used in savoury Chinese cuisine but never desserts or sweets, as it has a full-bodied, smoky flavour. In Arabic cultures, the ground seeds are added to coffee.

## COSMETIC USES

Macerated cardamom oil has antimicrobial, anti-inflammatory, and antifungal actions. These attributes help boost hair growth, prevent dandruff, and protect the scalp from dryness and inflammation.

## HOME REMEDIES

Drinking cardamom tea or eating the seeds is a remedy for digestive complaints such as indigestion, IBS, and constipation. The tea is a moderately effective painkiller, especially for the treatment of mild muscular pains and spasms. Use an oil or salve for arthritis or rheumatism, dermatitis, and fungal infections. The infusion may be used as a medicated wash for various skin disorders, and it may also be gargled for bad breath, mouth ulcers, and sore throats.

> *Caution:* To be on the safe side, do not take large amounts of cardamom if you are pregnant or breastfeeding. Only use small amounts of cardamom if you have gallstones, as large amounts can trigger gallstone colic.

# Carnation

*Dianthus spp.*

. . . . . . . . . . . . . .

PLANETARY RULER: Sun

ELEMENT: Fire

ASSOCIATED DEITIES: Jupiter, Zeus

MAGICAL VIRTUES: Protection, energy, love, marriage, mourning

## LORE

Carnations are native to the Mediterranean. Theophrastus (371–287 BCE) called them *dianthus* from the Greek words *dios* (divine) and *anthos* (flower). The common name, *carnation*, comes from the Latin *corona*, meaning "a crown."

## MAGICAL USES

Use carnation petals in protection incense, sachets, and talismans. You can also use carnation oil to protect possessions (just wipe a little on). Plant carnations in the garden or keep them in pots by your door as a magical safeguard against harm. Add carnation petals to incenses of love, use them in love spells, or drink carnation-infused wine with a lover. Carnations vibrate with the energy of the sun, strength, and health. Use them in spells, potions, and rituals of healing and calling for power, vitality, and wellness.

## CULINARY AND HOUSEHOLD USES

All carnation petals are edible, but the clove-scented pinks (*Dianthus caryophyllus*) are best. Using the petals only, removed from the calyx, sprinkle them over salads, or use them to garnish fruit dishes, to flavour summer drinks, or to make carnation vinegar, conserves, or syrup. The petals can also be candied for cake decoration.

## COSMETIC USES

Carnation petals stimulate the healing and softening of the skin. Use a carnation infusion as a wash for wrinkles, inflamed skin, acne, rashes, rosacea, and eczema. Carnations are naturally quite high in saponins (soap); simmer the leaves in water, strain them out, and use the liquid to cleanse your skin.

## HOME REMEDIES

Carnations have mild pain-relieving properties, and you can soak in a warm bath to which a carnation infusion has been added for muscular aches and menstrual cramps. Carnation flower tea can be taken for nervousness, stress, and mild depression, and it may be of use in cases of seasickness.

> *Caution:* Carnations may cause allergic symptoms in sensitive people or contact dermatitis in pets. Avoid use during pregnancy, as it may cause uterine contractions in sufficient doses. Excess use may cause toxicity. It should be avoided in cases of spleen/kidney deficiency.

# Catmint

### a.k.a. Catnip

*Nepeta cataria*

. . . . . . . . . . . . .

PLANETARY RULER: Venus

ELEMENT: Water

ASSOCIATED DEITIES: Bast, Ceridwen, Freya, Sekhmet

MAGICAL VIRTUES: Fertility, shape-shifting,
psychic work, love, friendship, peace

## LORE

The genus name is derived from the old Etruscan city of Nepeta, and the species name, *cataria*, comes from the Latin word for cats. The French call catnip *herbe aux chats* (herb of cats). It is well-known that the bruised leaves emit a scent that is stimulating to cats, which respond by licking it, chewing it, and rolling in it. Rats, however, hate it. Before the introduction of India and China teas, it was a common herbal tea in both Britain and France.

## MAGICAL USES

Drink catnip tea or use it as incense to help with shape-shifting work or to connect with a cat spirit animal. It can also be used as a gift for your own pet cat to create a psychic bond between you. Grown near the home, planted in the garden, or hung over the door, catnip attracts good luck. To attract friendship, hang up a charm bag with catmint or use the herb in spells and incenses. You can also use it in love, peace, and fertility spells, incense, charms, sachets, amulets, and talismans. Add it to the bath or carry a herb bag containing catnip to attract love, and sprinkle it at the corners of your bed to attract a lover.

## CULINARY AND HOUSEHOLD USES

Catmint leaves and flowers make a pleasant tea. The leaves and shoots may be used in sauces, soups, and stews. Lay catmint in linen drawers to repel insects.

## COSMETIC USES

Catnip is an astringent that tightens sagging skin; use it as an infusion in the bath or as a facial wash. You can also add it to homemade creams and toners. For hair care, a catnip rinse will condition and moisturize the hair and help treat dandruff.

## HOME REMEDIES

The leaves and flowering tops are used, and an infusion aids colds, flu, and fevers, inducing sweating and reducing the temperature. The tea calms headaches of a digestive or nervous origin and is generally relaxing. It helps stomach upsets, dyspepsia, colic, and flatulence. An infusion can also be used externally to soothe scalp irritations, and a poultice of mashed leaves and flowering tops can be applied to bruises. The tincture can be used as a rub for arthritis and rheumatism. Catnip can be made into a salve for treating haemorrhoids. A catnip pillow aids sleep.

> **Caution:** *Catnip is safe for most adults in small amounts, though smoking it or excessive use may cause headaches and vomiting. It should not be taken by children, epileptics, individuals with pelvic inflammatory disease or heavy periods, or those who are pregnant or breastfeeding. Do not take it two weeks before scheduled surgery.*

# Cedar, True

*Cedrus* spp.

· · · · · · · · · · · · ·

PLANETARY RULER: Sun

ELEMENT: Fire

ASSOCIATED DEITIES: Anu, Artemis, Bel, Diana,
Ea, Isis, Jehovah, Osiris, Persephone, Sezh

MAGICAL VIRTUES: Purification, consecration,
protection, immortality, funeral rites

## LORE

True cedars belong to the genus *Cedrus* and are native to the Mediterranean and Asia Minor. Cedarwood from Lebanon (*lubbunu* meaning "incense") was highly prized in the ancient world for use as a building material and for making idols, and the fragrant heartwood was used as an incense. It is mentioned more often than any other tree in the Bible. Like other evergreens, it represents incorruptibility and eternal life. The ancient Celts embalmed the heads of their noblest enemies in cedar resin, while the Egyptians used cedar resin for the mummification process, as well as medicines, perfumes, incenses, and cosmetics.

## MAGICAL USES

Cedar is associated with power, longevity, and the immortality of the soul. The primary use of cedarwood or essential oil is in incense, which is often used in funeral rites or to purify and consecrate the working area and magical tools. You can also use an incense of the wood or ritual fumigation/sain of the burning leaves. Cedarwood chips can be used in charms for long life and growth or added to spells to increase their potency.

## CULINARY AND HOUSEHOLD USES

Cedarwood can be used as an insect repellent in clothes' drawers and wardrobes.

## COSMETIC USES

A decoction of the bark may be dabbed on the under-eye area to reduce bags and wrinkles or used as a wash to treat skin redness or itchiness. A glycerite of the young leaves, diluted with rose water, is a moisturising toner for mature skin.

## HOME REMEDIES

The oil, resin, and heartwood have all been used in traditional medicine. The plant is a strong disinfectant, and a poultice of the crushed leaves may be applied to small wounds. A salve, macerated oil, or glycerite of the leaves applied topically may aid dry eczema, dermatitis, and psoriasis. A tea of the leaves can be taken for coughs and colds.

> *Caution:* Contact with the leaves or bark can cause contact dermatitis in some sensitive people. Do not take the essential oil internally.

# Cedar, Thuja

*Thuja* spp.

. . . . . . . . . . . . . .

PLANETARY RULER: Sun

ELEMENT: Fire

MAGICAL VIRTUES: Purification, protection

## LORE

The *Thuja* genus of evergreen coniferous cedar are native to eastern Asia and North America, where Indigenous peoples used it as a herb of purification in sacred ceremonies, such as in sweat lodges and the Lakota sun dance ritual. It is one of the four sacred medicines of many Native Americans, along with sweetgrass, sage, and tobacco.

## MAGICAL USES

Cedarwood or leaves may be burned as incense or used for a ritual fumigation/sain for the purification and protection of a place or person. Add the leaves to a ritual purification bath to cleanse the aura. Burn cedar incense or essential oil in the bedroom to prevent nightmares (extinguish it before you go to sleep). Hang some above the door and windows of your home to repel negativity. Carry a little in a herbal charm bag when you need protection.

## CULINARY AND HOUSEHOLD USES

Use the fragrant, fresh twiggy branches as a besom to sweep and perfume your home. Keep some leaves in your clothes' drawer or wardrobe to discourage moths and other insects.

## COSMETIC USES

Add a decoction of the leaves to a footbath to treat sore and swollen feet.

## HOME REMEDIES

The leaves are used. For home use, it is best to stick to external applications only. Made into a macerated oil or salve, thuja may help sore muscles. The tincture may be applied to warts.

. . . . .

A decoction of the leaves can be added to the bath for the treatment of rheumatism and osteoarthritis, improving the removal of toxins and relieving stiffness. A steam of the leaves may be used for colds and flu.

> **Caution:** *Do not use if pregnant or breastfeeding. Avoid if you have an autoimmune disease or take immunosuppressants. An overdose of thuja taken internally can cause nausea, vomiting, diarrhoea, asthma, seizures, and death. Do not take the essential oil internally or use at all if pregnant or breastfeeding.*

# Centaury

*Centaurium erythraea*

. . . . . . . . . . . . . . .

PLANETARY RULER: Sun

ELEMENT: Fire

ASSOCIATED DEITIES: Chiron

MAGICAL VIRTUES: Herb-cunning, healing, protection, exorcism

## LORE

The botanical name *Centaurium* comes from the Roman writer Pliny's association of the plant with Chiron, a centaur (half man, half horse) who had been wounded by an arrow poisoned with the blood of the monstrous Hydra. He used centaury to treat his wound, and though he was never completely cured, it gave him greater insight into the suffering of others, and he became a great healer. The *erythraea* part of the name indicates "red" and comes from the colour of the flowers. It is a bitter-tasting herb, known in ancient Rome as *fel terrae*, or "bile of the earth." It was much used in classical and mediaeval times for treating digestive complaints and fevers, hence its folk name of feverwort. It was also used to counter evil spirits and witches.

## MAGICAL USES

If you are studying herb craft, centaury tea may be taken as a dedicatory drink to mark your intention towards the herb kingdom and to commune with Chiron, the patron of herbalists. Use centaury in incenses and charms in exorcism rites and to dispel negativity and to repel evil.

## CULINARY AND HOUSEHOLD USES

Centaury can be used to flavour wines, liqueurs, gins, and vodkas.

## COSMETIC USES

Use a centaury infusion as a hair rinse to treat head lice and dandruff. Add to shampoos to cleanse the hair and enhance white hair. As a skin toner, a centaury infusion will reduce the appearance of enlarged pores; it will also tighten the skin. It may fade freckles and lighten the skin.

## HOME REMEDIES

Centaury is a digestive tonic; it contains a bitter glycoside that stimulates digestive secretions. Taken before a meal, the tea is useful for dyspepsia, to stimulate the appetite, and to aid digestion. One of its folk names is feverwort: taken as a tea, it is a diaphoretic that stimulates sweat and helps break fevers. An infusion of the aerial parts may be used as a wash or compress for wounds and sores.

> **Caution:** *Centaury may cause mild abdominal discomfort in some people. It should not be taken by those with peptic ulcers or by individuals who are pregnant or breastfeeding.*

# Chamomile/Camomile

*German Chamomile—Matricaria recutita*
(syn. *Matricaria chamomilla* or *Chamomilla recutita*)
*Roman chamomile—Chamaemelum nobile*

PLANETARY RULER: Sun

ELEMENT: Water

ASSOCIATED DEITIES: Baldur, Cernunnos, Hecate, Ra, sun gods

MAGICAL VIRTUES: Protection, healing, sun, motherhood, peace, harmony

## LORE

The name *chamomile* is derived from the Greek *kamai*, meaning "on the ground," and *melon*, meaning "apple," because the scent is reminiscent of apples. The genus name *Matricaria* comes from the Latin *matrix*, meaning "womb," or from *mater*, meaning "mother," recalling the plant's reputation in ancient Europe for healing women's complaints.

## MAGICAL USES

Chamomile is a solar herb, vibrating with the sun's powers of regeneration, healing, and protection. Mindfully drink a cup of chamomile tea to absorb these energies. Put the dried flowers in your Midsummer incense or in incense used to invoke sun gods. For protection, and to prevent negativity entering your home, smear chamomile oil around the doors and windows. In the garden, chamomile acts as a guardian herb.

## CULINARY AND HOUSEHOLD USES

Make a soothing herbal tea from chamomile flowers. The fresh flowers can be frozen into ice cubes and dropped into refreshing summer drinks. The fresh flowers can also be used to make wine and mead or infused into jams. Eat the young, fresh leaves in a salad, or use them as a garnish.

## COSMETIC USES

Chamomile is good for sensitive skin prone to inflammation. Place cold, damp chamomile tea bags on tired, puffy eyes. Used as a skin wash, chamomile tea is a natural skin lightener that also fades spots and acne scarring. Use a chamomile infusion as a lightening rinse for blond hair.

## HOME REMEDIES

Chamomile tea has a relaxing and sedative effect. It has been used for centuries to aid sleep and relieve stress and anxiety. It is a gentle remedy for digestive problems, indigestion, and stomach acid. Added to the bath, it will relax tense, aching muscles and period pain. Used externally, chamomile's anti-inflammatory and antibacterial properties make it useful for eczema, insect bites, rashes, and sore, itchy skin. Gargle for canker sores and other mouth irritations. Apply a chamomile poultice to haemorrhoids.

> *Caution:* *Chamomile is generally considered a very safe herb, but people sensitive to members of the Asteracea family may want to avoid chamomile. Avoid medicinal amounts of chamomile if you are taking blood-thinning medication, sedatives, or non-steroidal anti-inflammatory drugs (NSAIDs), such as aspirin, and if you are pregnant or breastfeeding. It may interact with Ginkgo biloba, garlic, saw palmetto, St. John's wort, and valerian.*

# Cherry, Sweet

*Prunus avium*

. . . . . . . . . . . . . . .

PLANETARY RULER: Venus

ELEMENT: Water

ASSOCIATED DEITIES: Aphrodite, Demeter, Venus, Xi Wang Mu

MAGICAL VIRTUES: Love, lust, fertility

## LORE

Cherry trees symbolise eroticism, sexuality, and fertility with their luscious, red fruits. In France and Sweden, a garland of cherry branches was hung on the door of any girl thought to be of easy virtue. In Germany, a barren cow would be led around a cherry tree. However, if fertile cherry trees are auspicious, old and barren cherry trees have an ominous reputation, and even the shadow of such a tree was considered unlucky or evil. In Lithuania, an old cherry tree is home to the devil Kirnis; in Albania, evil spirits called Aërico live there; and in Denmark, forest demons hid themselves in old cherry trees and did harm to those who approached them. Fall asleep beneath such a tree and you will wake up with swollen hands and feet. In Scotland, it is a witch tree and unlucky to fell, use for any purpose, or take indoors.

## MAGICAL USES

Use cherry wood, bark, stones, and blossoms in charm bags, incense, and so on for spells and rituals of love, seduction, lust, fertility, and Beltane. Eat cherries or drink cherry wine with a lover.

## CULINARY AND HOUSEHOLD USES

Cherries are rich in fibre, vitamins, and minerals. They may be eaten fresh; made into jams, pies, jellies, ice creams, sauces, and compotes; added to smoothies or yoghurt; or made into wine and liqueurs, such as cherry brandy. They may be used to flavour alcoholic drinks, such as whisky or gin.

## HOME REMEDIES

The fruit, stems, and resin are used. The fruits are a mild laxative. They are high in antioxidants and anti-inflammatory compounds, which may promote overall health, benefit those with arthritis and gout, and reduce muscle stiffness and soreness after exercise. A decoction of the stems can be used as a diuretic and astringent in cases of cystitis, nephritis and urinary problems, arthritis, and gout. Cherry bark resin may be sucked on for a sore throat or cough.

*Caution:* Do not eat the stones; they contain toxic compounds.

# Chervil

*Anthriscus cerefolium*

. . . . . . . . . . . . . . .

PLANETARY RULER: Jupiter

ELEMENT: Air

ASSOCIATED DEITIES: Ceridwen

MAGICAL VIRTUES: Women's mysteries, immortality, ancestor contact

## LORE

The specific name, *cerefolium*, refers to chervil's powerful reputation as a brain stimulant, and even today many think that chervil is a good restorative for the elderly and those whose memory has begun to fail. The first known references to chervil come from Columella, a Roman writer on agriculture, and from Pliny. Chervil was a valued medicinal plant during the Middle Ages when it was used as a diuretic and for cleaning the liver and kidneys. Women in labour were bathed in chervil. Witches were said to use the black seeds to produce "double vision." Traditionally the herb was eaten after Lent, on Maundy Thursday, because of its restorative qualities after fasting.

## MAGICAL USES

Chervil is primarily a herb used in women's mysteries. Drink chervil tea or add some chervil to the ritual cup to commune with the divine feminine. Burn it as an incense. Chervil also reminds us of the immortality of the soul throughout the cycle of life, death, and rebirth, and it may be used to become in tune with the higher self when used as a tea or incense. Use it to contact ancestor spirits at Samhain. Chervil tea also helps to heighten your awareness and promote clarity of mind before any ritual or magical working. It may also be taken as a restorative after a period of fasting.

## CULINARY AND HOUSEHOLD USES

Chervil, a good source of potassium and calcium, has a slight anise flavour. It may be used fresh in salads, as a garnish, or in combination with other herbs (it enhances their flavour)

for soups, sauces, and meat, fish, or egg dishes. It is best used fresh. Infuse some in vinegar to use as a dressing.

## COSMETIC USES

Use a chervil infusion as a wash to purify and improve the texture of your skin in cases of acne or inflammation and to reduce lines and wrinkles. Dip some cotton pads in the infusion and apply them to sore or inflamed eyelids; use them to reduce dark circles. The crushed stems can be rubbed straight onto blemishes.

## HOME REMEDIES

The aerial parts are used. Chervil tea has anti-inflammatory and expectorant properties, making it useful for colds, flu, catarrh/mucus, and the expulsion of phlegm from the respiratory tract. It is also a diuretic and may aid the removal of toxins to benefit rheumatism and arthritis. Add a strong chervil infusion to the bath to treat varicose veins and circulatory problems. The bruised leaves may be applied as a poultice to painful joints.

> **Caution:** *To be on the safe side, avoid medicinal amounts if pregnant or breastfeeding.*

# Chickweed, Common

a.k.a. Stitchwort

*Stellaria media*

. . . . . . . . . . . . . . . .

PLANETARY RULER: Moon

ELEMENT: Water

ASSOCIATED DEITIES: Astraea

MAGICAL VIRTUES: Love, protection, balance

## LORE

The botanical name, *Stellaria media*, means "between the stars" and was given to the plant because of the tiny white flowers that nestle into the bright green foliage. Though it is native to Europe, chickweed has been naturalised in many parts of the world and long used as a medicinal plant, pot herb, and animal feed, particularly for chickens (hence the name *chick*weed).

## MAGICAL USES

Chickweed resonates with the energy of cosmic balance—of the natural law of *themis*, which comes from the gods, as opposed to *nomoi*, the laws created by humans. The plant is assigned to Dike Astraea (star maiden), who holds the scales of justice in the stars—the constellation Libra. Taking chickweed in the form of tea or food opens us up to the universal energies of the gods and cycles of existence. The star-shaped (pentacle-shaped) flowers of chickweed are gently but powerfully protective. If your cause is just (and the goddess of justice will know), use it in the form of talismans and charm bags, add it to home wards, or just carry some. Allow it to grow in your garden, which shows you respect the natural balance. To attract loving energies, carry some chickweed or bathe in a chickweed infusion.

## CULINARY AND HOUSEHOLD USES

Chickweed is highly nutritious and rich in calcium, magnesium, manganese, zinc, iron, phosphorus, potassium, and A, B, and C vitamins. It can be added fresh to salads, cooked as a leafy vegetable, or included in soups and stews. Try making chickweed pesto. If you keep chickens, they will love the occasional leafy handful of fresh chickweed.

## COSMETIC USES

A wash of chickweed infusion will relieve sore and inflamed skin.

## HOME REMEDIES

Chickweed is useful for cooling inflammations, whether internal or external. Use a poultice of chickweed or a chickweed salve to soothe minor burns, skin irritations, bruising, abscesses, ulcers, and rashes. Try adding a strong chickweed infusion to your bath to relieve itching. Chickweed tea can be drunk for colds and flu and to treat iron-deficiency anaemia, as chickweed is rich in iron. Chickweed tea is diuretic and may help relieve water retention. Chickweed is a gentle laxative, so don't over consume. Apply a cool compress to varicose veins and haemorrhoids.

> **Caution:** *Be sure to identify your plant correctly, as several other plants are called chickweed. Avoid internal use if you are pregnant or breastfeeding.*

# Chilli/Cayenne

*Capsicum annuum var. annuum/Capsicum frutescens*

PLANETARY RULER: Mars

ELEMENT: Fire

ASSOCIATED DEITIES: Alakshmi, Lakshmi, Uchu

MAGICAL VIRTUES: Shamanic travel, counter
magic, protection, love, aphrodisiac

## LORE

When Christopher Columbus sailed across the ocean, his aim was to find a better route
and a cheaper way to get black pepper, but instead he found the New World and another
culinary delight—chillies. He named them pimiento (red pepper), which still causes confusion, as they are not really peppers at all but part of the Solanaceae, or nightshade, family.
As well as eating them, the Indigenous peoples of South and Central America used chillis,
combined with hallucinogenic plants, to travel to other realms and pursue vision quests.

## MAGICAL USES

Chillies are burned with garlic or sprinkled around the house for protection, exorcism, and
counter magic. A string of dried chillies hung in the kitchen or a wreath of chillies hung
on your front door is protective. Small amounts of chilli powder (too much and your eyes
may water) may be added to protection and banishing incenses, as well as Mars and fire
incenses. Adding chilli boosts the power of magical preparations.

## CULINARY AND HOUSEHOLD USES

Add fresh chilli to curries, chillies, soups, stews, sauces, chutneys, and pickles. Chilli powder may be added to meat or vegetable dishes, pasta, and eggs.

## HOME REMEDIES

Chilli is a sialagogue (stimulates saliva), which will help the digestive process and combat bad breath. It contains a compound called capsaicin, which gives it its hot and spicy taste and is a natural painkiller. Chillies may be made into an oil or salve to relieve osteoarthritis, rheumatoid arthritis, fibromyalgia, shingles, diabetic peripheral neuropathy, and muscle and back pain. If you have a sinus headache or cold, eating chillies or drinking chilli tea will help loosen congested mucus, as well as provide a rich hit of vitamin C to boost the immune system.

> **Caution:** *Side effects of topical application can include skin irritation, burning, and itching. Don't use capsicum on damaged or broken skin. Do not use on children. Eating very hot chillies can cause stomach irritation. Do not use if you are breastfeeding or pregnant. Avoid if you take anticlotting medications, including aspirin, as capsicum may increase the effect. Avoid if you take theophylline.*

# Cinnamon

*Cinnamomum verum* syn. *Cinnamomum zeylanicum*

. . . . . . . . . . . . . . .

PLANETARY RULER: Sun

ELEMENT: Fire

ASSOCIATED DEITIES: Aesculapius, Aphrodite,
Apollo, Dionysus, Helios, Ra, Venus

MAGICAL VIRTUES: Warming, energising, love, passion,
protection, healing, regeneration, divination

## LORE

Cinnamon was known in the ancient world and is recorded in the Old Testament as one of the costly spices given to the Queen of Sheba by Solomon. Its use was essentially for spiritual purposes, and it was employed in anointing oils and incenses.

## MAGICAL USES

Cinnamon vibrates with solar energies, which are warming, energising, protective, and healing. They also aid divination. Cinnamon sticks and powder may be added to incense used in such rituals or incorporated into spells, potions, sachets, and charm bags for those purposes. When you need to end one cycle and begin a new one, add cinnamon to incense and spell formulations. Use it in charms to draw love, happiness, and money.

## CULINARY AND HOUSEHOLD USES

Cinnamon is used to flavour sweets and desserts, drinks, stews, casseroles, and curries. Add ground cinnamon to cakes and biscuits; sprinkle it on baked apples, custards, and toast. Add cinnamon sticks to mulled wine and punches.

## COSMETIC USES

Cinnamon contains antioxidants and nutrients that stimulate hair growth, plump the skin, stimulate collagen growth, and tighten loose skin. Use cinnamon in facial scrubs and hair rinses. Brush powdered cinnamon on your teeth and gums to protect against oral bacteria.

. . . . .

## HOME REMEDIES

Cinnamon tea is slightly astringent and good for nausea and diarrhoea, indigestion, bloating, and flatulence. Cinnamon contains eugenol, a natural anaesthetic, so it may be beneficial for pain management in cases of arthritis, muscle soreness, and menstrual cramps when taken as a tea. A cinnamon compress applied to affected areas may also be helpful. A natural antiseptic, sprinkle cinnamon powder on cuts and small wounds after they have been washed. For coughs and colds, cinnamon helps to dry and clear mucus from the sinuses and lungs. Taken regularly, cinnamon helps to reduce high cholesterol.

> *Caution: Cinnamon is considered safe for most people, though continued use can irritate the mouth, and skin applications may cause redness and irritation. It should not be used in very large amounts by people with liver problems, diabetics (it lowers blood sugar) unless levels are carefully monitored, individuals who are pregnant or breastfeeding, or young children.*

# Clary Sage

*Salvia sclarea*

PLANETARY RULE: Moon/Mercury

ELEMENT: Air

ASSOCIATED DEITIES: Moon goddesses

MAGICAL VIRTUES: Clairvoyance, visions, women's mysteries

## LORE

The common name is from the Latin *clarus*, which means "to clear." The genus name, *Salvia*, comes from the Latin *salvere*, meaning "to cure" or "to save." This reflects the medicinal use of clary sage. Culpeper called it clear eye, as a mucilaginous preparation from the seeds was used to draw impurities from the eye. Clary was used in the brewing industry, and as an additive to wine or beer, it was famous for making a very intoxicating drink.

## MAGICAL USES

Clary sage helps to clear the third eye and induce visions. Take as tea or wine, or use clary sage oil to anoint the third eye directly before meditation and divination. A sleep pillow stuffed with clary sage will encourage visionary dreams. Clary sage may be used in incense, anointing oil, tea, wine, or women's mysteries, particularly croning rituals.

## CULINARY AND HOUSEHOLD USES

The young leaves (the older ones become bitter) may be added to salads, soups, stews, and omelettes. You can also try coating the leaves in batter and deep-frying them. The flowers may be added fresh to salads. Use the flowers or leaves to flavour jellies, gins, vermouths, wines, and liqueurs. The leaves and flowers may be infused to make a tea, which was a popular drink in Europe before the arrival of China tea. Add the aromatic flowers and leaves to potpourri blends.

## COSMETIC USES

Clary sage contains antifungal, antimicrobial, and anti-inflammatory compounds. Adding clary sage to homemade creams and serums may help moisturise; it may also soothe irritated skin and rosacea. Used as a hair rinse, a clary sage infusion helps control dandruff and excess oil.

## HOME REMEDIES

The leaves and flowers are used. A leaf poultice will draw out splinters, and it may be applied to swellings, boils, and ulcers. Clary sage tea is helpful for stress, insomnia, and digestive problems. It is rich in phytoestrogens and useful for treating menopausal symptoms, especially hot flushes (try sipping cold clary tea if you experience one). The tea may also help symptoms of premenstrual syndrome (PMS) and menstrual cramps.

> *Caution:* Do not use during pregnancy or after consuming alcohol. Avoid if you take other sleeping herbs or medications. Avoid the essential oil if you are epileptic. It is not recommended for children.

# Cleavers

a.k.a. Goosegrass

*Galium aparine*

. . . . . . . . . . . . . .

PLANETARY RULER: Moon

ELEMENT: Water

ASSOCIATED DEITIES: Gods of spring

MAGICAL VIRTUES: Renewal, revitalisation, binding

## LORE

Cleavers has dozens of common names in different places, and most of them refer to the plant's clinging habit: catchweed; everlasting friendship; sticky buds; scratch-weed; and grip-grass, to name a few. The Anglo-Saxons called it *hedge rife*, meaning "tax gatherer" or "robber," from its habit of plucking wool from sheep as they passed by. The plant is thought to have acquired the folk name of goosegrass from the fact that geese are very fond of the leaves. During the Middle Ages, cleavers was used as a strewing herb.

## MAGICAL USES

Cleavers is very much associated with renewal at springtime. It can be taken as a spring tonic to refresh and revitalise the body after the winter. Cleavers can be added to the ritual cup and food during Ostara rites. It may also be used for divination at this time. Use cleavers in binding magic, either winding it around a poppet or written spell or putting it in charm bags.

## CULINARY AND HOUSEHOLD USES

The whole plant is rich in vitamin C. The plant's hooklike bristles soften when cooked. The young leaves and whole, tender shoots can be cooked and eaten as a vegetable or added to soups and stews. The aerial parts may be juiced as a spring tonic drink. Cleavers belongs to the coffee family, and its seeds may be roasted and ground to make a coffee substitute. A mesh can be made by overlapping cleaver shoots, resulting in a sieve for straining hot oil ointments. The roots yield a red dye when mixed with alum.

## COSMETIC USES

A strong infusion of cleavers is a good deodorant.

## HOME REMEDIES

A cleavers infusion or the juiced plant makes a cleansing spring tonic; it has diuretic properties and is good for the lymphatic system. This may benefit rheumatism in particular.
Cleavers tea may help induce a relaxing sleep. Applied topically, a cleavers infusion or oil
will help relieve itching, and it may benefit skin conditions such as eczema. A poultice of
cleavers may be applied to staunch bleeding and treat wounds, scalds, burns, sunburn, and
irritated skin.

> **Caution:** *None known, but avoid using medicinal amounts during pregnancy or if
> breastfeeding as a precaution.*

# Clove

*Syzygium aromaticum* syn. *Caryophyllus aromaticus*
*Eugenia aromatica* /E. *caryophyllata*/E. *caryophyllus*

PLANETARY RULER: Sun/Jupiter

ELEMENT: Fire

MAGICAL VIRTUES: Protection, banishing,
exorcism, love, prosperity, astral travel

## LORE

The Latin word for nail is the origin of *clove* since the buds resemble little nails and one of the primary uses of cloves in magic is in "nailing," or stopping, the effects of the evil eye, which is a very widespread belief throughout the world.

## MAGICAL USES

Clove may be used in spells and rituals to "nail" malicious magic and spiteful gossip sent against you. A necklace of cloves is protective. Clove may also be added to love potions or carried in the pocket to attract a lover. A ritual cup containing clove may be shared with friends to deepen kinship. Cloves can be added to money-drawing and good luck charm bags, and clove oil can be smeared on a green candle in a prosperity spell. Lightly ground cloves may be added to sun and Jupiter incenses and incenses of fire, love, astral travel, or prosperity and protection.

## CULINARY AND HOUSEHOLD USES

Cloves add flavour to curries, meat dishes, casseroles, and stews, and they are also used in marinades and some condiments, such as Worcestershire sauce. They are popular in desserts, often paired with cinnamon and nutmeg, and work especially well with apples, pears, and pumpkins. They are a vital ingredient of beverages such as mulled wine and eggnog.

## COSMETIC USES

Clove is a natural antiseptic and can be used to combat pimples and breakouts. Simply combine ground cloves with honey and apply to spots. Leave the mix on for 15 minutes and rinse off.

## HOME REMEDIES

Cloves contain eugenol, which is an anaesthetic and the reason clove oil is used in some commercial toothache remedies. Clove tea as a mouth rinse will aid gum diseases, such as gingivitis, periodontitis, and oral thrush, controlling the growth of oral pathogens with its powerful antifungal properties. For respiratory infections, rub clove salve or clove oil onto your chest. For arthritis and sore muscles, a compress works as a topical anaesthetic, dulling pain and acting as a strong anti-inflammatory.

> *Caution:* *Frequent and repeated application of clove oil or clove buds to the tissues of the mouth can sometimes cause damage and should never be used on children. Stay on the safe side and avoid larger amounts of clove if you are pregnant or breastfeeding. Avoid it if you have a bleeding disorder and do not take it for three weeks before surgery, as eugenol slows blood clotting.*

# Clover

*Trifolium* spp.

. . . . . . . . . . . . . .

PLANETARY RULER: Mercury

ELEMENT: Earth

ASSOCIATED DEITIES: Aphrodite, Freya, Hathor, Venus.

MAGICAL VIRTUES: Luck, visionary herb, Beltane,
faithfulness, love, fairy contact, abundance

## LORE

The word *clover* is possibly from the Latin *clava*, meaning "club." In Anglo-Saxon the plant
was called *cloeferwort* (a wort is a medicinal herb). It is wonderful for nitrogen fixation in
the soil, and clover makes good hay, hence the phrase "be to in clover," meaning abundance. Clovers generally have three leaves, and four leaves are rare, so finding one is often
considered lucky.

## MAGICAL USES

Clover may be employed in teas, wines, incenses, salves, and potions to aid access to the
spirit world. Use a clover oil, incense, or infusion in rituals and spells for increase, abundance, and prosperity. Use clover oil to consecrate your pentacle. Carry a clover for luck.
Use clover for rituals and spells of love as an anointing oil, in charm bags, or in the incense.

## CULINARY AND HOUSEHOLD USES

Red clover and white clover are both edible. The fresh flowers may be added to salads,
infused for a herbal tea, or made into wine. Freeze them in ice cubes, then drop them into
summer drinks and cocktails. Dust them with flour and fry them in oil until they are crispy
for a tasty nibble. Add the fresh leaves to salads, stews, sauces, and soups.

## COSMETIC USES

Red clover oil helps slow down signs of skin ageing, increases collagen production, and
adds moisture. Add some to homemade face creams, oils, and lip balms.

## HOME REMEDIES

Red clover flower infusions are used to treat PMS and menopausal symptoms. Red clover flower oil or salve contains calcium and magnesium, which can help ease muscle pain and tension, rashes, eczema, and psoriasis. White clover tea may be useful in alleviating fever, coughs, and colds, while its pain-killing properties make it helpful for rheumatic aches, arthritis, and gout. Cool the tea and use it as an eyewash and to soothe and cleanse wounds. A poultice of mashed white clover flowers will reduce the swelling of insect bites and wounds.

> *Caution:* Do not take medicinal amounts if you are pregnant, breastfeeding, or have hormone-dependent conditions, such as endometriosis, uterine fibroids, or cancers of the breasts, ovaries, or uterus. Individuals with prostate cancer should also avoid taking red clover. Do not use medicinal amounts if you are undergoing oestrogen replacement therapy or if you are taking antiplatelet or anticoagulant drugs, oral contraceptives, or tamoxifen.

# Cohosh, Black

*Actaea racemosa* syn. *Cimicifuga racemosa*

. . . . . . . . . . . . . . .

PLANETARY RULER: Sun/Pluto

ELEMENT: Fire

ASSOCIATED DEITIES: Crone goddesses

MAGICAL VIRTUES: Protection, courage, strength, women's mysteries

## LORE

The name *cohosh* comes from the Algonquian word for "rough." Native Americans used the root to treat snake bites and for pain management, menstruation problems, childbirth, and menopausal symptoms.

## MAGICAL USES

Also known as black snake root, cohosh root may be used in celebrations of women's mysteries, especially to mark menopause and rituals of cronehood. It can be taken as a tea, carried, or used in incense. Add cohosh to sachets and herbal charms carried for strength and courage in difficult circumstances. The powdered root can be sprinkled around a room, or across the threshold, for protection and to dispel negative influences.

## CULINARY AND HOUSEHOLD USES

The leaves can be cooked as a vegetable (see the caution section).

## COSMETIC USES

Add black cohosh root to homemade creams to moisturise, protect, and lighten the skin.

## HOME REMEDIES

A decoction or tincture of the root is used, and black cohosh root is best known for its use in combatting menopausal symptoms. It contains phytoestrogen compounds, which can help during hot flushes and induce restful sleep. Its anti-inflammatory actions may be of use in the treatment of arthritis.

**Caution:** Do not confuse with blue cohosh (Caulophyllum thalictroides), which has different properties. Avoid if you are pregnant, breastfeeding, or taking antidepressants. Do not take if you have liver problems, have heart problems, or have or have had breast cancer or other hormone-dependant cancers. Do not take for more than six months. Stop if you experience any side effects, such as jaundice, skin rash, upset stomach, dizziness, or heart arrhythmias.

# Coltsfoot

*Tussilago farfara*

. . . . . . . . . . . . . . . .

PLANETARY RULER: Venus

ELEMENT: Water

ASSOCIATED DEITIES: Spring deities

MAGICAL VIRTUES: Visions, peace, tranquillity, love

## LORE

An old name for coltsfoot was the son before the father, as the yellow flowers appear in early spring and before the leaves. The genus name, *Tussilago*, is from the Latin for cough, as coltsfoot was commonly used to treat chest complaints. The Roman naturalist Pliny recommended it for excess mucus and catarrh, while the ancient physicians Dioscorides and Galen recommended smoking the leaves for the same purpose. For many years, coltsfoot formed the basis of a British herbal tobacco.

## MAGICAL USES

Coltsfoot may be used as the base for shamanic smoking mixtures or added to incenses that promote tranquillity and induce visions. The flowers may be made into a ritual wine for the spring equinox or dried and added to incenses of Ostara and spring deities. Add coltsfoot to herbal sachets and charms to attract a new love.

## CULINARY AND HOUSEHOLD USES

The flowers and leaves may be made into a tea, and the flowers may be used to produce a lovely spring wine. Commercially available coltsfoot rock can be used for the treatment of coughs. In the past, the down that grows on the underside of the leaves was soaked in saltpetre and used in tinder boxes.

## COSMETIC USES

Coltsfoot contains anti-inflammatories, antioxidants, and antimicrobial compounds. Add it to homemade skin toners and skin washes to treat acne. Coltsfoot also contains agents that help soften and moisturise the skin when added to homemade skin creams. Use a coltsfoot infusion as a final hair rinse to strengthen the hair, fight dandruff, and prevent split ends.

## HOME REMEDIES

A tea or infusion can be made of the flowers or leaves to soothe a dry, irritated cough and to help relieve chest and upper respiratory complaints and symptoms of bronchitis. Use as an antibacterial wash when treating external wounds and insect bites. A coltsfoot poultice will soothe sores, boils, and skin ulcers.

> **Caution:** *Coltsfoot contains alkaloids, so it should not be taken long term; do not take for more than two weeks. Do not use if you have liver disease. To be on the safe side, avoid coltsfoot if pregnant or breastfeeding.*

# Comfrey

*Symphytum officinale*

. . . . . . . . . . . . . . . .

PLANETARY RULER: Saturn

ELEMENT: Air/water

ASSOCIATED DEITIES: Hecate

MAGICAL VIRTUES: Safety when travelling, healing

## LORE

The name *comfrey* is derived from the Latin *confervere*, which means "to grow together," and the genus name, *Symphytum*, which means "to unite." Both words and their meanings are references to the plant's reputation as a healer of broken bones—hence its folk name of knitbone. The grated root was used for a plaster that set hard over the broken bone. Greeks and Romans used comfrey to stop heavy bleeding, treat bronchial problems, and heal wounds and broken bones. Poultices were made for external wounds, and comfrey tea was consumed for internal ailments. It was carried by soldiers to treat wounds.

## MAGICAL USES

In folk magic, comfrey is most closely associated with protection when travelling. Put some in your shoe, place a piece in your suitcase, or hang some in your car. Add comfrey to incenses, herbal charms, or sachets for healing. Add comfrey tea to the bath and bathe in it to promote healing.

## CULINARY AND HOUSEHOLD USES

The young leaves can be eaten as a vegetable, either cooked or kept raw in salads. The dried or roasted roots can be combined with dandelion and chicory roots and used as a coffee substitute. Comfrey, when used with alum, gives a bright yellow dye. Soak the leaves in water for a few days to make a liquid feed for your plants.

## COSMETIC USES

Comfrey is rich in mucilage, which softens the skin. Add it to homemade moisturisers or use a comfrey infusion in the bath. Add to homemade skin toners to firm the skin.

## HOME REMEDIES

The leaves and roots are used, and as a poultice, it will soothe bruises, sprains, varicose veins, and mild skin irritation. Do not use on broken skin though. Comfrey has some mild pain-relieving properties, so a poultice, macerated oil, or salve may help arthritis, rheumatism, bursitis, pulled muscles, back injuries, and strained tendons and ligaments.

> *Caution:* *Comfrey contains alkaloids. Do not use medicinal amounts of the root internally, and do not use the leaves for more than four weeks. Do not give it to young children, and do not use internally if pregnant or breastfeeding.*

# Coriander

*Coriandrum sativum*

. . . . . . . . . . . . . . . . . . .

PLANETARY RULER: Mars

ELEMENT: Fire

ASSOCIATED DEITIES: Ana, Anahita, Anatu, Aphrodite, Ariadne, Venus

MAGICAL VIRTUES: Love, passion, peace, protection

## LORE

The name *coriander* comes from the Greek *koris*, which means "a bedbug," thought to be a reference to the strong scent of the leaves. The Roman naturalist Pliny described it as an aphrodisiac, and this reputation has persisted down the ages. Coriander seeds were placed in Egyptian tombs as a symbol of timeless love and passion. In Europe, during the Middle Ages, it was widely believed to provoke lust and was thus often added to love spells and potions.

## MAGICAL USES

Use coriander seeds instead of confetti at weddings and handfastings. Add to spells to incite passion or to love charms, potions, and incense. Use coriander oil to anoint candles for love magic. Coriander seeds can be included in the ritual cup at handfastings and Great Rite celebrations. Add to the handfasting cake.

## CULINARY AND HOUSEHOLD USES

Sprinkle fresh coriander (cilantro) leaves on curries and stir-fries or add them to salsas. Substitute coriander leaves for basil to make a zingy pesto. The crushed seeds can be added to curries, breads, sauces, soups, stews, pastries, and sweets.

## COSMETIC USES

With their minerals and vitamins, antioxidant-rich coriander leaves can be used as a face mask that may help minimise wrinkles, tighten sagging skin, and fight the free radicals that damage your skin. Make a paste of fresh leaves by mixing them with a little honey in a pestle and mortar. Apply the paste to the face, leave on for 15–20 minutes, then rinse off with warm water. A hair rinse made from coriander leaf tea will promote new hair growth.

## HOME REMEDIES

The leaves and fruit are carminative, meaning they are useful for bloating, gas, and indigestion. Coriander is a natural treatment for high cholesterol levels; add some coriander to your diet and try combining the fresh leaves with fruits and vegetables in your juicer.

> *Caution:* Fresh coriander leaves may cause an allergic reaction in some people. Coriander seeds can have a narcotic effect when consumed in excessive quantity, which is perhaps how it came to be known as dizzycorn.

# Cornflower

*Centaurea cyanus*

· · · · · · · · · · · · · · · · · · · ·

PLANETARY RULER: Saturn

ELEMENT: Water

ASSOCIATED DEITIES: Chiron, Flora, harvest goddesses

MAGICAL VIRTUES: Hope, fidelity, love, protection, clairvoyance

## LORE

The genus name, *Centaurea* (centaur), comes from the legend that this plant was used by Chiron to heal a wound he sustained. *Cyanus* means "blue," after Cyanus, a youthful follower of the goddess Flora. When he died, she turned him into the flower. The common name, *cornflower*, tells us that it used to grow profusely in cornfields. It was hated by farmers because the plant depletes the soil, and in the days of hand reaping, it would blunt the sickles and dye them blue, giving the plant the folk name of hurt sickle.

## MAGICAL USES

The cornflower, like the field poppy, represents the gifts of the Harvest Goddess at Lughnasa and the autumn equinox; wear garlands of cornflowers and add the petals to incenses and the ritual cup. An infusion of cornflowers may be used to bathe the third eye chakra to clear clairvoyant sight. Use cornflower in love potions and spells.

## CULINARY AND HOUSEHOLD USES

The dried flowers are added to herbal tea blends to impart a lovely blue colour. They can be added fresh to salads. They yield a blue dye and may be used to make a blue herbal ink when mixed with alum water.

## COSMETIC USES

Add a cornflower infusion to shampoos and hair rinses to treat dandruff and add shine to grey hair. Soak a pad in a cornflower infusion and apply to the area under the eyes to treat dark circles. Used in homemade skin toners or washes, cornflower will dry out excess oil and treat acne.

## HOME REMEDIES

An infusion of the petals may be drunk to aid digestion and for constipation, water retention, and nervous problems. Use as a mouthwash for mouth ulcers and bleeding gums. Use as a compress for wounds, bruises, and skin ulcers. Bathe sore eyes with cornflower tea.

> *Caution:* Cornflower is generally considered a safe herb but avoid it if pregnant or breastfeeding. Do not use it if you are sensitive to the Asteraceae/Compositae plant family.

# Cumin

*Cuminum cyminum* syn. *Cuminum odorum*

. . . . . . . . . . . . . .

PLANETARY RULER: Mars

ELEMENT: Fire

MAGICAL VIRTUES: Love, faithfulness, fidelity

## LORE

Cumin is frequently confused with caraway (*Carum carvi*), and many European languages do not differentiate between the two, which makes untangling the mythology of both difficult. In mediaeval Europe, it was said that cumin seed prevented lovers from straying. Young women gave their sweethearts bread or wine seasoned with cumin, and it was baked into the loaves of bread given to soldiers sent off to war. The plant was often featured at weddings, and it was believed that a happy life awaited a bride and groom who carried cumin seeds throughout the wedding ceremony.

## MAGICAL USES

Cumin is used in spells and rituals of faithfulness and fidelity. Cumin seeds may be baked into cakes and breads, added to handfasting or wedding food and wine, or popped into a pocket to keep a lover faithful.

## CULINARY AND HOUSEHOLD USES

In Greece and Rome, cumin seeds were used as a condiment in the same way pepper is today. Cumin seeds may be added sparingly to pickles, sausages, soups, stews, curries, stuffing, rice and bean dishes, biscuits, and cakes. Cumin is used as a flavouring agent in some liqueurs.

## COSMETIC USES

Cumin is a rich source of vitamin E, making it wonderful for the skin, combatting free radical damage, combatting wrinkles and sagging, and fading age spots. Grind the seeds, mix them with a little honey, and use as an exfoliator.

## HOME REMEDIES

Cumin may help with minor digestive problems, reducing bloating and wind with its anti-spasmodic action, while stimulating bile secretion and improving digestion. As an expectorant, cumin is useful for coughs and colds in the form of cumin seed tea or cumin honey.

> **Caution:** *Cumin is considered safe in food amounts and nontoxic in moderate doses. Allergic reactions to the herb can occur in people who are allergic to other plants in the Apiaceae family. To be on the safe side, it should not be used in medicinal doses during pregnancy or if breastfeeding. It should be avoided by those suffering from oestrogen receptor positive tumours.*

# Cypress, Mediterranean

*Cupressus sempervirens*

. . . . . . . . . . . . . .

PLANETARY RULER: Saturn

ELEMENT: Earth

ASSOCIATED DEITIES: Ahuramazda, Aphrodite, Apollo, Artemis, Athene, Ashtoreth, Athene, Bhavani, Cupid, Cyparissus, Demeter, Diana, The Fates, Freya, The Furies, Hades, Hecate, Hera, Herakles, Isis, Jupiter, Mithras, Mut, Nephthys, Persephone, Pluto, Rhea, Saturn, Silvanus

MAGICAL VIRTUES: Death, mourning, immortality of the spirit

## LORE

The cypress is named after Cyparissus, a favourite friend of the god Apollo. Having accidentally killed Apollo's favourite stag, he died of grief, and Apollo changed him into a cypress tree. The specific name, *sempervirens*, means "everlasting" and refers to the evergreen nature of the tree, its long life span (some are more than 1,000 years old), or perhaps to the tree's association with death and the afterlife. It was the custom to plant the trees by graves and to place cypress in front of a house in mourning. In Turkey a cypress planted on a grave symbolised the ascension of the soul into heaven.

## MAGICAL USES

Cypress speaks of the inevitability of death and may be used at funerals and memorial services as incense, as firewood, or in mourning wreaths. It may also be planted in memory of the dead. However, it is an evergreen and also reminds us of the incorruptible nature of the spirit. Use at Samhain in the form of incense to honour the ancestors.

## COSMETIC USES

A decoction of the cones and shoots applied to the scalp and hair will stimulate hair follicles, make the hair glossy, and help eliminate dandruff. The decoction may be dabbed on the skin to combat acne or under the arms as a deodorant.

. . . . .

## Home Remedies

The leaves, cones, branches, and essential oil are used externally only. Rub diluted essential oil on the chest to treat nasal congestion. An astringent decoction of the leaves and cones may be applied to varicose veins and haemorrhoids to tighten up the blood vessels. An antifungal footbath of a cone decoction may be used to cleanse the feet and to counter excessive sweating and athlete's foot.

*Caution:* Do not take internally.

# Daisy

*Bellis perennis*

· · · · · · · · · · · · · · · · · ·

PLANETARY RULER: Venus

ELEMENT: Water

ASSOCIATED DEITIES: Alcestis, Aphrodite, Apollo, Artemis, Belenos, Belidis, Flora, Freya, Jesus, Saule, St. Margaret, Thor, Venus

MAGICAL VIRTUES: Protection (especially for children), innocence, purity, fidelity, youth, love, spring, childhood

## LORE

Daisies bloom from spring to autumn. The common name, *daisy*, comes from the Old English *daeges eage*, meaning "day's eye," since the flower, with its yellow centre and row of white or pale pink petals, looks like a little rayed sun that opens and closes its petals in response to the light. One of its folk names is bairnswort, and it is a plant very much associated with the protection of young children and babies, often used in the form of daisy chains (necklaces of the flowers).

## MAGICAL USES

The dried flowers and leaves can be added to incenses and herbal talismans of protection, solar deities, Ostara, Midsummer, etc. Place a daisy chain in a child's bedroom for protection.

## Culinary and Household Uses

The fresh young leaves can be added to salads, soups, stews, and sandwiches. Daisy flowers make pretty, edible garnishes for salads and cocktails. Daisy flower tea has a slight lemony flavour. Pick the flower buds before they open and pickle them in vinegar; use them as you would capers.

## Cosmetic Uses

*Bellis perennis* lightens and brightens the complexion. Use as a wash, oil, or cream on age spots and uneven skin tone. Add dried daisy petals to exfoliating preparations to remove dead cells from the surface of your skin, leaving it looking radiant. You can refresh the skin of your whole body by putting the flowers in a muslin bag and dropping it in your bath.

## Home Remedies

Daisies are astringent and contain antibacterial agents. Use as a wash or salve on sores, fresh wounds, scratches, and bruises. Daisy tea may be used to treat coughs, colds, and bronchitis and will help loosen catarrh and mucus. If you have a mouth ulcer, try chewing a daisy leaf. Daisy has anti-inflammatory and pain-killing properties, and drinking daisy flower tea or rubbing on daisy salve may help in cases of arthritis, inflamed joints, and sore muscles. Daisy tea is a mild diuretic (promotes urination) and will help eliminate toxins from your body, which may help with gout, acne, and boils. If you have a fever, use a daisy compress on your forehead or drink daisy tea to promote sweating and lower the fever.

> **Caution:** *Daisies are generally considered safe, and there are no known side effects. It is wise to avoid medicinal amounts if pregnant or breastfeeding. However, some people are allergic to the daisy or Asteraceae family, so use with caution if there is any risk of a reaction.*

# Damiana

*Turnera diffusa syn. Turnera aphrodisiaca*

· · · · · · · · · · · · · · · ·

PLANETARY RULER: Pluto

ELEMENT: Water

ASSOCIATED DEITIES: Gods of love and lust

MAGICAL VIRTUES: Love, lust, meditation

## LORE

The common name comes from the Greek *damia*, meaning "to tame or subdue." In 1699, Father Juan Maria de Salvatierra, a Spanish missionary, reported that the Mexicans made a beverage from damiana leaves, added sugar, and drank it for its love-enhancing properties and its mild euphoric effect on the mind. In the 1870s, it was imported to the United States and advertised as a powerful aphrodisiac, a controversial claim that remains to this day.

## MAGICAL USES

Damiana may be added to charms and potions of love and lust. A tea of the leaves may be drunk prior to tantric rituals, sex magic, and the Great Rite. The tea can also be used as an aid to divination and meditation or to improve psychic powers.

## CULINARY AND HOUSEHOLD USES

Damiana leaves may be dried and used as a minty-tasting tea. Damiana is an ingredient in a traditional Mexican liqueur that is sometimes used in margaritas.

## COSMETIC USES

Damiana contains antioxidants and helps heal, firm, and tighten the skin. Use a damiana infusion as a skin wash, add it to homemade toners, or add a macerated damiana oil to homemade face creams.

## HOME REMEDIES

Damiana is a well-known antidepressant, relaxant, and nervine. Take the tea for anxiety, mild depression, or nervous exhaustion. The tea also has diuretic and urinary antiseptic actions, which may be of benefit in cases of urinary infections.

> **Caution:** *Do not take during pregnancy or if breastfeeding. Damiana may lower blood sugar levels, so monitor them carefully if you are diabetic. Do not take two weeks before or after surgery. Very large doses may result in seizures.*

# Dandelion

*Taraxacum officinale*

. . . . . . . . . . . . . . .

PLANETARY RULER: Jupiter

ELEMENT: Air

ASSOCIATED DEITIES: Hecate, George, Theseus, Brighid, sun gods

MAGICAL VIRTUES: Solar rituals, healing, divination, increase

## LORE

Dandelion's sunny yellow flowers bloom in late spring and are followed by the fluffy seed heads in summer. The common name comes from the French *dent de lion*, or "lion's tooth," though the name is possibly a corruption of "rays of the sun."

## MAGICAL USES

Associated with solar energies, energy, and vitality, the petals can be added to sun incenses to increase their power or used in incenses, potions, spells, and rituals for strength and healing. Drink dandelion leaf tea to enhance psychic powers; the dried flowers may be added to divination incenses. Add the fluffy seed heads to moon preparations.

## CULINARY AND HOUSEHOLD USES

The young spring leaves (the older ones get bitter) can be eaten fresh in salads, boiled as a vegetable, or infused in boiling water to make a tea. The root can be cooked like carrots, added raw to salads, or roasted and ground as a substitute for coffee. The flowers may be eaten raw, used as a garnish for salads, or dipped in batter and deep-fried. Dandelions can be added to tonic beers and wines. These beverages will aid digestion.

## COSMETIC USES

Dandelions have antiaging and anti-inflammatory properties, encouraging healthy skin cell production, evening out skin tone, and stimulating circulation. Add dandelion oil to homemade face creams and salves. Use dandelion flower tea as a hair rinse to stimulate growth or as a wash to treat large pores, age spots, blemishes, sunburn, and chapped skin.

. . . . .

## HOME REMEDIES

Dandelion is a good all-round health tonic that's rich in vitamins and minerals. The bitter leaves promote the secretion of digestive fluids, aiding digestion. Dandelion root is a safe liver herb, which stimulates bile production, and may be helpful in cases of jaundice, hepatitis, and urinary tract infections. Dandelion tea stimulates urination and may be used to treat swollen ankles and fluid retention but without the consequent loss of potassium caused by orthodox drugs. Dandelion leaf tea or dandelion coffee will aid the removal of acid deposits in arthritic joints. Rub dandelion flower oil on tense muscles and stiff joints. Smoothed on the skin, dandelion flower oil will reduce the irritation of eczema, psoriasis, acne, and skin rashes.

> **Caution:** *Avoid if you take lithium or diuretics or if you have gallstones, gallbladder complaints, obstructed bile ducts, gastroesophageal reflux disease (GERD), gastritis, or ulcers. Dandelions slightly lower blood sugar and may decrease the efficacy of some antibiotics.*

# Date

*Phoenix dactylifera*

PLANETARY RULER: Sun

ELEMENT: Air

ASSOCIATED DEITIES: Amon-Ra, An, Anubis, Apollo, Artemis, Ashur, Clio, Demeter, Hathor, Helios, Herakles, Hermes, Inanna, Ishtar, Isis, Lat, Leto, Mullissu, Mylitta, Nepthys, Nike, Thoth

MAGICAL VIRTUES: Aphrodisiac, potency, virility, love, fertility, abundance, good luck, wealth, victory, counter magic, immortality, peace

## LORE

The species name, *dactylifera*, is based on the Greek words *daktylos* (digit) and *fero* (I bear) because dates resemble fingers as they grow. Cultivated for at least 5,000 years, there are many references to the date palm in the ancient world, as well as in the texts of Judaism, Christianity, and Islam. In Mesopotamian art, the palm tree was used to symbolize Mylitta, the goddess of love and fertility. The Babylonian goddess Inanna was called Our Lady of the Date Clusters. The tree is also a symbol of immortality; the Egyptian goddess Nepthys was sometimes depicted as a palm tree with two arms, one hand presenting a tray of dates to the deceased soul and the other hand presenting the waters of life. Excavations have uncovered mummies robed in date palm leaves.

## MAGICAL USES

Pieces of dried date can be added to incenses, herbal talismans, and amulets used for fertility magic and abundance. Dates, or incenses containing dried dates, may be used as offerings in rites of any of the plant's associated deities. Use dates in funeral and memorial rites to acknowledge the immortality of the soul.

## CULINARY AND HOUSEHOLD USES

Dates are eaten fresh or dried and may be added to both sweet and savoury dishes. Fresh dates can be pressed to extract a sweet juice. Date mash ferments into an alcoholic drink called arak. The tree sap is used as a beverage, fresh or fermented, and a type of sugar can be extracted from it. The tender terminal buds may be eaten as a vegetable.

## COSMETIC USES

Used as a fruit mask, dates possess antibacterial, antifungal, and moisturising properties, which may help rosacea. An oil extracted from date kernels reduces wrinkles.

## HOME REMEDIES

Dates can be used to relieve constipation. Simply soak a handful of dates in water overnight and consume both the dates and the liquid. The same remedy may relieve a hangover.

*Caution:* None known.

# Dill

*Anethum graveolens* syn. *Peucedanum graveolens*

PLANETARY RULER: Mercury

ELEMENT: Air/fire

ASSOCIATED DEITIES: Hermes, Mercury

MAGICAL VIRTUES: Protection, communication,
mental activity, study, love, peace, harmony

## LORE

The name comes from the Old German *dilla*, meaning "to soothe," a reference to its well-known soothing effect on the digestive system but also an allusion to the belief it was soothing in general; ancient Greeks covered their heads in dill to induce sleep. Ancients believed dill would heal wounds more quickly, and Roman gladiators rubbed the plant's oil into their skin. In the Middle Ages, it was known as St. John's Eve herb, providing protection from evil spirits at the summer solstice.

## MAGICAL USES

Hang up dill to ensure harmony or burn an incense of dill to cleanse an angry atmosphere. Use dill for love spells and potions. Dill seeds can be used for spells and rituals to aid communication, study, mental clarity, magical writings, and travel, including shamanic and trance journeys. Dill is a protective herb used to counter magical attacks and negative energy; dill oil can be used to seal protective talismans, doorways, and so on. You can also simply hang the seed heads in the home.

## CULINARY AND HOUSEHOLD USES

The aromatic leaves are best used fresh with tomato dishes, soups, and sauces or to garnish sandwiches, potato salad, and coleslaw. The seeds may be used to flavour stews, sauces, breads, cakes, pastries, and pickles.

## COSMETIC USES

Dill seed stimulates the production of elastin in the skin. Use dill oil as a moisturiser. Put an infusion of dill into your bath water. Soak your hands in a dill infusion to strengthen your nails and improve the appearance of the skin.

## HOME REMEDIES

To aid digestion and prevent flatulence, drink dill seed tea. Chewing the seeds will also freshen the breath. Drink a cup of dill seed tea before bed to promote sleep. Dill tea can also relieve tension headaches.

> *Caution:* *Do not take medicinal amounts during pregnancy or if breastfeeding. Dill lowers blood sugar slightly, so if you are diabetic, you should monitor your levels carefully. Do not take dill if you are on lithium. Fresh dill can cause contact dermatitis in some sensitive people or increase the photosensitivity of the skin.*

# Dittany of Crete

*Origanum dictamnus* syn. *Amaracus dictamnus*

PLANETARY RULER: Venus

ELEMENT: Water

ASSOCIATED DEITIES: Aphrodite, Artemis,
Britomartis, Dictynna, Eilithia, Eros, Venus

MAGICAL VIRTUES: Love, aphrodisiac, protection

## LORE

The species name, *dictamnos*, is probably derived from the Greek *dicti*, the Cretan mountains where it grows (and where the god Zeus was born), and *thamnos*, meaning "shrub." The name may also come from its association with Dictynna (also called Britomartis), a goddess of mountains worshipped on Crete. She was sometimes syncretised with the moon/huntress goddess Artemis. In the Cretan dialect, the plant is known as *erontas*, meaning "love," as the pink blooms were presented as love tokens on the island, the effort of their perilous acquisition from the mountains demonstrating a true depth of feeling.

## MAGICAL USES

Use the leaves and flowers in incenses, spells, herbal talismans, and so on for protection, the invocation of the associated deities, or love and lust magic. It is traditionally given to newlyweds to ignite their passion.

## CULINARY AND HOUSEHOLD USES

Many consider the taste too medicinal for culinary uses, but the leaves and flowers can be made into a refreshing tea, and the leaves can be added sparingly to soups, sauces, and stews or used to flavour liqueurs.

## COSMETIC USES

Add a macerated oil or infusion to homemade antiaging skin care preparations. To diminish cellulite, try using the infusion with a soft brush in brisk motions on the affected area. Chew the leaves or gargle the tea for bad breath.

## HOME REMEDIES

The herb has antibacterial, antimicrobial, and antifungal properties. The tea may be used for coughs, sore throats, stomach ache, and menstrual pains. An infusion or compress may be used externally on wounds, bruises, and skin irritations.

> **Caution:** *This herb should not be confused with dittany (Dictamnus albus), a fairly common herb in northern Europe. To be on the safe side, avoid medicinal amounts if pregnant or breastfeeding.*

# Echinacea

*Echinacea* spp.

. . . . . . . . . . . . . . .

PLANETARY RULER: Mars

ELEMENT: Earth

ASSOCIATED DEITIES: Gods of healing

MAGICAL VIRTUES: Magic boosting, strength, protection, healing, purification, clairvoyance

## LORE

Echinacea is the name of a group of flowering plants native to North America. First Nations people used echinacea extensively to treat various ailments, such as wounds, snakebites, sore throats, and painful teeth. The Western tribes called it elk root, as it was believed that wounded elk sought it out as medicine.

## MAGICAL USES

Echinacea adds strength to charm bags, incenses, and spells of healing, purification, and protection. Carry a root with you when you need strength. Drink the tea to aid clairvoyance and psychic abilities.

## CULINARY AND HOUSEHOLD USES

The flowers and leaves make a pleasant tea.

## COSMETIC USES

Use a skin wash of echinacea tea as a facial toner; its anti-inflammatory and antibacterial properties may help treat acne. Incorporated into homemade creams, an infusion or macerated oil will help hydrate skin, boost collagen production, and diminish wrinkles.

## HOME REMEDIES

The flowers, leaves, and roots of Echinacea purpurea, E. pallida, and E. angustifolia are used as immune boosters and herbal antibiotics. Take the infusion or tea for colds and flu, and use the tea as a gargle for sore throats, mouth ulcers, and tonsillitis. Use a decoction of the root at the start of an infection. The tincture may be taken for urinary infections. An echinacea salve may be used on cuts, boils, and skin sores.

> Caution: High doses can cause nausea or dizziness. Some people experience allergic reactions to topical applications.

# Elder

*Sambucus nigra*

. . . . . . . . . . . . . .

PLANETARY RULER: Venus

ELEMENT: Air

ASSOCIATED DEITIES: Crone goddesses, death goddesses, dryads, earth goddesses, fairies, Holda, Hulda, Lady Elder, Venus

MAGICAL VIRTUES: Protection, honouring crone goddesses, fairy contact

## LORE

Elder's name comes from the Anglo-Saxon *aeld*, meaning "fire," as hollowed elder branches were blown through to kindle fires. The genus name, *Sambucus*, indicates a musical instrument, as the Greeks and Romans made flutes from its hollow stems. It is a tree widely associated with magic, witches, and crone goddesses, and consequently it is both treated with great caution and surrounded by warnings and taboos.

## MAGICAL USES

The blossoms are used in workings for fairy contacts, and the twigs, leaves, and berries are used for rituals associated with crone goddesses. The dried flowers make a good fixative for herbal incenses, and the berries make a potent ritual wine for the autumn equinox or Samhain. Carry the wood and twigs or hang them in the home for protection. The berry juice may be used to make a magical ink for writing spells.

## CULINARY AND HOUSEHOLD USES

The flowers are used in cordials and wines or can be coated in batter and deep-fried. The berries can be made into wine and jellies. The bark and roots yield a black dye for wool, and the leaves, when used with alum, make a green dye. The berries will dye articles purple or blue.

## COSMETIC USES

Elder flowers are used to make elder flower water, an astringent skin toner. The flowers incorporated into a cream are especially beneficial for mature and sallow complexions. They soften the skin, smooth wrinkles, fade freckles, and soothe sunburn. The Romans used the berries to make a black hair dye.

## HOME REMEDIES

The flowers and berries are used. Elderflower tea is effective in bringing down the temperature and therefore is useful when it comes to the flu and other infections where high temperature is a problem, such as measles. It also has antiviral properties and may benefit cases of bronchitis, sinusitis, and other catarrh/mucosal inflammations of the upper respiratory tract. Elderberry vinegar and glycerite have been used for centuries for coughs, colds, and flu. They can help boost the immune system and lower cholesterol, as well as benefit rheumatism and diarrhoea.

> *Caution:* Only use Sambucus nigra *as unripe berries of other* Sambucus *varieties can cause nausea and diarrhoea when uncooked. Elderberry might cause the immune system to become more active, so do not take if you are on immunosuppressant medication. Stay on the safe side and avoid medicinal use if you are pregnant or breastfeeding.*

# Elm

*Ulmus* spp.

· · · · · · · · · · · · ·

PLANETARY RULER: Saturn

ELEMENT: Earth

ASSOCIATED DEITIES: Ceridwen, Danu, Dionysus,
Gaia, Hecate, Hel, Holle, Loki, Odin, Ran, Woden

MAGICAL VIRTUES: Protection, fertility, death, underworld, transition

## LORE

In Norse myth, Odin created Embla, the first woman, from the elm and Ask, the first man, from the ash. Elsewhere, elms are associated with death and passage to the underworld. In Greek myth, Orpheus, having returned from the underworld, stopped to play his harp, and a grove of elms sprang up. In Celtic counties, elm trees guarded burial mounds. Elm was widely used for protective magic from supernatural forces. A guardian elm was often grown on Swedish farms, where twigs were fixed to clothes or horse bridles and a sprig of elm was put in the churn so the fairies could not steal the butter.

## MAGICAL USES

Elm connects the worlds of the living, the dead, and the yet to be born. Use at rituals celebrated at liminal times (initiations, death, Samhain, and dark moons), in incense, as a wand, or in spells. Elm is also used for protection from supernatural forces; a twig or piece of wood may be sewn into the clothes, carried, or fixed in the home. Add chips of elm bark to incenses of protection.

## CULINARY AND HOUSEHOLD USES

Elm bark can be ground to make flour. The ground inner bark may be used as a thickener for soups. The young leaves and developing fruits may be added to salads, and the leaves and flowers can be cooked as vegetables or added to soups and stews. The leaves may be made into a herbal tea.

· · · · ·

## COSMETIC USES

Elm bark has emollient properties that improve the softness and suppleness of skin when used in homemade creams. Use a decoction of elm bark as a rinse to treat dandruff and improve the strength and volume of your hair.

## HOME REMEDIES

A decoction of elm bark may be used to wash wounds. The powdered inner bark of the slippery elm (*Ulmus fulva*) mixed to a paste with water has demulcent properties that protect the gastrointestinal tract from irritation, which is useful in the treatment of gastritis, enteritis, colitis, and diarrhoea. It can be applied as a poultice to wounds, boils, ulcers, burns, and inflamed skin.

*Caution:* Do not use medicinally during pregnancy or if breastfeeding.

# Eucalyptus

*Eucalyptus* spp.

. . . . . . . . . . . . .

PLANETARY RULER: Moon/Pluto/Mercury

ELEMENT: Water/air

MAGICAL VIRTUES: Purification, protection, healing, dispelling negativity

## LORE

There are some 700 varieties of eucalyptus, a fast-growing tree that can reach 200 feet tall. The name means "well-covered," which is a reference to the cap that protects the developing flower. The leaves produce an oil that is released in warm weather, creating a haze in the air. Every part of the tree is highly flammable—so much so that the trees have been known to burst into flames. It is a sacred plant for Australian Aboriginals, representing the division of underworld, earth, and heaven. They use the wood to make ritual didgeridoos and the leaves and their oil for medicine.

## MAGICAL USES

A eucalyptus leaf incense or ritual fumigation/sain may be used for the purification of a home, a sacred space, or the aura of a person. Add the dried leaves or essential oil to incense burned in sick rooms or use it in healing magic, adding it to talismans and spells. The leaves may be added to herbal amulets and wards for protection and dispelling negativity.

## CULINARY AND HOUSEHOLD USES

The leaves act as an insect repellent. Hang them in doors and windows, put them in a muslin bag in drawers and wardrobes, or burn them to ward off mosquitoes. Dry the leaves and add them to potpourri.

## COSMETIC USES

Antiseptic eucalyptus leaves can help cleanse, repair, moisturise, and strengthen the skin. A wash of an infusion helps acne. In the bath or shower, eucalyptus boosts circulation—put some leaves in a muslin bag and hang it beneath the bath taps as they run or suspend it in the shower. For the hair, a eucalyptus leaf rinse will boost shine and stimulate growth.

. . . . .

## HOME REMEDIES

The leaves are used, and the oil extracted from them is a common ingredient in commercial chest rubs used to relieve congestion, mouthwashes, and cough lozenges. Add the leaves to a steam for clearing congestion from the upper respiratory tract to treat coughs, colds, hay fever, and blocked sinuses. A macerated oil or salve may be used as a rub for sore or stiff muscles, rheumatism, arthritis, and neuralgia. The infusion may be used topically to bathe wounds, burns, and cuts. It may also be used as an antiseptic mouthwash or gargle for sore throats.

> **Caution:** *The leaves, when ingested in larger amounts, are toxic. Animals eating them may suffer diarrhoea and vomiting. Stick to topical applications for home use. Handling the leaves can cause skin irritation and contact dermatitis in sensitive individuals. The essential oil should never be taken internally and always used very well diluted.*

# Evening Primrose

*Oenothera biennis*

. . . . . . . . . . . . . . .

PLANETARY RULER: Moon

ELEMENT: Water

ASSOCIATED DEITIES: Moon deities

MAGICAL VIRTUES: Moon magic, women's rituals

## LORE

Native to North America, the evening primrose is so called because the faintly phosphorescent flowers open in the evening and are pollinated by night-flying insects. The botanical name is derived from *oinos* (wine) and *thera* (a hunt), borrowed from a name given by the ancient Greek Theophrastus to an unrelated European plant said to provoke a relish for wine. Native Americans used this plant as a food staple, as well as a herbal medicine.

## MAGICAL USES

As a night-blooming flower, the evening primrose is closely connected to the energies of the moon. It may be employed in rituals and spells of the moon, and while it has no direct association with any European moon deities, like Diana, it may honour moon deities in decorations, chaplets, incenses, and other herbal preparations. It connects us to the female energies of ebb and flow and the cycles of life, and it may be used in rituals of acknowledging menopause, motherhood, and female puberty.

## CULINARY AND HOUSEHOLD USES

The whole plant is edible. The leaves can be used as a potherb when young, and the sweet flowers make a pretty garnish for salads or cocktails. The flower buds can be peeled and eaten, while the roots may be boiled and eaten like parsnips. You can even steam the young seedpods. The seeds may be used as a substitute for poppy seeds on baked goods.

## COSMETIC USES

The aerial parts can be used in infusions and poultices for the improvement of a variety of skin conditions, hence evening primrose's use in many cosmetic products. Evening primrose oil has moisturizing and softening effects, so it is often included in cosmetics such as face cream. It improves acne, eczema, and psoriasis.

## HOME REMEDIES

A poultice of the leaves and stems may be used to relieve rheumatism. An infusion of the leaves and stems may be drunk for digestive upsets and diarrhoea. A syrup made from the leaves and stems is helpful for coughs. The oil (capsules are commercially available) may help the symptoms of menopause, rheumatoid arthritis, and eczema and dermatitis. It may also lower blood pressure. Use the macerated oil on dry, flaky skin.

> *Caution:* *Evening primrose oil has a shelf life of six months or less. Do not take it if pregnant or if you are on drug or herbal anticoagulants or antiplatelet agents. It may increase the risk of seizures when taken with certain nonprescription cough and cold products, herbals, or prescription drugs for schizophrenia. It may also interfere with anti-epileptic drugs.*

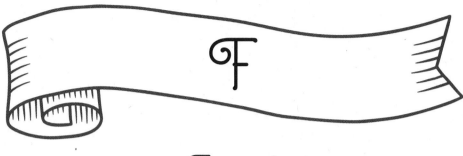

# Fennel

*Foeniculum vulgare syn. Anethum foeniculum*

. . . . . . . . . . . . . . .

PLANETARY RULER: Mercury

ELEMENT: Fire

ASSOCIATED DEITIES: Adonis, Apollo, Dionysus, Prometheus

MAGICAL VIRTUES: Protection, purification,
fertility, shamanic travel, courage, joy

## LORE

In Greek myth, the Titan Prometheus stole fire from the gods. Hiding it in a fennel stalk, he brought it down to earth for the benefit of humankind. Believing fennel seeds to promote strength and courage, Roman soldiers mixed them with their meals. Fennel is one of the sacred herbs mentioned in the tenth-century CE Anglo-Saxon Nine Herbs Charm. During the Middle Ages, people hung fennel over their doors on the dangerous Midsummer Eve to ward off evil spirits. They also pushed the seeds into keyholes, believing the seeds would stop ghosts from entering.

## MAGICAL USES

To rekindle your inner fire, call on the magic of fennel. Use it in teas, incense, oils, and talismans for spells and rituals of fertility, creative endeavour, vision quests, and shamanic travel. Fennel is a protective herb that dispels baneful influences; infuse fennel leaves in boiling water and use the cooled water as a wash to cleanse your home, sacred space, and magical tools. Use fennel oil to ritually seal doorways and windows to prevent bane entering.

## CULINARY AND HOUSEHOLD USES

The flowers and leaves can be added to salads, soups, stews, and sauces. The stems can be chopped raw into salads or added to soups, stews, and stir-fries. Fennel seeds will add an aniseed flavour to breads, cakes, pastries, soups, stews, sweet pickles, apple pie, and sauces.

## COSMETIC USES

Use a fennel seed infusion as a wash to cleanse and firm the skin, tighten pores, and reduce wrinkles. You can also add fennel to moisturising creams and lotions for similar purposes. Use fennel seed tea as a final hair rinse to treat dandruff and scalp problems. A paste of ground fennel seeds and water can be rubbed onto patches of cellulite.

## HOME REMEDIES

Drinking fennel tea or chewing fennel seeds 20 minutes before a meal aids digestion and prevents gas pains, indigestion, IBS symptoms, and heartburn. Fennel can also be used for treating coughs, sore throats, hoarseness, and catarrh/mucus in the form of tea or syrup. For sore eyes, blepharitis, and conjunctivitis, apply a fennel compress over closed eyes. A cup of fennel seed tea may ease the effects of a hangover.

> *Caution:* *Do not use medicinal amounts on children. Avoid if you have bleeding disorders, endometriosis, uterine fibroids, hormone-sensitive cancers, or take tamoxifen. Large amounts of fennel may slightly decrease the effectiveness of birth control pills. Pregnant individuals should not take fennel as a medicinal herb, though small amounts are considered safe if used in cooking.*

# Fenugreek

*Trigonella foenum-graecum*

. . . . . . . . . . . . . .

PLANETARY RULER: Mercury

ELEMENT: Air

ASSOCIATED DEITIES: Apollo, Shitala

MAGICAL VIRTUES: Increase, health, protection, banishing negativity, love

## LORE

Both the common and the botanical names come from *foenum-graecum*, meaning "Greek hay," as the plant was frequently added to hay. The cavalry units of imperial Rome took it with them to treat sick horses.

## MAGICAL USES

Utilise fenugreek in spells, rituals, and charms when you want something to increase. Add fenugreek to a money-drawing incense or oil or anoint a green candle with fenugreek oil and burn it. To attract prosperity, place fennel in sachets, charm bags, and talismans. Try adding some fenugreek to food and drink or use in spells and rituals for love. Along with attracting positivity, fenugreek also repels negativity.

## CULINARY AND HOUSEHOLD USES

Fennel seeds are primarily used to flavour curries and may be sprinkled on bread crusts. They can be roasted and used as a caffeine-free coffee substitute. Try sprouting the seeds and adding the shoots to salads.

## COSMETIC USES

Fenugreek seeds have antibacterial and anti-inflammatory properties. They are also rich in vitamin B3. Add fenugreek oil to homemade skin preparations (creams and salves); the actions of fenugreek will soften the skin and help the repair and regeneration of damaged skin cells. You can also make a facial scrub by mixing the ground seeds with honey. Use a fenugreek infusion as a final hair rinse to soothe the hair shafts and leave it shining.

. . . . .

## HOME REMEDIES

The seeds are used. Fenugreek seed tea is a mild but effective laxative. Fenugreek has soothing mucilage, and used as a gargle, it will help relieve a sore throat and hoarseness. Fenugreek contains the chemicals diosgenin and oestrogenic isoflavones; they are similar to the female sex hormone, oestrogen. Loss of oestrogen causes menopausal symptoms, and eating fenugreek and drinking fenugreek tea can help ease them. A fenugreek compress may relieve rheumatic and arthritic pain.

> *Caution:* *Fenugreek is considered safe in food amounts and in medicinal amounts for a period up to six months. Side effects may include diarrhoea, stomach upset, bloating, gas, and a "maple syrup" odour in urine. Pregnant individuals should not take medicinal amounts of fenugreek. Large amounts of fenugreek should not be taken with antiplatelet or anticoagulant drugs. Individuals who have allergies to peanuts or soybeans may also be allergic to fenugreek. Repeatedly applying topical fenugreek to the same areas may cause itching, redness, rashes, or other reactions.*

# Feverfew

*Tanacetum parthenium* syn. *Chrysanthemum parthenium/*
*Matricaria parthenium/Leucanthemum parthenium*

. . . . . . . . . . . . . .

PLANETARY RULER: Venus

ELEMENT: Water/fire

ASSOCIATED DEITIES: Danu

MAGICAL VIRTUES: Protection, women's mysteries

## LORE

Feverfew was described in the works of the ancient Greek physicians Pedanius Dioscorides and Claudius Galenus under the name *parthenium* (from the Greek *parthenos*, meaning "virgin"). This, along with its old genus name *Matricaria*, meaning "mother," denotes its use for female complaints. It was a widespread country remedy for a variety of ailments, including fevers, hence the common name feverfew. The Anglo-Saxons believed it was a remedy against being elf shot—attacked by the invisible darts of malicious fairies, which caused illness. In the Middle Ages, it was planted around houses and carried as a protection against the plague.

## MAGICAL USES

Plant feverfew near the home for protection, or include it in herbal protection talismans and wards to prevent magical attack. Smear a macerated oil around your doors and windows to keep out negativity. An amulet of feverfew may be carried to protect you when you travel. Add it to Midsummer incense and decorations. Use it in women's circles and rites of female mysteries.

## CULINARY AND HOUSEHOLD USES

Feverfew is not recommended as a culinary herb as it tastes rather unpleasant, and too much fresh feverfew can cause sores in the mouth. Sprigs of feverfew can be hung in the house to keep away insects.

. . . . .

## Cosmetic Uses

A wash of feverfew infusion can help reduce facial redness and skin irritation.

## Home Remedies

The leaves and flowers are used. A feverfew tea, a feverfew tincture, or one or two leaves eaten daily between bread (this stops irritation from the plant) can be used to prevent migraines (it won't ease the pain of migraines once they've begun). A poultice of the leaves may be applied to the stomach for colic. Feverfew tea may relieve menstrual pain and discomfort. It also has an anti-inflammatory effect and has been used to relieve the pain and inflammation of arthritis.

> *Caution:* *Feverfew may cause miscarriages, so pregnant individuals should not take it. It should also be avoided by small children and those who are breastfeeding. Chewing the fresh leaves of feverfew may result in mouth irritation and temporary loss of taste. Do not use if taking anticlotting drugs or herbs.*

# Fig

*Ficus carica*

. . . . . . . . . . . . . . . . .

PLANETARY RULER: Jupiter

ELEMENT: Fire

ASSOCIATED DEITIES: Aphrodite, Bacchus, Brahma, Demeter, Dionysus, Hathor, Inanna, Ishtar, Isis, Juno, Pan, Saturn, Shiva, Venus

MAGICAL VIRTUES: Love, fertility, sex, abundance, aphrodisiac, protection

## LORE

The fig is native to Iran, Asia Minor, and Syria, but now it is widespread across the Mediterranean. The succulent, many-seeded fruit has been valued since the most ancient times and appears in many mythologies as a symbol of abundance, sex, fertility, blessing, and protection and dedicated to a variety of gods. They were widely considered aphrodisiac.

## MAGICAL USES

The energy of the fig is nurturing and protective. A fig tree in your garden will bring luck and ward off negativity. Add figs to the ingredients of spells and charms for love and lust or workings designed to draw prosperity. Eat figs in feasts of love and sharing to benefit all present. Use a fig wand or incense containing figs in rites of fertility. Offer figs to the plant's associated deities or add dried fig to incenses used to invoke them.

## CULINARY AND HOUSEHOLD USES

Figs are highly nutritious, containing dietary fibre and a plethora of vitamins and minerals. Eat your figs fresh or dried; serve them in a salad; pair them with feta or ricotta cheese; make them into jam; add them to cakes and pastries; grill or bake them to add to savoury dishes; make them into a syrup for desserts and cocktails; or ferment them into a potent wine.

## COSMETIC USES

A fresh fig face mask (mix with honey) will help balance sebum production and reduce the appearance of wrinkles by promoting collagen production.

. . . . .

## HOME REMEDIES

Figs are used for their mild laxative and stool-softening action in cases of constipation. They can be eaten fresh or made into syrups for this purpose. For warts, apply the milky juice from a freshly broken fig stalk to the affected area. The leaves may be applied as a poultice to boils and sores. A tea made from fig leaves helps lower blood sugar. Early research shows it may reduce insulin requirements in type 1 diabetics.

> *Caution:* Skin contact with fig fruit or leaves can cause rashes for some sensitive people. Fig leaf may decrease blood sugar, so monitor your levels carefully if you are diabetic.

# Flax

*Linum usitatissimum*

. . . . . . . . . . . . . .

PLANETARY RULER: Mercury

ELEMENT: Fire

ASSOCIATED DEITIES: Arachne, Arianrhod, Brighid, Fates, Freya,
Hulda, Inanna, Neith, Norns, Thor, Uttu, weaver goddesses

MAGICAL VIRTUES: Fertility, women's mysteries, weaving magic, divination

## LORE

Flax is one of the oldest known cultivated plants. The priests of Rome, Egypt, India, Asia
Minor, and Israel wore white robes of fine, white linen. In Norse myth, the goddess Freya
was often depicted spinning, and the cats that pulled her chariot had reins of linen. At
Yule, she would travel round, and all the distaffs would be left wound around with flax. The
German goddess Hulda was said to have shown humans the art of spinning and weaving
flax into cloth. Offerings of flax continued to be made to various spirits well into Christian
times. In Russia, for example, on the Feast of St. Paraskeva, people would make offerings to
the saint of flax skeins by throwing them into a well or sacred spring.

## MAGICAL USES

Flax is associated with female mysteries, the spinning of magic, the Goddess who weaves
creation, and the Fates and Norns who weave fate, so flax flowers and thread are suitable for
all such rites. Make your magical cords or witch's ladders from flax thread, weaving in spells
as you go, weaving the thread of what is to be. Flaxseeds may be scattered on the threshold
of your home for protection or scattered around your bed if you suffer from nightmares
sent against you. Carry flaxseeds to ward off the evil eye and magical attacks.

## CULINARY AND HOUSEHOLD USES

During times of hardship, flaxseeds were roasted and used as a food. Flaxseed tea was popular in the eighteenth century.

## COSMETIC USES

Mix flaxseed powder with boiling water to form a gel, and use it as a soothing face pack that will tighten skin and soften fine lines. It can also be used as a setting gel for the hair. Flaxseed oil will soften dry skin (use medical grade only if you purchase it).

## HOME REMEDIES

The seeds are used, and they can be added to the diet to reduce high blood pressure and cholesterol. They can be mixed with boiling water to make a thick gel to use as a poultice on boils, ulcers, cuts, and inflammations. A decoction can be used for the treatment of catarrh/mucus, bronchitis, urinary infections, and pulmonary infections.

> *Caution:* Flax is unsuitable for pregnant and breastfeeding individuals, small children, and individuals with hormone-dependent conditions or oesophageal or intestinal blockages.

# Foxglove

*Digitalis* spp.
· · · · · · · · · · · · ·

PLANETARY RULER: Venus

ELEMENT: Water

ASSOCIATED DEITIES: Fairies, Flora, Juno, Mars

MAGICAL VIRTUES: Protection, fairy contact, baneful magic

## LORE

The botanical name, *Digitalis*, comes from the Latin *digitabulum*, which means "a thimble," a reference to the shape of the flowers. The common name is a corruption of "folk's glove," implying the mittens of fairies who, like the flowers, were believed to inhabit woody dells. Indeed, many of the plant's folk names emphasise its association with the fairy folk—goblin gloves, fairy's glove, fairy caps, fairy thimbles, fairy petticoats, fairy fingers, and fairy weed. In folklore, like other fairy flowers, it is unlucky to pick foxgloves or take them indoors. In Roman mythology, the queen of the gods, Juno, was jealous that her husband, Jupiter, had given birth to Minerva without a mother. When she complained to Flora, goddess of flowers, Flora slipped a foxglove flower onto her finger and lightly touched Juno on her breasts and belly with it. Juno was immediately impregnated and gave birth to Mars, the fatherless god of war, which perhaps brings us to the other side of foxglove: its association with death and darkness. Some of its other folk names tell us about its highly poisonous nature and its association with witchcraft and baneful magic—witches' gloves, dead men's bells, bloody fingers, witches' bells, and witches'-thimbles.

## MAGICAL USES

Foxglove flowers, or the dew collected from the flowers at dawn, may be used in charm bags, talismans, and spells to contact fairies—providing your intentions are pure. You can also plant foxgloves in your garden to attract fairies, and growing foxglove will protect the home and garden. Grow one near the door to repel evil influences. Use the leaves in protective talismans and wards hung around the home or carried on the person. Naturally, because of its poisonous nature, foxgloves were used for cursing and baneful magic in the past.

· · · · ·

## Home Remedies

Foxglove is highly poisonous and not suitable for home use, though it has provided a pharmaceutical drug, digitalis, which has been used for the treatment of heart failure for the last two hundred years. It was one of the few native plants to be included in the British Pharmacopoeia.

> **Caution:** *Toxic—do not ingest! Digitalis is poisonous, and symptoms include vomiting, headache, irregular heartbeat, and convulsions leading to death in some cases.*

# Frankincense

*Boswellia thurifera*

. . . . . . . . . . . . .

PLANETARY RULER: Sun

ELEMENT: Fire

ASSOCIATED DEITIES: Adonis, Aphrodite, Apollo, Bel,
Demeter, Hades, Helios, Jehovah, Jesus, moon goddesses,
Pluto, Ra, sun gods, Venus, Vishnu, Vulcan, Yama

MAGICAL VIRTUES: Purification, consecration, meditation, love, aphrodisiac

## LORE

Frankincense has been in use as a religious and magical herb for thousands of years. It was burned in the temples of ancient Egypt and at sunrise in honour of the sun god Ra. In ancient Greece, the ritual of sacrifice was opened with grains of frankincense and myrrh thrown onto the fire as a bloodless offering to the gods. It is still used today in churches and religious ceremonies around the world.

## MAGICAL USES

In incense, frankincense resin cleanses, purifies, consecrates, and raises vibrations. It may be added to most incenses but is particularly useful in purification and meditation blends; the fragrance concentrates the mind and drives away negativity. Frankincense may be used to invoke any of the associated deities, but it is particularly sacred to sun gods and may be used in all rituals to do with the sun. It is also associated with moon goddesses, and its milky tears may be used at full moon rituals. It is sacred to Aphrodite, goddess of love, and may be used in love incenses and rituals.

## CULINARY AND HOUSEHOLD USES

The resin is edible and can be chewed like gum but only if you use food-grade grains. The burning resin repels insects.

## COSMETIC USES

Add frankincense extract to creams to minimise wrinkles and to tighten sagging skin. The resin can be powdered and added to baking soda to make an antiseptic tooth powder. You can also dab this powder under the arms as a naturally deodorising talc.

## HOME REMEDIES

The essential oil and resin are used. The essential oil, however, should never be taken internally, but the resin can be—in moderation. The resin can be made into a tincture with alcohol, infused with boiling water, or infused in a carrier oil and taken to treat coughs, colds and congestion, and cystitis. Any of these mixes can also be used externally to promote the healing of wounds. The resin can be chewed like gum to treat digestive ailments. A few drops of the essential oil can be used in a steam inhalation to clear a cold.

> **Caution:** *Do not ingest frankincense if you take medication to prevent blood clotting. Do not use the essential oil internally at all.*

# Fuchsia

*Fuchsia* spp.

. . . . . . . . . . . . .

PLANETARY RULER: Venus

ELEMENT: Water

ASSOCIATED DEITIES: Fairies, Inti

MAGICAL VIRTUES: Love, fairy magic,
solar magic, blessing

## LORE

The *Fuchsia* genus consists of around 105 species of flowering shrubs and trees with numerous varieties and hybrids. Most are native to the tropical and subtropical regions of Central and South America. Imported into Europe in the eighteenth century, they soon became popular ornamental plants and assigned in Christian lore to the Virgin Mary.

## MAGICAL USES

In Europe, fuchsias are considered to be fairy flowers. To use them to connect with fey energies and bring good fortune to your home and garden, plant fuchsias or grow them in containers. Employ the flowers in love spells, charms, herbal talismans, incenses, and potions. Add the dried flowers and berries to Venus planetary incense and water incense.

## CULINARY AND HOUSEHOLD USES

Every part of the fuchsia is edible. Garnish salads with the pretty flowers, freeze the blossoms in ice cubes to add to drinks and cocktails, or candy the flowers to decorate cakes. The berries are rich in vitamin C and may be used as a substitute for most kinds of soft fruit (strawberries, raspberries, blackberries, etc.) in ice creams, jellies, jams, pies, cheesecakes, muffins, cookies, and cakes. Though all varieties of fuchsia berries can be eaten, it has to be said that some varieties taste better than others.

## HOME REMEDIES

Fuchsia has anti-inflammatory properties. Scrunch up a fresh fuchsia leaf and use it as a poultice for inflamed skin, bites, and stings.

**Caution:** *None known.*

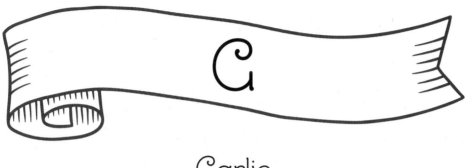

# Garlic

*Allium sativum*

. . . . . . . . . . . . . . .

PLANETARY RULER: Mars

ELEMENT: Fire

ASSOCIATED DEITIES: Aesculapius, chthonic deities,
Hecate, Mars, Osiris, Ptah, Sokar, Zeus Kasios

MAGICAL VIRTUES: Apotropaic, exorcism, protection,
healing, strength, courage, aphrodisiac

## LORE

There is a widespread belief that garlic and onions are tied to the underworld forces, death, darkness, and evil, and they are often associated with death and chthonic deities. The ancient Greeks made offerings of garlic to the witch-goddess Hecate. They believed that garlic was a powerful counter-force to the evil eye. Garlic was also used as protection from the evil attentions of fairies, demons, vampires, and baneful spirits. In Rome, garlic was sacred to Mars, the god of war, and it was thought that eating copious amounts of garlic made soldiers more courageous.

## MAGICAL USES

Garlic is a suitable offering for the underworld forces, whether to seek their protection, divine their intentions, or repel them and eliminate the evils they bring. Garlic is used as a herb of protection; ropes of garlic may be hung up in the home to ward off negativity and magic sent against you. Garlic cloves can also be added to protective charms and wards. Add garlic powder to incense employed in exorcisms or to drive out negativity.

## CULINARY AND HOUSEHOLD USES

Garlic is often sautéed with onions to form the basis of soups, casseroles, stews, curries, pasta dishes, vegetable dishes, and so on. The whole bulb can be wrapped in foil and roasted. It may be used raw when making garlic mayonnaise (aioli).

## COSMETIC USES

Strongly antiseptic, a clove of garlic may be rubbed on pimples to get rid of them. Massage garlic oil into your hair and scalp to prevent hair loss and reduce dandruff.

## HOME REMEDIES

A broad-spectrum antibiotic, garlic is capable of killing a wide variety of bacteria. Eat plenty of garlic or take a garlic aceta or electuary for coughs, colds, and urinary infections or to combat diarrhoea, stomach cramps, flatulence, and sluggish bowels. Externally, garlic can be applied to insect bites, boils, and unbroken chilblains. Taken regularly, garlic can also help reduce cholesterol and lower blood pressure. Regular use may help to regulate intestinal flora. Garlic may also help reduce the symptoms of rheumatism and arthritis.

> *Caution: Garlic is considered safe for most people, though it can cause bad breath, heartburn, and gas. It should not be applied in high concentrations to the skin as it may cause a reaction. Avoid large amounts if you are on blood-thinning medications. Garlic can decrease the effectiveness of some HIV/AIDS medications and oral contraceptives.*

# Geranium (Pelargonium), Scented

*Pelargonium spp.*

. . . . . . . . . . . . . . .

PLANETARY RULER: Venus

ELEMENT: Water

MAGICAL VIRTUES: Fertility, love, aura cleansing,
protection, happiness, health

## LORE

While true geraniums are native to Europe and frost hardy, pelargoniums, which come from the subtropical regions of South Africa (and elsewhere), are tender. Both plants were originally classified in the genus *Geranium* by Linnaeus in 1753, though, and the confusion continues today, as pelargoniums are still called geraniums. Scented-leafed pelargoniums come in a wide variety of fragrances.

## MAGICAL USES

Pelargoniums can be employed in spells, incenses, talismans, oils, and potions to bring about happiness, prosperity, and fertility. For love magic, add the dried leaves and petals to incenses, spells, talismans, and sachets. Add to Venus and water incenses. Scented pelargonium leaves and oil can be used to make protection oils and charms.

## CULINARY AND HOUSEHOLD USES

The flowers and leaves of scented pelargoniums can be eaten, though some smell better than they taste; the rose-, lemon-, and mint-scented pelargoniums are the varieties most commonly used for culinary purposes. Like other scented ingredients, use only small amounts or the taste will be unpleasant. The leaves make a pleasing herbal tea. Incorporate the leaves in cakes, jellies, fruit punches, syrups, iced tea, herb butter, baked puddings, pie toppings, cookies, rice dishes, cobblers and fruit crumbles, cheesecakes, sorbets, and ice cream, or just use them as a garnish. The leaves can also be macerated in wine overnight or infused in gin or vodka for 5–7 days. Candy the flowers and use them to decorate cakes.

## COSMETIC USES

Rose-scented geranium is especially moisturising, and it is beneficial for mature skin, dry skin, acne, and dry eczema. Use it in the form of a wash, oil, or cream. To make a natural deodorant, dry and powder the leaves, combine them with baking soda (bicarbonate of soda), and apply the mix beneath your armpits.

## HOME REMEDIES

An infusion may be added to the bath to treat cellulite, water retention, and stiff or sore muscles. To treat chilblains, add it to a footbath. For a headache, soak a cloth in a cooled infusion and apply it to the forehead or drink a cup of rose-scented pelargonium tea. The leaves have an antibacterial action, helping to soothe itchiness. If you are bitten by an insect or scratched while gardening, simply crush a leaf and press it on the affected area.

> *Caution:* *There have been some rare cases of contact dermatitis with scented-geraniums (pelargoniums) or rose geranium essential oil. To be on the safe side, do not use medicinal amounts of any scented geranium if you are pregnant or breastfeeding, and do not consume the coconut-scented geranium (Pelargonium grossularioides) at all if you are pregnant—it had historic use as an abortifacient.*

# Ginger

*Zingiber officinale*

. . . . . . . . . . . . . . . . .

PLANETARY RULER: Mars

ELEMENT: Fire

MAGICAL VIRTUES: Energy, passion, love, lust, protection, courage

## LORE

According to traditional Chinese medicine, ginger restores yang, or hot energy, which includes sexual energy. Ginger has been widely used as an aphrodisiac since ancient times. The Greeks, Romans, and even the mediaeval abbess Hildegard of Bingen believed it excited male sexual arousal. In ancient India, people ate ginger as a spiritual cleanser, the sweet smell of the root on the breath making them acceptable to the gods.

## MAGICAL USES

Ginger galvanizes all acts of magic; add it to any spells, rituals, incenses, charms, and talismans you want to accelerate and make stronger in action. Eat ginger before ritual as an act of purification and to increase spiritual energy. Use ginger for tantric rituals and spells of lust, passion, and love. Use ginger oil to seal talismans of protection. Incorporate powdered ginger into protection charms and incense.

## CULINARY AND HOUSEHOLD USES

For cooking, ginger may be used fresh, powdered, or preserved in the form of candied ginger. Its warm, spicy taste makes it good in sweet dishes such as cakes and gingerbread, savoury dishes such as curry, drinks such as ginger beer, and some pickles.

## COSMETIC USES

Ginger invigorates the skin, improves its elasticity, and helps even out skin tone. Use a regular ginger and honey face mask. To treat thinning hair, stimulate scalp circulation by massaging your scalp with diluted ginger oil. Use ginger tea as a final hair rinse. Add ginger to a body scrub to combat cellulite and improve blood flow to the skin.

. . . . .

## HOME REMEDIES

Ginger tea can be sipped for nausea and diarrhoea, motion sickness, indigestion, wind, and irritable bowels. Ginger is a powerful anti-inflammatory and has some pain-killing properties; apply it as a compress, salve, or oil for osteoarthritis and rheumatoid arthritis, bursitis and tendonitis, and muscle aches and sprains. Ginger tea loosens phlegm and helps clear mucus from the throat when dealing with colds and flu. For a sore throat, gargle with ginger tea.

> **Caution:** *Natural ginger is considered safe for most people. However, if you have acid reflux, it may exacerbate symptoms. Large amounts of ginger should be avoided by those with gallstones.*

# Ginseng

*Panax* spp.

. . . . . . . . . . . . . .

PLANETARY RULER: Sun

ELEMENT: Fire

MAGICAL VIRTUES: Strength, power, energy,
sexual potency, lust, love, protection

## LORE

Ginseng refers to the roots of plants in the *Panax* genus. The name *Panax* means "all-healing" in Greek, and the plant has been used in Asian and Native American traditional medicine for hundreds of years. Like the mandrake, the roots often resemble a human being, marking them out as something magically potent.

## MAGICAL USES

The energy of ginseng is fortifying, restoring both physical and spiritual energy. It can be taken as a tea when you feel depleted of either of these. Add ginseng to spells and potions to give them an extra boost and add it to herbal charm bags to increase their power. You can also carry a piece of the root when you need to draw on its strength and protection. Ginseng has a reputation as an aphrodisiac; drink the tea or use the root in spells of love and lust.

## CULINARY AND HOUSEHOLD USES

The fresh roots can be eaten raw, steamed, added to stir-fries, or made into tea. Powdered *Panax* ginseng may be added to cooked foods or beverages.

## COSMETIC USES

*Panax* ginseng is great for your skin. It reduces wrinkles, puffiness, and inflammation; boosts elasticity and collagen production; and generally brightens the skin. Add the powder to face packs or the extract to homemade oil serums and face creams.

## Home Remedies

*Panax* ginseng root tea (or commercially available capsules and extract) may help reduce damaging inflammation in the body. Compounds in ginseng such as ginsenosides and compound K help protect the brain from free radical damage and may help boost cognitive function and mood. Some find that *Panax* improves symptoms of erectile dysfunction in men and sexual desire in post-menopausal women. Taking *Panax* boosts the immune system and helps reduce incidents of colds and flu. It may reduce fatigue by increasing energy production in cells.

> **Caution:** Panax ginseng should not be confused with Eleuthero (*Siberian ginseng*), as they cannot be used interchangeably. Panax *should not be used if pregnant or breastfeeding, given to small children, or consumed by those with hormone-dependant cancers. Do not take with antipsychotic drugs or antiplatelet or anticoagulant drugs. Do not take for more than six months. Do not use if you have an autoimmune condition.*

# Goldenrod

*Solidago* spp.

. . . . . . . . . . . . . .

PLANETARY RULER: Venus

ELEMENT: Air

ASSOCIATED DEITIES: Gods of abundance

MAGICAL VIRTUES: Luck, prosperity, money drawing, love

## LORE

The genus name comes from the Latin *solida*, meaning "to make whole," referring to its use as a medicine; the Chippewa called it *gizisomukiki*, which means "sun medicine." Its medicinal properties and sunny golden flowers make it a very lucky and beneficent plant in folklore, and when the yellow flowers suddenly bloom near a house, the inhabitants are said to have good luck. Even better, if an abundance of goldenrod appears, there may be hidden treasure nearby. In England, the stiff stem of the plant was used as a divining rod to detect this treasure, but it was only successful if the right person used it.

## MAGICAL USES

Grow goldenrod in your garden to attract luck and prosperity. Use the flowers in spells, herbal charms, and so on to draw money to you. The stiff stem may be used as a wand in spells and rituals of prosperity and abundance. Add the leaves and flowers to love-drawing incenses and spells.

## CULINARY AND HOUSEHOLD USES

Young goldenrod leaves are edible. After the Boston Tea Party, when the rebellious American colonists dumped all the imported tea into Boston Harbor, they found that an excellent substitute could be made from the leaves of North American goldenrod. They named it liberty tea, which has a mild aniseed flavour.

## Cosmetic Uses

Use a goldenrod rinse to treat dandruff. Use a goldenrod wash or vinegar as a skin toner to reduce enlarged pores.

## Home Remedies

The aerial parts are used. Taken internally, a goldenrod infusion is a valuable diuretic for urinary tract disorders, such as cystitis. Goldenrod has antifungal properties; use an infusion as a douche for vaginal thrush and as a mouthwash for oral thrush. Gargle the tea for sore throats (or just chew the leaves), or take the tea to combat allergic rhinitis. Topically, a tincture or infusion can be used to wash wounds to prevent infection and speed healing.

> *Caution:* *Be careful with your plant identification, as goldenrod resembles some toxic plants. Goldenrod should not be taken by those with high/low blood pressure, heart disease, or osteoporosis.*

# Gooseberry

*Ribes uva-crispa* syn. *Ribes grossularia*

· · · · · · · · · · · · ·

PLANETARY RULER: Moon/Venus

ELEMENT: Water

ASSOCIATED DEITIES: Arianrhod, Brighid

MAGICAL VIRTUES: Fertility, release, change, ancestral wisdom

## LORE

No one really knows why this plant is called gooseberry. It may come from serving a sauce of the berries with goose or be from the Old Norman *groses* or *grosier*, meaning "redcurrant." Alternately, it may derive from the German *Krausbeere*, which comes from *krus* (curl), referring to the curl of the flower petals. Indeed, it was formerly called feaberry, dewberry, and wineberry too. It is sometimes given as the sacred tree I*phin* in the Irish ogham alphabet, and the 1390 CE In *Lebor Ogaim* called it "the sweetest of woods" and "most wonderful of tastes."[1] Not surprisingly, it is surrounded by folklore, ranging from the idea of children being found under gooseberry bushes to the curing of warts by pricking them with a sharp gooseberry thorn and passing it through a wedding ring. To dream of luscious, ripe gooseberries is lucky—unless you are a sailor, when it means danger on your next voyage.

## MAGICAL USES

Sacred to both Arianrhod and Brighid, gooseberry may be used in rituals, charms, and spells of female fertility or as offerings to the goddesses who protect and oversee the cycles of women. The thorns of gooseberries may be used to prick poppets or to transfer disease, grief, and grievances away from the body. Take gooseberry wine to connect to ancestral wisdom.

---

1  Folkard, *Plant Lore, Legends and Lyrics.*

## CULINARY AND HOUSEHOLD USES

Unripe gooseberries are used to make a tart sauce to accompany oily fish. Ripe gooseberries may be made into jams and jellies, baked in pies, and whipped up with cream and milk to make gooseberry fool. I find gooseberry wine is delicious.

## COSMETIC USES

Gooseberries are a rich source of vitamin C and antioxidant-rich compounds. Use a gently cleansing fresh-fruit mask to leave your skin looking revitalised and rejuvenated. This is especially good for oily skin. Add gooseberry tincture to shampoos to cleanse the scalp and help strengthen the hair. A wash of a gooseberry leaf infusion is astringent and may be used as a skin toner.

## HOME REMEDIES

The fruit and leaves are used. The stewed fruit is a gentle laxative, making it useful in cases of constipation. Topically, a leaf infusion may be used to wash and treat wounds.

*Caution:* None known.

# Gorse

a.k.a. Furze

*Ulex europaeus*

. . . . . . . . . . . . . . .

PLANETARY RULER: Sun/Mars

ELEMENT: Fire

ASSOCIATED DEITIES: Lugh, spring goddesses, Thor

MAGICAL VIRTUES: Love, fertility, luck, protection, health

## LORE

According to folklore, when the gorse is in flower, kissing is in season (i.e., most of the year!). A gorse branch was traditionally added to a bride's bouquet for luck and fertility. It is a symbol of good fortune and fecundity for its abundant, long-lived blossoms. Moreover, when burned to the ground in autumn, it comes back even stronger in spring, demonstrating its potent life force. It was thrown onto the Midsummer fires, and blazing branches were carried round the herd to bring health and luck to the animals. In Wales a sprig of gorse is considered a protection against witches.

## MAGICAL USES

The energy of gorse is hope and positivity. The tea or flower essence is useful if you are depressed, helping you to find your true path and the energy and personal strength needed to take positive action. Use the flowers for decorations and incense at Ostara, Midsummer, and Lughnasa and for spring goddesses and the god Lugh. You can colour decorative Ostara eggs with a gorse flower infusion. A sprig of gorse blossoms is protective and a good luck gift. Use them in bridal bouquets to confer great fortune. The flowers may be used as a purifying agent, taken as a tea, used as a ritual wash, or scattered in the ritual bath.

## CULINARY AND HOUSEHOLD USES

The flowers are edible. They make one of the best country wines and were once used to flavour whiskey (try infusing them in spirits for a couple of days). The flower buds can be pickled like capers, baked in cakes, added to salads, or used for decoration. A tea can be made from the flowers or shoot tips. The sharp spines of gorse were once used as a comb for cleaning wool. A yellow dye is obtained from the flowers.

## COSMETIC USES

Used as an astringent wash, gorse has a skin-firming and tightening effect.

## HOME REMEDIES

Though used in folk medicine for coughs, sore throats, and jaundice, gorse plays little part in modern herbalism.

> *Caution:* Do not overconsume the flowers, as the plant contains slightly toxic alkaloids. The long pods and dark seeds are not edible whether they are raw or cooked.

# Grapevine

*Vitis vinifera*

. . . . . . . . . . . . . . . .

PLANETARY RULER: Moon

ELEMENT: Water/earth

ASSOCIATED DEITIES: Bacchus, Bona Dea, Dionysus,
Hathor, Juno, Liber, Libera, Maron, Meditrina, Orthosia,
Osiris, Priapus, Rhea, Satyrs, Silvanus, Three Graces

MAGICAL VIRTUES: Fertility, rouses magical powers,
prediction, divine ecstasy, immortality

## LORE

All plants that had the ability to change consciousness were considered sacred in antiquity.
Moreover, the vine grows in a spiral pattern, which is a very ancient symbol of immortality. The natural fermentation of grapes must have seemed magical. The Greek god of wine
Dionysus (Roman Bacchus) was a death and resurrection vegetation god who defied the
social order, broke taboos, and gained knowledge through divine madness. Wine was seen
as his blood.

## MAGICAL USES

Wine plays a part in many magical rituals; it is drunk as the blood of the God, which
imparts divine consciousness, and used as a libation to the gods and spirits. Grapes are
a symbol of immortality through death and resurrection, and they are offered at rituals/
sabbats with this theme, including funerals. They are symbols of fertility and plenty, and
they may be planted in the garden, placed on the altar, and used in spells, talismans, and so
on to attract the same. Dried grape leaves or raisins may be added to incenses to invoke the
plant's associated deities.

## CULINARY AND HOUSEHOLD USES

Grapes contain many vitamins and minerals and make a healthy snack. They can be
blended into smoothies, used to make jam and vinegar, and added to breakfast yoghurt or

oats, salads, and desserts. They can be juiced for a refreshing drink, or dried to make raisins. Vine leaves may be stuffed with rice and other fillings and baked. And, of course, grapes are used to make wine!

## Cosmetic Uses

Crushed grapes can be used as an antiaging fresh-fruit face mask that contains valuable antioxidants and alpha hydroxy acids. Use it to get rid of minor acne and other blemishes. The commercially available grapeseed oil is a component in many beauty preparations.

## Home Remedies

Grapes contain the antioxidant resveratrol, which may protect against cancer, reduce cholesterol, lower blood pressure, improve the memory, and protect the eyesight. In addition, grapes contain anti-inflammatory compounds that help protect against chronic diseases. A handful of grapes is rich in fibre and may ease constipation. Grapes also contain the hormone melatonin, so a few grapes before bed may help you sleep. They are a good source of potassium, which helps balance fluid in the body and lower high blood pressure.

*Caution:* None known.

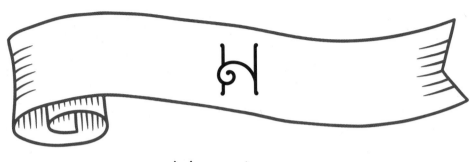

# Hawthorn

*Crataegus monogyna*

PLANETARY RULER: Mars

ELEMENT: Fire

ASSOCIATED DEITIES: Blodeuwedd, Cardea, Creiddylad,
Fairies, Flora, Hymen, Maia, Olwen, Thor

MAGICAL VIRTUES: Marriage, love, exorcism, protection, warding

## LORE

Hawthorn is a renowned magical plant surrounded by taboos. It is said to be unlucky to take the flowers indoors, except on May Day, and cutting down a hawthorn will result in the death of cattle. When the oak, ash, and thorn grow together, it is a favourite haunt of the fairies. Hawthorn branches drive off evil spirits, witches, ghosts, vampires, and lightning. In Greece and Rome, it was the marriage wood, providing wedding garlands and torches.

## MAGICAL USES

At Beltane, the sacred marriage of the Lord and Lady, use it in the incense, chaplets, wine, or decorations. It may be used at handfastings and weddings. Use the wood for warding magic, in protection amulets, for rituals of exorcism, and in protection oils and incense. Use the flowers for fairy magic and fairy contact.

## CULINARY AND HOUSEHOLD USES

The leaves are good in a salad, and the berries can be made into jams and jellies, fruit leather, relishes, sauces, and vinegars. The flowers or berries can be made into wine, and a liqueur can be made from hawthorn buds and brandy. In War World II, the berries were ground up and used to bulk out bread flour. Dry the fruits and mix them with your breakfast porridge or muesli.

## COSMETIC USES

A wash made from an infusion of hawthorn leaves is mildly astringent and can be used as a skin toner to treat oily skin or acne and inflammatory skin diseases. It can also be used as a final rinse for greasy hair.

## HOME REMEDIES

Herbalists use hawthorn to increase the flow of blood to the heart muscles, reducing the symptoms of angina, improving the heart rate, and lowering blood pressure. This can help with circulatory problems, such as Raynaud's disease, and may also help to improve poor memory by improving the circulation of the blood to the brain. In addition, it is used to treat nervous conditions like insomnia and nervous diarrhoea, aid digestion, and lower LDL (bad) cholesterol.

> **Caution:** *It is considered safe for most adults when used at the recommended dose short term (four months). In some individuals it can cause nausea, stomach upset, headache, dizziness, palpitations, and insomnia. It should not be used by individuals who are pregnant or breastfeeding. It can interact with prescription drugs for heart problems.*

# Hazel

*Corylus avellana*

. . . . . . . . . . . . . . .

PLANETARY RULER: Mercury

ELEMENT: Air

ASSOCIATED DEITIES: Aengus, Arianrhod, Artemis, Asclepius,
Bacchus, Boann, Chandra, Connla, Daphne, Demeter, Diana,
Donar, Fionn, Hecate, Hermes, Lleu, Llew, Lugh, Mac Coll,
Manannan, Mercury, Odin, Ogma, Taliesin, Thor, Woden

MAGICAL VIRTUES: Peace, wisdom, fertility, protection, luck

## LORE

Hazel, as a symbol of authority and wisdom, provided the wand or staff for several deities.
The Greek god Hermes, for example, carried a winged hazel wand (caduceus), which had
the power of filling human hearts with peace, and the wand of Asclepius, god of medicine,
was hazel. The priests of the goddess Demeter carried hazel staffs, and Irish heralds carried
hazel wands to denote their mandate. In folklore, hazelnuts are associated with fertility,
luck, and protection. A good nut year is thought to be a bonus year for babies. As the saying
goes, "Plenty of nuts, plenty of cradles." Devon brides were greeted by an old woman offering a gift of hazelnuts. At Roman weddings, hazelnuts were burned for luck. In England,
three hazel pins driven into a wall protect a home from fire.

## MAGICAL USES

Hazel provides the wood most used for magic wands, and it should be cut from a one-year-
old tree using a new knife. Forked hazel twigs make the ideal divining rods to search for
water and hidden treasure. A divining rod should be cut at the summer solstice or on Twelfth
Night. The nuts may be used in fertility spells and charm bags. You can also carry hazelnuts
in your pocket for luck. According to English folklore, if you find a double hazel (two nuts
in one shell), it brings riches. Hazel protects against bewitchment; carry a hazel twig on your
person or in your vehicle. Beat the bounds of your property with hazel branches to drive out

negativity and protect them. Fasten a hazel cross on the house wall or stable. Place a hazel cross on the hearth ashes. At the autumn equinox, use hazelnuts in the cakes.

## CULINARY AND HOUSEHOLD USES

Hazelnuts can be eaten raw, cooked, ground into flour, pounded into nut butter, or liquidised into nut milk. A commercially available hazelnut oil is available. A frayed hazel twig makes a good natural toothbrush. A fresh nut can be rubbed onto wood as a furniture polish.

## COSMETIC USES

The finely ground nuts can be used in face masks and facial scrubs.

## HOME REMEDIES

Hazelnuts are a natural food source and are rich in potassium, phosphorus, magnesium, copper, protein, and unsaturated fatty acids. They can be powdered and mixed with honeyed water and drunk to help a chronic cough. Pepper can be added to the mixture to draw mucus from the sinus passages.

*Caution:* *None known unless you have a nut allergy.*

# Heather

a.k.a. Ling

*Calluna vulgaris*

. . . . . . . . . . . . . . . . .

PLANETARY RULER: Venus

ELEMENT: Water

ASSOCIATED DEITIES: Aphrodite Erycina, Astarte, Attis,
bee goddesses, Butes, Cybele, Dana, Isis, Nechtan Mac Labraid,
Osiris, goddesses of high summer, Uroica, Venus Erycina

MAGICAL VIRTUES: Fairy contact, protection, luck, money, death and
mourning, regeneration, resurrection, community harmony, initiation

## LORE

The genus name, *Calluna*, comes from the Greek meaning "to sweep," since heather twigs
were commonly used to make brooms and besoms and often credited with magical powers
of protection. Because heather could survive the annual heath burnings that used to take
place, it was a plant symbolic of regeneration and resurrection. Naturally growing white
heather is very rare, making finding some lucky.

## MAGICAL USES

Heather is a plant of regeneration and renewal, of life through death and initiation. It contains the power of fire, which transforms, purifies, and renews. Utilise heather in wines,
teas, incenses, and anointing oils. Burn heather to clear negativity, and use a heather broom
to sweep negative influences away. Carry heather when you need protection. Plant heather
around the garden to attract friendly spirits.

## CULINARY AND HOUSEHOLD USES

Heather flowers can be infused in honey or made into herbal syrups, both of which can be
used to flavour baked goods. A pleasant tea can be made from the flowering stems. Common heather is used as a flavouring agent for beer and wine.

## COSMETIC USES

Heather is cleansing, detoxifying, disinfecting, anti-inflammatory, nourishing, conditioning, and soothing for the skin. Heather tea makes a good tightening and cleansing face wash. You can also grind dried heather flowers and mix them with a little honey and water to make a skin exfoliator. Put heather flowers in a muslin bag and use it in the shower as an exfoliating skin scrub. Heather has a mild bleaching effect; apply pads soaked in a weak heather tea to the under-eye area for dark circles.

## HOME REMEDIES

Heather tea is a urinary antiseptic that disinfects the urinary tract and mildly increases urination. A heather salve or macerated heather oil can be rubbed on the affected parts in cases of rheumatism, gout, arthritis, and chilblains. A heather infusion poured into a warm bath helps joint problems. Heather tea is mildly sedative and useful for insomnia and nervous exhaustion. Dip a compress in a heather infusion and apply it to the forehead to relieve headaches.

> *Caution:* To be on the safe side, avoid medicinal amounts if pregnant or breastfeeding.

# Holly

*Ilex* spp.

. . . . . . . . . . . . . .

PLANETARY RULER: Saturn/Mars

ELEMENT: Fire

ASSOCIATED DEITIES: Bacchus, Cailleach Bheur, Christ, Dionysus, Frau Holle, Freya, Holda, Holde, Lugh, Mars, Saturn, Tannus, Taranis, Thor

MAGICAL VIRTUES: Protection, fire magic, immortality, endurance, strength

## LORE

Any plant that bears fruit in the winter seemed especially magical to northern Europeans. Holly was used for decoration at the Roman Saturnalia (winter solstice), which is a tradition that continues to this day with the modern Christmas. Many superstitions accompany the Yuletide holly; it is unlucky to bring it into a house before Christmas Eve or to allow it to remain after Twelfth Night. The wood and prickly leaves were considered to offer protection from bewitchment and evil spirits.

## MAGICAL USES

Holly plays an important part in the Yule ritual and is used as decoration, wands, and firewood. It represents the persistence of life—and the God—through the death time of winter. Its kindling at this time is sympathetic magic for the renewal of the sun. Holly is a tree of fire magic (the waxy wood burns hot), so it was accordingly called *tinne* (fire) in the Irish Ogham tree alphabet, from which we get our word *tinder*. For the kindling of a sacred fire, holly can be used as a drill in the fire bow. For protection against lightning, bewitchment, and evil spirits, plant a holly tree near the front door, place holly branches and leaves in the windows, or use a holly wand to banish those malevolent forces. A sprig in the bedroom protects against nightmares.

## CULINARY AND HOUSEHOLD USES

The leaves are edible. They contain caffeine and were used during World War II as a coffee substitute. A tea can be made from some varieties, including English holly (*Ilex aquifolium*)

and American holly (*Ilex opaca*). The latter was popular during the American Civil War. The flowering stalks give soups and stews an aromatic flavour. Branches of holly were latterly used to sweep chimneys.

## COSMETIC USES

An infusion of European holly leaves or flowers is hydrating and conditioning for the skin. Use it as an anti-inflammatory toner, or use it for the water part of a homemade cream.

## HOME REMEDIES

Holly is not commonly used by modern herbalists. Holly leaf tea has a weak diuretic effect. Tea from American holly may be drunk for colds and flu or used as an external wash or compress for sores and itching.

Caution: *The berries are poisonous and should not be consumed.*

# Honeysuckle

*Lonicera* spp.

. . . . . . . . . . . . . . .

PLANETARY RULER: Jupiter

ELEMENT: Earth

ASSOCIATED DEITIES: Ceridwen, fairies, Pan

MAGICAL VIRTUES: Binding, protection, love, lust, counter magic

## LORE

Honeysuckle climbs by winding itself clockwise around trees, fences, or other supports in order to ascend, giving it its folk name of woodbind. Its winding and binding habit made it a symbol of constancy, devotion, and the bonds of love or even of erotic desire. The plant was very much tied to witchcraft, and it was seen as a tool that protected against the attentions of evil witches and as a herb used by them. Honeysuckle is commonly used in binding spells, which shouldn't come as a surprise.

## MAGICAL USES

Honeysuckle flowers follow the path of the sun from east to west during the day, turning towards it. Using the energy of honeysuckle, in the form of tea, wine, or flower essence, helps us connect to the cycles of life and to accept change. For protection, grow honeysuckle around your door, carry some in a herbal amulet, or add it to protection incense and oil. The stems are used in binding spells; you can wrap them around an image of a person you wish to stop from doing you further harm.

## CULINARY AND HOUSEHOLD USES

The flowers are edible and can be made into tea, used as an edible garnish, or made into syrup (use poured on desserts, on ice cream, or in drinks). The flowers can also be used to flavour gin or be made into wine.

## Cosmetic Uses

The flowers are used. They have antibacterial and anti-inflammatory properties, which are used to treat inflamed skin. Use it in the form of a cream or oil. Honeysuckle oil can be warmed and used as a treatment for dry flyaway hair.

## Home Remedies

The flowers contain salicylic acid (like aspirin) and have pain-killing and anti-inflammatory properties. Take honeysuckle flower tea for headaches or make a stronger infusion and pour it into the bath for rheumatism and arthritis. Make a glycerite or syrup for coughs, colds, sore throats, and catarrh/mucus. To use honeysuckle as an antiseptic first aid treatment for bites and stings, crush up some flowers, apply them directly to the affected area, and cover with a clean cloth.

> **Caution:** *Most varieties of honeysuckle berries, stems, and leaves are slightly toxic and will upset the gastrointestinal tract if consumed in sufficient amounts. Skin contact with honeysuckle can cause a rash in sensitive people. To be on the safe side, avoid medicinal quantities of honeysuckle if pregnant or breastfeeding and for two weeks before surgery.*

# Hop

*Humulus lupulus*

PLANETARY RULER: Mars

ELEMENT: Air

ASSOCIATED DEITIES: Ceridwen, Cernunnos,
Hel, Inanna, Leto, underworld deities

MAGICAL VIRTUES: Vision quests, connection with underworld deities

## LORE

The first record of hops comes from Egypt in the first century CE, where it was mentioned as a salad herb and medicine. Strangely, Egyptians didn't use it to make beer, though they did have ale (beer uses hops, ale doesn't). Hops clear, flavour, and preserve beer. The botanical name is derived from *humus*, meaning "earth" (it likes deep soil), and *lupulus*, meaning "wolf," which is a reference to the strangling habit of the plant as it climbs, similar to the way in which a wolf strangles its prey. The common name *hop* comes from the Anglo-Saxon *hoppon*, meaning "to climb."

## MAGICAL USES

When used in the ritual cup, beer has a different energy to that of wine; it is more earthy and basic. A beer or hop infusion helps to connect with the animal energy within, particularly wolf spirits. It makes a suitable libation or drink in rituals of underworld deities. Beer may be used as the ritual drink from Samhain to Imbolc. Use a hop infusion prior to meditation or vision quests or take one before bed to invite prophetic and teaching dreams.

## CULINARY AND HOUSEHOLD USES

The young shoots may be cooked and eaten like asparagus, and the leaves can be used as a garnish for salads and tomato dishes. The flowers make a calming tea. The shoots are fibrous and can be used to make a homemade paper. The plant yields a brown dye.

## Cosmetic Uses

Hops are a natural, antibacterial deodorant. Use the infusion as a bodywash or powder the dried leaves and flowers and use as an underarm talc. Hops contain phytoestrogens and anti-inflammatories. An infusion, macerated oil, or cream can be used for mature skin to increase collagen and elastin production and to combat dryness, wrinkles, and redness.

## Home Remedies

The flowers make a sedative and calming tea for nervous tension, which may also relieve tension headaches. A stronger infusion can be used for insomnia. A hop pillow may help induce a natural sleep. The bitter principles in hops stimulate the gastric juices and aid digestion, and the antispasmodic actions may relieve the symptoms of IBS and Crohn's disease. The tannins in hops may stem mild diarrhoea. Its phytoestrogens may help with menopause. Externally, hops may be used in a wash, poultice, or compress for neuralgia, arthritis, rheumatism, boils, rashes, and bruises.

> **Caution:** *Avoid if you have depression; it may cause drowsiness. Do not take with other sedatives or anticonvulsants.*

# Horehound, White

*Marrubium vulgare*

. . . . . . . . . . . . . .

PLANETARY RULER: Mercury

ELEMENT: Air

ASSOCIATED DEITIES: Horus, Isis, Osiris, Thor

MAGICAL VIRTUES: Protection, counter magic, exorcism

## LORE

The genus name comes from the Hebrew word *marrob*, meaning "bitter juice," since the plant is very bitter. It is one of the five bitter herbs of the Mishna eaten by the Jews at Passover to commemorate the exodus from Egypt. In Egypt it was dedicated to the god Horus and known as the Seed of Horus. On holy days his statue would be anointed with horehound oil. It has long been used as a medicinal herb, and it was mentioned by the Roman writer Pliny and the Greek physician Hippocrates. In the Middle Ages, it was viewed as a magical herb for protection against the spells of witches.

## MAGICAL USES

Horehound is used for protection and warding magic; hang a sprig in the house, use it in protection oils and herbal amulets, or carry some for protection. A macerated oil can be used to anoint the body or tools used specifically in rituals of Horus. Use horehound in incenses for temple and aura cleansing or for exorcisms.

## CULINARY AND HOUSEHOLD USES

The leaves and the flowers can be added in moderation to salads, stir-fries, soups, and stews. The leaves can be made into a herb tea or used to flavour beer. The calices can be used for wicks in clay lamps, and the stems can be floated on oil used for nightlights.

## COSMETIC USES

Horehound is antiseptic and skin soothing, helping to protect the skin from free radical damage from environmental sources and blue light pollution from computer screens. Use the infusion as a facial wash or add to homemade skin care products.

## HOME REMEDIES

The leaves are used, and an infusion, a syrup, or lozenges are useful for sore throats, respiratory tract infections, bronchitis, wheeziness, asthma, and nonproductive coughs (it is an expectorant and helps thin mucus, making it easier to cough up). Horehound tea taken before meals contains bitter principles that stimulate the appetite and may help prevent gas and indigestion. Use the infusion as a wash for skin conditions.

> *Caution: Large amounts can cause cardiac arrhythmia or vomiting, diarrhoea, and an upset stomach. Avoid medicinal amounts if pregnant or breastfeeding.*

# Horse Chestnut

*Aesculus hippocastanum*

. . . . . . . . . . . . .

PLANETARY RULER: Jupiter

ELEMENT: Fire

ASSOCIATED DEITIES: Summer goddesses

MAGICAL VIRTUES: Fertility, meditation

## LORE

The genus name, *Aesculus*, comes from the Latin *esca*, which means "food," though the horse chestnut is poisonous. This name was originally given to an oak, whose acorns were used to make a type of flour. All British schoolchildren know the famous game of conkers, which is played by drilling a hole in a nut, attaching a length of string to it, holding the other end of the string, and then swiping at your opponent's conker (nut) as hard as you can.

## MAGICAL USES

Added to any incense, horse chestnut will deepen the experience of the ritual or meditation at hand. The flowers are sacred to the Summer Goddess and may be used to invoke her when used in incense, garlands, or decorations. The chestnut is a fertility symbol, and individuals who wish to conceive can use them in charm bags and fertility spells.

## CULINARY AND HOUSEHOLD USES

Horse chestnuts contain saponins, a soapy substance that can be used for washing natural fibres. Peel and grate the nuts, then simmer them in hot water for 10 minutes. Strain. The soapy liquid can then be used for washing, though it may add a slightly blue/green tinge to the cloth.

## COSMETIC USES

Horse chestnut oil and salve can be used topically to treat spider veins and dark circles under the eyes, boost circulation and improve skin appearance, and reduce blotchiness and the appearance of wrinkles and cellulite. The oil can be used on the hair to prevent heat damage when drying or added to shampoos and conditioners to prevent breakages.

## HOME REMEDIES

The nuts are used, and aescin, the main active ingredient, has anti-inflammatory properties. It is used externally as an oil, salve, or tincture for treating varicose veins, haemorrhoids, and swollen veins (phlebitis).

> **Caution:** *This information applies to Aesculus hippocastanum and not to related species. It is for external use only, and it should only be applied to unbroken skin. Raw horse chestnuts are toxic, as are the flowers and bark of the tree. Do not take internally. The pollen from the flowers may cause allergic reactions in sensitive individuals. People who are allergic to latex might also be allergic to horse chestnut.*

# Horsetail

*Equisetum arvense*

PLANETARY RULER: Saturn

ELEMENT: Darth

ASSOCIATED DEITIES: Smith gods

MAGICAL VIRTUES: Survival, endurance, protection,
past-life work, magical smithcraft

## LORE

For more than 400 million years, horsetail has existed, and the plant has barely changed during that time. The name *equisetum* means "horse bristle." Spores emerge from the earth in spring and are replaced later in the season by the distinctive segmented, sterile stalks, which look like green horse tails or bottle brushes.

## MAGICAL USES

Horsetail is an ancient species that survived a mass extinction, which speaks of a powerful, enduring strength. When you need that kind of strength, use horsetail in spells, incense, amulets, and pouches. Horsetail tea, with its prehistoric connections, may be employed in workings designed to link with the long-distant, ancestral past. Horsetail is a herb of Saturn, and it can be used in rituals of ending and releasing. Dried horsetail stems will clean and polish metal magical tools.

## CULINARY AND HOUSEHOLD USES

The young spore stems were a popular spring delicacy in ancient Rome. Treat as you would asparagus or coat with flour and fry. Mature horsetail contains high amounts of silica (about 30 percent), and the plant becomes very hard when dried; it was historically used for the polishing of tools and wood. The fresh plant can be used as a pan scourer.

## Cosmetic Uses

Horsetail boosts collagen and skin elasticity and stimulates hair growth and shine. Horsetail infusion is a healing astringent when used in a skin toner, bath, or lotion and will reduce cellulite when applied to the affected area. A rinse of horsetail infusion gives hair shine and strength. Dab the infusion on weak nails to strengthen them.

## Home Remedies

Horsetail contains water-soluble silica, which helps rebuild connective tissues and stimulates the production of bone cells. The tea can be of benefit in treating weak and broken bones, pulled tendons, osteoarthritis and rheumatoid arthritis, and weak skin, hair, and nails. A fresh horsetail poultice applied to the affected area may reduce arthritic pain. Astringent components in horsetail reduce bleeding when applied directly to minor injuries such as cuts and scrapes.

> **Caution:** *Do not use an incorrect species* (Equisetum palustre, *for example, is poisonous), and do not take internally for longer than two weeks. Avoid if you have low vitamin B levels; take prescription diuretics, laxatives, or antiretroviral drugs; have heart or kidney problems; or are alcoholic, pregnant, breastfeeding, or under eighteen.*

# Houseleek

*Sempervivum tectorum*

· · · · · · · · · · · · · · ·

PLANETARY RULER: Jupiter

ELEMENT: Air

ASSOCIATED DEITIES: Jupiter, Thor, Zeus

MAGICAL VIRTUES: Protection, luck, love, aphrodisiac

## LORE

Houseleek has many mythological associations with protection from thunder and lightning. In lore, it was *diopetes*, a gift from the sky god Zeus/Jupiter that protected against storms and fire. In Norse myth, it was a plant of the thunder god Thor. In the Middle Ages, it was firmly believed that houseleek growing on the roof would keep a house safe from lightning.

## MAGICAL USES

Houseleek will give good protection to those in its vicinity. Grow it in pots and baskets or on the roof of your house and shed. The plant will even flourish in cracks in the pavement by the front door. Carry some in a herbal talisman. To honour and invoke thunder and sky gods, use it in incense and magical oils. Add houseleek to incense, oils, charm bags, and spells of love.

## CULINARY AND HOUSEHOLD USES

The fresh young leaves are edible. Eat them in salads. Pop some leaves in your water bottle to make a refreshing infusion.

## COSMETIC USES

Houseleeks produce a healing gel with similar properties to aloe vera, making it a viable alternative. This gel can help skin repair and regeneration. It moisturises and firms the skin and can be used in antiaging preparations. To treat age spots on the hands, add houseleek to creams; it has a mild skin-lightening effect. Its leaves are cooling and astringent. Houseleeks

· · · · ·

may be added to homemade skin toners, and houseleek tea may be used as a skin toner by itself. Add the leaves to a facial steam or bath.

## HOME REMEDIES

Herbalists consider houseleek, with its similar properties to aloe vera, to be one of the safest treatments for inflammations, burns, scalds, swellings, bruises, cuts, stings, bites, and ulcers. The juice or bruised leaves of the fresh plant can be applied as a poultice. Simply remove a thick, fleshy leaf from the plant. It can then be peeled or pressed and applied directly to the affected area. Use houseleek in a salve for burns, scalds, and skin inflammations.

*Caution: Large doses taken internally are emetic.*

# Hyssop

*Hyssopus officinalis*

. . . . . . . . . . . . . . . .

PLANETARY RULER: Jupiter

ELEMENT: Fire

ASSOCIATED DEITIES: Pluto, Zeus

MAGICAL VIRTUES: Purification, protection, cleansing

## LORE

The genus name, *Hyssopus*, is believed to come from the Hebrew *ezob*, which means "holy herb." It is mentioned in the Bible with "purge me with hyssop and I shall be clean," and according to the Bible, when the seven plagues were upon Egypt, the Hebrews used brushes made of hyssop to paint their doorways with lamb's blood to protect their children. Hyssop was a religious herb for both the Hebrews and the Greeks, who used bunches of it to sweep and purify temples.

## MAGICAL USES

Hyssop is a herb of purification. It can be used in a wash or an incense to purify the sacred space. Bunches of hyssop may also be employed to sweep the circle or temple, or sprinkle cleansing potions around a room or ritual area. Hyssop dispels negativity and is excellent when added to the ritual bath. It can be burned as an incense to dispel negativity both during personal meditation and in ritual. An infusion of this herb can be used to consecrate ritual tools. Hyssop hung in small bunches above windows and doorways will protect the property and prevent any negative energy from entering.

## CULINARY AND HOUSEHOLD USES

Hyssop flowers and leaves may be used as a flavouring in soups, stews, and casseroles. The young leaves can be added to salads. A refreshing and relaxing herbal tea may be made from the leaves or flowers. The leaves and flowers may be added as a flavouring for liqueurs. Add the fragrant leaves to potpourri or scented sachets.

. . . . .

## Cosmetic Uses

In manufacturing, hyssop oil is often used as a fragrance in soaps and cosmetics.

## Home Remedies

An infusion of the flowering tops can be used as an aid to digestion and for the treatment of coughs, catarrh/mucus, rheumatism, and sore throats. Used externally, the leaves can be made into a poultice or lotion for the treatment of bites, stings, cuts, bruises, and ear and eye infections.

> *Caution:* *Do not use if pregnant or breastfeeding, on small children, or if you have seizures.*

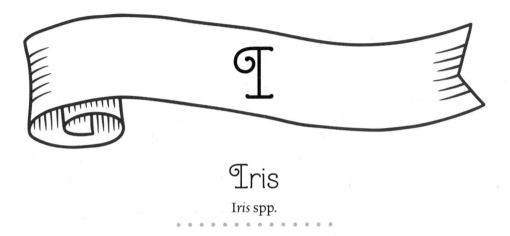

# Iris

*Iris* spp.
· · · · · · · · · · · · · ·

PLANETARY RULER: Venus

ELEMENT: Water

ASSOCIATED DEITIES: Aphrodite, Chloris, Hera,
Iris, Isis, Juno, Osiris, Venus, Perun

MAGICAL VIRTUES: Protection, messages, aphrodisiac

## LORE

Iris takes its name from the Greek word for rainbow and its goddess, who brought messages from heaven to humankind. She took the souls of dead women to the afterlife, just as Hermes took the souls of dead men. In Greece, irises were planted near graves, which is something still done in the Middle East. The ancient Egyptians used it as a symbol of eloquence, placing it on the brow of the sphinx and on the king's sceptre.

## MAGICAL USES

Orris, the fragrant root of the iris, is a fixative for natural perfumes, herbal sachets, and incenses. The root must age for three years before the violet-like scent develops. It can be sprinkled on bed sheets as an aphrodisiac. The sword-shaped leaves make it a defensive or protective plant, and the roots and leaves can be hung about the home and added to the bath-water for personal protection. Iris may serve as a funeral herb, either placed in wreaths and flower arrangements or planted on the grave of the departed, signifying hope for new incar-nations.

## CULINARY AND HOUSEHOLD USES

Powdered and aged orris may be used as a fixative for potpourris and sachets and for per-fuming linens. It may be added to the rinsing water of laundry to impart a violet scent. Some varieties, such as *Iris germanica*, have culinary uses, and their roots can be used to fla-vour brandies and liqueurs, ice cream, sweets, and baked goods. It is one of the ingredients in the Moroccan herb and spice blend ras el hanout.

## COSMETIC USES

The fresh juice of orris may be used as a facial wash to diminish freckles and treat wrinkles. Powdered orris may be used as a substitute for talc. Orris tea can be used as a mouthwash to strengthen gums and freshen the breath.

## HOME REMEDIES

Both the peeled, dried, and powdered root (aged at least three years) and the fresh root juice are used. It stimulates the appetite and digestion, combatting constipation and bloat-ing. Externally, orris can be applied to wounds.

> **Caution:** *There are no known side effects as long as the root is carefully peeled and dried. However, both the fresh plant juice and the root can cause severe irritation of the mouth, stomach pain, vomiting, and bloody diarrhoea.*

# Ivy, English

*Hedera helix*

· · · · · · · · · · · ·

PLANETARY RULER: Saturn

ELEMENT: Water

ASSOCIATED DEITIES: Ariadne, Arianrhod, Attis, Bacchus,
Bran, Ceridwen, Christ, Cissia, Cronos, Dionysus, Feronia,
Gorgopa, Hercules, Hymen, Isis, Kundalini, Lakshmi, Mars,
Osiris, Pan, Persephone, Priapus, Psyche, Rhea, Saturn, Zeus

MAGICAL VIRTUES: Changing consciousness, prophecy,
vision, rebirth, regeneration, initiation, protection

## LORE

Ivy is a tenacious climbing plant that attaches itself very firmly to whatever it grows up, producing aerial roots along its stems that change shape to fit the surface of whatever it climbs. Most of ivy's symbolic associations come from the fact it is an evergreen, flowering late in the year and staying alive and vibrant throughout the winter while other plants around it lie dead or dormant. This made it a sign of life continuing and hope for the future.

## MAGICAL USES

Ivy is protective. Grow it up your garden walls or on the house to safeguard your property. Place sheafs of ivy near your front door or hang an ivy wreath on it. Decorate the altar with ivy during the dark time between the autumn equinox and Yule to house the continuing life force of the spirits of nature. At Yule, ivy represents the power of rebirth and the Sun God reborn at the winter solstice. Ivy represents the path of the sun and the labyrinth dance of life with its spiral growth and arrangement of leaves.

## COSMETIC USES

The chief cosmetic use of ivy is in the treatment of cellulite, used in the form of poultices and wraps, compresses, creams, and lotions. Massage the affected areas with ivy salve, oil, or infusion to encourage the dispersal of toxins and stored fluid. For sunburn, make the leaves into a lotion or salve to rub onto affected areas. An ivy toner or lotion will tighten skin.

## HOME REMEDIES

Stick to using ivy (*Hedera helix*) for external remedies only. A lotion or salve may be made from the leaves to soothe tired muscles, or you can pour some ivy infusion into a warm bath and soak. For neuralgia, rheumatism, and neuritis, apply a pain-killing poultice of ivy leaves.

> **Caution:** *For external use only. Ivy (Hedera helix) is mildly toxic when eaten and can cause vomiting, abdominal pain, and diarrhoea. The berries are more poisonous than the leaves, but both contain toxic saponins. Contact with ivy can cause skin reactions in those who are sensitive.*

# Jasmine

*Jasminum* spp.

. . . . . . . . . . . . .

PLANETARY RULER: Moon/Jupiter

ELEMENT: Water

ASSOCIATED DEITIES: Artemis, Diana, Ganesha, Kamadevi,
mother goddesses, Quan Yin, Vishnu, Zeus

MAGICAL VIRTUES: Positivity, sensuality, aphrodisiac, luck, love, beauty

## LORE

Jasmine is a name that covers many tropical and subtropical plants of the genus *Jasminum*.
The two kinds most commonly grown in gardens are *Jasminum officinale*, which has fragrant, white blossoms, and the larger-flowered *Jasminum grandiflorum*. The name *jasmine* is
derived from the Persian word *yasmin*, meaning "gift from God," indicating just how highly
the plant is valued for its intoxicating, heady perfume.

## MAGICAL USES

The incense smoke of jasmine flowers can be directed around the aura, boosting it after
depletion incurred during illnesses or emotional stress. It also gives psychic protection
to the aura. Jasmine oil or incense can be used for creating a relaxed, romantic, and sexual
atmosphere. Use the oil for a couples massage. Add the dried flowers to love sachets and

incenses. Take jasmine tea before meditation, or drink it before bed to promote psychic dreams. Apply jasmine oil to the third eye.

## CULINARY AND HOUSEHOLD USES

Jasmine flowers can be used to flavour beverages, ice cream and sorbets, sweets, cakes, cookies, jellies, and puddings. Perhaps the best-known culinary use of jasmine is the delicate aromatic tea. To make jasmine rice, add jasmine tea or a jasmine tea bag to the water the rice is cooked in.

## COSMETIC USES

Jasmine is wonderful for softening and moisturising the skin, increasing its elasticity and decreasing the appearance of wrinkles. Add jasmine oil to your homemade skin preparations, such as moisturising creams and lotions. Give your hair a treat and brush slightly warmed macerated jasmine oil through the length of your hair. Wrap your head in a warm towel and leave for 30–60 minutes before washing.

## HOME REMEDIES

Jasmine is antispasmodic. A cup of jasmine tea aids digestion and relieves flatulence, abdominal pain, diarrhoea, dyspepsia, and IBS. Jasmine tea has a sedative effect on the nervous system and promotes peaceful sleep. Take a cup when you are feeling stressed or before bed. Jasmine tea is also antiseptic and can be administered externally as a wash to treat cuts and scrapes. A compress dipped in a jasmine infusion and applied to the forehead can be soothing for headaches.

> *Caution:* *Make sure you identify your species of jasmine correctly. Some plants are called jasmine but are not members of the Jasminum genus at all, and some of these are toxic. Jasmine is an emmenagogue and therefore should not be used during pregnancy. The scent of jasmine can worsen some migraines.*

# Juniper

*Juniperus communis*

. . . . . . . . . . . . . . . . . .

PLANETARY RULER: Sun/Mars/Saturn

ELEMENT: Fire

ASSOCIATED DEITIES: Apollo, Artemis, chthonic
deities, Furies, Hecate, Medea, Pan

MAGICAL VIRTUES: Justice, purification, underworld contact

## LORE

In the ancient world, juniper was connected with the dead and the underworld, perhaps because its fragrance was used to cover the scent of death. The ancient Egyptians used it in the embalming process, while in ancient Greece, it was used to invoke Hecate and other chthonic deities. In Christian lore, it was believed that fumigations of juniper had the power to eradicate evil, a reward to the tree for having once sheltered the infant Jesus. In mediaeval Europe, the home of a dead person was smoked with juniper. In Scotland, it was used as a sain at Hogmanay (New Year), while in Czechoslovakia stables were fumigated with juniper to expel demons.

## MAGICAL USES

Juniper's energy is one of purification, and it can be used in healing rituals and for banishing negativity. The berries may be used in amulets and teas, and the fresh needles can be used as an incense or in the bath. A branch hung above the front door wards off evil. Juniper also resonates with justice and truth, so it may be used in rites concerning these matters as long as your cause is just. The dried berries and needles can be burned to invoke or honour Hecate and other underworld deities.

## CULINARY AND HOUSEHOLD USES

The berries have a spicy taste and are used to flavour gin. They can also be used in cookery to flavour casseroles, pickles, marinades, and stuffings or added in moderation to fruitcake. A purple-brown dye can be obtained from the berries and roots.

. . . . .

## COSMETIC USES

Commercially, juniper essential oil is used in perfumes, aftershaves, cosmetics, and soaps. A homemade macerated oil or salve made from the crushed berries will aid irritated skin conditions. A berry decoction can be brushed or lightly scrubbed onto cellulite-prone areas of the skin to help eliminate toxins.

## HOME REMEDIES

Juniper berry tea can be useful for frequent urinary tract infections such as cystitis and fluid retention. It may also be used for digestive problems, including upset stomach, flatulence, heartburn, and bloating. Juniper has anti-inflammatory properties and can be taken internally as a tea or applied externally as a salve for arthritis, gout, and other rheumatic conditions.

*Caution: Juniper is considered safe in food amounts or when taken medicinally short term. Taking large amounts long term may cause kidney problems. Avoid if pregnant or breastfeeding, for two weeks before and after surgery, or if you take diuretics. Juniper may lower blood sugar, so monitor your levels carefully if you are diabetic.*

# Lavender

*Lavandula* spp.

- - - - - - - - - - - - - -

PLANETARY RULER: Mercury

ELEMENT: Air

ASSOCIATED DEITIES: Cernunnos, Circe, Hecate, Medea, Saturn

MAGICAL VIRTUES: Love, apotropaic, cleansing, purification, fairy magic

## LORE
Lavender's name comes from the Latin *lavare*, meaning "to wash," which explains its ancient purpose. The Greeks, Romans, and Carthaginians all used lavender in bathwater and laundry for both its scent and its therapeutic properties, a practice that continued throughout the Middle Ages in Europe, when it was also thought to drive off ghosts.

## MAGICAL USES
Lavender purifies and cleanses. Use a lavender infusion to wash ritual robes and cleanse ritual equipment and spaces. It can also be added to purification baths. Prior to meditation, drink lavender tea or burn lavender incense to foster stillness and peace. Use the incense in rituals that explore the element of air and to develop the intellect and powers of logical thought. Add lavender to love spells or use it in incense, oils, sachets, and charm bags for love. Use lavender to attract fairies, elves, and nature spirits.

## CULINARY AND HOUSEHOLD USES

Lavender flowers are edible, and small amounts may be used in cakes, biscuits, ice creams, and desserts. Too much lavender can taste unpleasant, so an alternative is to make lavender sugar by layering dried lavender flowers and sugar in an airtight container for a couple of days. Sift off the sugar and use it for baking. Lavender syrup may be added to lemonade, smoothies, and cocktails. Pop a few stems of fresh lavender in a bottle of vodka or gin, leave overnight, and strain.

## COSMETIC USES

Lavender helps skin heal and renew. It also fights wrinkles and acne. Add it to skin washes, toners, lotions, and creams or include lavender oil in your homemade cosmetics. Make a lavender bath bag by putting lavender flowers, fresh or dried, in a muslin bag and drop it into the bathwater. Use lavender oil on cleansed feet that are prone to sweatiness; it is a natural deodorant.

## HOME REMEDIES

An antiseptic lavender infusion can be used as a wash for minor cuts. Lavender salve may be used for cuts, bruises, and skin irritations. It helps minimise scarring and can be applied to varicose veins, burns, and other skin injuries. Drink lavender tea for a soothing effect on the central nervous system, for mild pain relief, to help headaches, to treat nervous tension, or to act as a mild sedative before bed. For inflamed skin and eczema, a lavender salve provides deep moisture while reducing the inflammation.

> **Caution:** *Lavender can cause irritation and headaches in some individuals. Do not use lavender essential oil on prepubescent boys. People with sensitive skin may find it irritating. Do not take in combination with other sedative or anticonvulsant drugs.*

# Lemon

*Citrus limon*

. . . . . . . . . . . . . . . . . .

PLANETARY RULER: Moon

ELEMENT: Water

ASSOCIATED DEITIES: Alakshmi

MAGICAL VIRTUES: Protection, dispelling negativity

## LORE

In lore, lemons have the reputation of dispelling poisons and other negative influences, including the evil eye. The emperor Nero consumed large numbers of citrus fruits as he was obsessed by the fear of being poisoned.

## MAGICAL USES

Because they resemble the shape of a human eye, lemons are used in sympathetic magic to repel the evil eye; hang lemons in the home or by the front door. You can also add dried lemon peel to protective sachets, charms, oils, and incense. Use lemon juice diluted in water as a wash to cleanse sacred spaces, robes, tools, the body, and aura (use in the bath). Add dried lemon peel to incense to drive away baneful magic sent against you. Lemon peel is also suitable for use in moon incenses.

## CULINARY AND HOUSEHOLD USES

Fresh, zingy lemon zest or lemon juice is commonly used in both sweet and savoury cooking in meat, fish, and vegetable dishes, as well as desserts. Lemon juice is added to drinks and used to make lemonade.

## COSMETIC USES

Lemon softens and brightens the skin, promotes new skin generation, diminishes wrinkles, and fades freckles and age spots. A lemon rinse will lighten hair and treat dandruff.

. . . . .

## HOME REMEDIES

High in vitamin C with fever-reducing properties, lemon is well known for the treatment of coughs and colds and often taken as a tea or syrup. Lemon has anti-inflammatory properties, which help reduce inflammation in arthritic and rheumatic conditions. Lemon aids digestion and encourages the production of bile. Treat wasp stings with fresh lemon juice. A cup of lemon tea will relieve a hangover.

*Caution:* *Lemon peel may cause contact dermatitis in sensitive individuals. Those with gastro-oesophageal reflux disease may experience an increase in symptoms when consuming citrus fruit. Eating lemon peel should be avoided by those with kidney or gallbladder problems.*

# Lemon Balm

*Melissa officinalis*

. . . . . . . . . . . . . . .

PLANETARY RULER: Moon

ELEMENT: Water

ASSOCIATED DEITIES: Artemis, Diana, moon goddesses

MAGICAL VIRTUES: Love, moon magic, joy, dreaming, visions, healing

## LORE

The genus name, *Melissa*, comes from the Greek word meaning "bee." Bees are particularly attracted to the lemon balm, and Pliny wrote that "bees are delighted with this herb above all others."[2] It was sacred to the moon goddess Artemis and used medicinally by the Greeks over two thousand years ago. Lemon balm has a happy reputation as a healing and refreshing plant. In Southern Europe it is called heart's delight and the elixir of life.

## MAGICAL USES

Uplifting lemon balm helps connect with the emotions and their tides and cycles. Add it to incenses, cakes, or wine for moon goddess and esbat rituals. Stuff a dream pillow with the dried leaves. Add lemon balm to sachets, incenses, and spells for joy and healing.

## CULINARY AND HOUSEHOLD USES

The lemon-scented leaves are used for flavouring food and drinks. Sprinkle them in salads, make a lemon balm herb butter, or add them to soups, vinegars, sauces, cakes, and cookies. Make a refreshing lemon balm leaf tea; add sprigs to iced tea and cocktails. Try flavouring gins and liqueurs with lemon balm leaves.

## COSMETIC USES

Lemon balm is antibacterial, astringent, anti-inflammatory, and slightly drying, which helps reduce skin irritation, particularly when treating acne, blocked pores, and blackheads. Add

---

2  Pliny the Elder, *Natural History*.

. . . . .

lemon balm leaves to homemade facial toners, use the infusion as a facial wash, or add the leaves to a facial steam. Add the infusion to homemade sun and after-sun lotions to protect from UV damage. Use an infusion as a rinse for greasy hair. A lemon balm infusion is also refreshing and reviving when added to the bathwater.

## HOME REMEDIES

The aerial parts are used. Lemon balm tea is calming to the central nervous system and can be used for anxiety, depression, tension, nervous palpitations, and anxiety caused digestive problems. An infusion or tincture can be used to treat nervous headaches, anxiety, and mild depression. It is antiviral and particularly good for cold sores; simply dab on the infusion. Apply the salve or fresh leaves to insect stings, insect bites, pimples, boils, and sores.

> *Caution:* *Lemon balm can cause side effects, including nausea, vomiting, abdominal pain, and dizziness, in some individuals. Avoid large amounts if pregnant, if breastfeeding, if you are taking sedative medications, for two weeks before surgery, or if you have an underactive thyroid.*

# Lemon Verbena

*Aloysia triphylla syn. Aloysia Citriodora/Lippia citriodora*

. . . . . . . . . . . . . .

PLANETARY RULER: Venus/Mercury

ELEMENT: Air

MAGICAL VIRTUES: Peace, joy, air magic, communication

## LORE

Lemon verbena was brought to Europe from Chile and Argentina by the Spanish, who grew it for the oil, which they used in perfume making. The botanical name comes from Maria Louisa, who was the princess of Parma and later the wife of King Carlos IV of Spain.

## MAGICAL USES

The leaves can be infused in candle wax to produce lemon-scented candles dedicated to the element of air and the direction of east. These can be used as Ostara altar candles or to help raise the vibrations to create a peaceful and joyous atmosphere. Use lemon verbena in spells, rituals, and herbal sachets and charm bags of communication. The leaves can be placed amongst robes and garments to scent and protect them. They can also be used in homemade herbal paper for magical use.

## CULINARY AND HOUSEHOLD USES

Lemon verbena makes a refreshing herbal tea. The lemon-scented leaves can be cooked like spinach, added to fish, chicken, and fruit salad, used to flavour ice cream, drinks, confectionery, cakes and puddings, or fruit jellies.

## COSMETIC USES

Lemon verbena has anti-inflammatory and antibacterial properties and makes a wonderful addition to your homemade skincare products. It will lessen reddening. Add the fresh leaves to a bath for a relaxing soak. Use lemon verbena in a compress for puffy eyes. As a hair rinse, it helps strengthen the hair and promotes growth.

. . . . .

## HOME REMEDIES

The leaves and flowers are used, and as a steam inhalation or tea, lemon verbena may aid nasal and bronchial congestion. Take the antispasmodic tea for nausea, indigestion, stomach cramps, bloating, and flatulence. The tea has a mood-lifting effect. It helps soothe anxiety, and a stronger dose will help insomnia. Lemon balm is a febrifuge; take the infusion to reduce fevers. Externally, use the infusion as a wash for boils, acne, and cysts.

> **Caution:** *To be on the safe side, avoid medicinal amounts if pregnant or breastfeeding. It can cause contact dermatitis in some people. Avoid large amounts if you have kidney disease.*

# Lemongrass

*Cymbopogon* spp.

. . . . . . . . . . . . . . . . . .

PLANETARY RULER: Mercury

ELEMENT: Air

MAGICAL VIRTUES: Communication, protection,
love, purification, psychic work

## LORE

Lemongrass is a tropical plant native to Southeast Asia, where it was used for cooking, medicine, and cosmetic purposes. Its use was little known outside of Asia until the seventeenth century, when it began to be exported—mainly for use in the perfume industry.

## MAGICAL USES

Lemongrass vibrates with the power of the element of air, and it can be used in rituals, spells, charm bags, and so on connected with communication, mental clarity, intellectual focus, and opening the psychic senses. During psychic work and divination, burn lemongrass incense or anoint a candle with lemongrass oil. Lemongrass incense can be used to cleanse your aura, home, or sacred space of negative vibrations. Use a lemongrass infusion to wash and purify your sacred space and magical tools.

## CULINARY AND HOUSEHOLD USES

Lemongrass adds a sweet, lemony flavour to food and drinks and is a common ingredient in Asian cuisine, especially Thai dishes. Lemongrass tea is a refreshing and uplifting summer drink. Try using lemongrass as a substitute for lemon or lime juice in cooking, or add it to stir-fries, soups, stews, and chicken or fish dishes. Tie some in a muslin bag and drop it in rice as it is cooking. Add the young leaves to salads. Make it into a syrup for cocktails and iced tea. Lemongrass is also useful as an insect repellent. Add lemongrass oil to homemade furniture polishes for a lovely scent.

. . . . .

## COSMETIC USES

Lemongrass contains nutrients such as vitamins A and C, potassium, calcium, magnesium, and phosphorous, plus antifungal, antibacterial, antiseptic, astringent, and antioxidant compounds, all of which make it a powerful cleanser and detoxifier for oily skin. To tighten the skin and treat acne, enlarged pores, and blackheads, add lemongrass to homemade skin toners, skin washes, and facial steams. Use a lemongrass infusion in the bath as a natural deodoriser and add to a footbath to treat sweaty feet. A lemongrass hair rinse may reduce dandruff; soothe irritated, flaky scalps; and stimulate hair growth.

## HOME REMEDIES

Lemongrass tea combats symptoms of stress, anxiety, and insomnia. It also aids digestion, reduces bloating, and may help relieve a headache. A lemongrass infusion acts to reduce fevers by promoting sweating. Used topically (infusion or oil), it has antimicrobial, antibacterial, and antifungal properties and may treat athlete's foot, ringworm, scabies, and yeast infections.

> **Caution:** *Avoid during pregnancy (it is an emmenagogue [i.e., brings on menstruation]) or if breastfeeding. Lemongrass essential oil might make people sleepy. Do not take with other sedative drugs or herbs.*

# Lilac

*Syringa* spp.

. . . . . . . . . . . . . .

PLANETARY RULER: Venus

ELEMENT: Water

MAGICAL VIRTUES: Renewal, apotropaic, warding,
banishing, death and mourning

## LORE

Lilacs were only introduced into Europe from Ottoman gardens in the sixteenth century and later taken to the Americas. The common name comes from the Arabic *lilak*, which means "dark blue." The genus name, *Syringa*, bestowed by Linnaeus in 1753, comes from the Greek word *syrinx*, which means a "pipe," referring to the pith-filled stems. Pipes and flutes used to be made by hollowing out the stems of wood or reed, though, ironically, lilac is very poor for this purpose. Our word *syringe* (another hollow tube) comes from the same root. The lilac has heart-shaped leaves, associating it in popular folklore with love. However, it is also considered unlucky to take indoors, and it was used as a funeral flower in the eighteenth and nineteenth centuries.

## MAGICAL USES

As it was introduced late into Europe, it has no genuine European deity associations (certainly not Pan) or traditional Western magical practices. However, it is used by modern witches for protection magic. To ward your home, plant a lilac near your door, smear lilac oil on the threshold, or scatter lilac petals on the doorstep as a barrier against evil.

## CULINARY AND HOUSEHOLD USES

Lilac flowers are edible, but they taste slightly bitter, so, as with all perfumed flowers, they should be used sparingly. Use them as an edible garnish for cakes, ice cream, and cocktails. Add a small number of fresh flowers to the batter of cakes, scones, and cookies. The flowers are best used to make lilac sugar, which can be added to your baking, or lilac syrup, which can be poured over ice cream or used as a base for cocktails. You might also make lilac-infused honey, which can be used in baking and making teas and other drinks. You can also crystallize the flowers for later use as decoration on biscuits and cakes.

## COSMETIC USES

Lilac is antimicrobial and antioxidant, has anti-inflammatory effects, stimulates cell regeneration, and helps repair oxidative damage. It may be utilised to minimise skin aging, prevent age spots, and stimulate cell renewal; mix some macerated lilac oil into your home-made moisturisers. If you have oily, acne-prone skin, lilac is your friend—the flowers and leaves are astringent, tightening and slightly drying the skin. Lilac is wonderful for your hair and scalp; massage a lilac infusion into your scalp to strengthen your hair at the roots and help reduce dandruff.

## HOME REMEDIES

Though it is rarely used in modern herbalism, a lilac compress will help reduce strains and bruises. Pop a few soothing lilac flowers into a muslin bag and drop it in your bath for a relaxing soak.

> **Caution:** *Do not use internally if pregnant, breastfeeding, or taking medicines that alter blood coagulation. The bark is toxic.*

# Lily

*Lilium* spp.

. . . . . . . . . . . . . . .

PLANETARY RULER: Moon

ELEMENT: Water

ASSOCIATED DEITIES: Aphrodite, Cybele, Hera,
Isis, Juno, Pudicitia, Rhea, Satyrs, Spes, Zeus

MAGICAL VIRTUES: Love, protection, purification,
harmony, funerals, mourning

## LORE

While many flowers are called lily, true lilies come from the genus *Lilium*, derived from the Greek *leírion*, meaning "true." Lilies have been cultivated for at least 4,000 years. They appear on ancient decorations and friezes from Egypt, Assyria, Crete, and Israel. In Greek myth, the lily is said to have been created when milk fell from the breast of the goddess Hera. The majority of the milk flowed into the heavens and became the stars of the Milky Way, but a few drops fell to earth and became lilies. The goddess Aphrodite made the large flower pistil look like a penis, so it has ancient associations with love and lust. In China and Japan, lilies are symbols of fertility. Conversely, in the Christian world, they were dedicated to the Virgin Mary, purity, death, and funerals (after which the deceased is returned to a state of spiritual purity).

## MAGICAL USES

Dedicated to Hera/Juno, the queen of the gods and patroness of marriage, the flowers may be incorporated in bridal wreaths or employed in spells of love magic. A higher resonance of this is in attracting spiritual love. The bulb of the Madonna lily (*Lilium candidum*) protects against sorcery and spells; hang the flowers above the door or place a pot of lilies in your window. Plant lilies in your garden to keep your property safe from magic sent against you.

## CULINARY AND HOUSEHOLD USES

Some kinds of *Lilium* bulbs are eaten in the Far East as root vegetables; however, some lily bulbs are too bitter to eat, and some are toxic. The flowers and bulbs of the Madonna lily are edible. Native Americans ate the flowers and roots of the Canada lily (*Lilium canadense*). The stems are used in Asian coookery. The Japanese use slices of the bulb in savoury dishes.

## COSMETIC USES

Crush lily petals in a pestle and mortar, add honey, and apply as a face mask to soften the skin and minimise wrinkles.

## HOME REMEDIES

Traditional Chinese medicine lists the properties of several *Lilium* species, but in Western herbalism, only the bulb, leaves, and flowers of the Madonna lily have been used. It is rarely employed today, and when it is, it is generally for topical application only, applied as a poultice to ulcers, calluses, abscesses, bruises, inflammation, rashes, burns, and wounds.

> **Caution:** *Some* Lilium *species are toxic to cats (as is the unrelated daylily* [Hemerocallis]) *and the effects can lead to kidney failure.*

# Linden

a.k.a. Lime Tree

*Tilia* spp.

. . . . . . . . . . . . . .

PLANETARY RULER: Jupiter/Mercury/Sun

ELEMENT: Air

ASSOCIATED DEITIES: Ceres, Demeter, fairies,
Freya, Frigg, Holda, Juno, Lada, Venus

MAGICAL VIRTUES: Protection, love, friendship, peace,
compassion, divination, justice, truth

## LORE

In Greek myth, the nymph Philyra, mother of Chiron the centaur, was transformed into a
linden. He grew up in its shade, where his mother taught him wisdom and compassion. In
the Northern tradition, it is associated with Freya, the goddess of fertility and love. Linden
trees were commonly planted in the town square in some northern European countries,
and under the linden tree, tribal judgment was made, marriages were conducted, and celebrations were held. In Poland, the linden tree was believed to have protective properties,
keeping people safe from lightning, evil spirits, and baneful magic.

## MAGICAL USES

Linden is a feminine tree of love, nurturing, and protection. Use the tea or incense in meditation or rituals to develop compassion. For protection, hang linden branches over doorways, plant a linden tree in the garden, or add the dried flowers to incenses, herbal amulets,
and wards. Use linden incense or sain/ritual fumigation to remove negative energies.

## CULINARY AND HOUSEHOLD USES

Linden flowers can be used to make a soothing tea, and the sap of the linden tree can be fermented into wine. The pressed seeds yield an oil that can be used for cooking. The young
leaves may be stuffed like grapevine leaves.

. . . . .

## COSMETIC USES

Added to homemade cosmetic creams and serums, linden provides antioxidant protection, and offers water-binding properties that help lock moisture into skin. In homemade toners, it is of benefit to oily skin, slowing down sebum production; it firms the skin and reduces pores.

## HOME REMEDIES

The flowers and leaves make a nerve tonic tea that is calming and sedative, making it useful in cases of anxiety and insomnia. It is diaphoretic (promotes sweating) and may help colds, flu, and fevers. It contains antioxidants (tiliroside and quercetin), which help reduce inflammation and pain.

> *Caution:* *Linden should not be used over an extended period. Do not take with other diuretics or if you are on lithium.*

# Liquorice/Licorice

*Glycyrrhiza glabra* syn. *Liquiritia officinalis*

. . . . . . . . . . . . . .

PLANETARY RULER: Mercury

ELEMENT: Fire

ASSOCIATED DEITIES: Asclepius, Chiron, Circe, Medea

MAGICAL VIRTUES: Fertility, love, protection, compelling

## LORE

The botanical name *Glycyrrhiza* comes from the Greek words *glukus*, meaning "sweet," and *rhiza*, meaning "a root." Liquorice was used medicinally by the Greeks, Egyptians, Romans, and the Scythians.

## MAGICAL USES

Liquorice root is used in love and lust spells. It can be carried on the person or added to charm bags, incense, oils, and so on to attract love. The root can be chewed for sexual potency or used in fertility rituals. Liquorice offers protection from negative energy; for this, it may be carried or powdered and sprinkled about the home and in doorways and windows. Keep liquorice with you when you need the upper hand in any situation.

## CULINARY AND HOUSEHOLD USES

Liquorice is 50 to 100 times sweeter than sugar, and natural liquorice root can be safely eaten by diabetics and used to sweeten diabetic desserts and sweets. (Sadly, the liquorice taste we get in commercial sweets is usually just an artificial flavouring.) Infuse the root in boiling water or milk and add the liquid to syrups, sauces, custards, ice cream, and panna cotta. Make liquorice sugar by putting the root in a container of sugar for at least two weeks, then use the sugar for baking. The root can be used to flavour beers, particularly stouts, as well as liqueurs and tobacco.

## COSMETIC USES

Liquorice is anti-inflammatory, antibacterial, and antifungal. It also contains saponins (soap). Use the infusion as a wash and add it to liquid castile soap for a shampoo to treat scalp problems. Try liquorice glycerite mixed with witch hazel as a toner to firm the skin and treat hyperpigmentation and skin irritation.

## HOME REMEDIES

The root is used, and the demulcent qualities of a cup of liquorice tea may help a sore throat, indigestion, heartburn, acid reflux, and peptic ulcers. Its expectorant (loosens phlegm) actions treat a cough and upper respiratory tract infections. Topically, in gels and creams, it may help soothe eczema, acne, and impetigo.

> *Caution:* *Liquorice should be used in moderation and for no longer than four weeks. Avoid if you have high blood pressure, liver disorders, kidney disease, or low potassium levels. Do not take if you are pregnant or breastfeeding. True liquorice can interfere with hormone replacement therapy and oral contraceptives.*

# Lotus

*Nelumbo* spp./*Nymphaea* spp.

. . . . . . . . . . . . . . .

PLANETARY RULER: Neptune

ELEMENT: Water

ASSOCIATED DEITIES: Aphrodite, Apollo, Astarte, Atum, Avalokitesvara, Brahma, Buddha, Demeter, Harpocrates, Ho Hsien-Ku, Horus, Isis, Kali, Kwan Yin, Lakshmi, Nefertum, Osiris, Padma, Quetesh, Ra, Sarasvati, Tara, Venus, Vishnu

MAGICAL VIRTUES: Purity, perfection, spiritual growth, compassion, enlightenment

## LORE

In antiquity, a variety of plants were called lotus. Today, lotuses are classified as five species of water lilies—three in the genus *Nymphaea* and two in *Nelumbo*. The lotus was a sacred flower to the peoples of Egypt, India, Tibet, and China, and it still is for Hindus and Buddhists today. The lotus roots on the bottom of a pond, in the mud, but its egg-shaped buds reach for the sun and open in its radiance, making it a symbol of creation from the primordial waters and spiritual flowering.

## MAGICAL USES

The lotus can help us work on our highest spiritual aspirations. It represents the totality of the Cosmos. The famous mantra *Om mani padme hum* means "Oh jewel of the lotus," and chanting it connects us to the All, purifying the mind, spirit, and body and leading us towards enlightenment. Each chakra, our bridges between the body and universal consciousness, has the lotus as an emblem, and the petals of each chakra can be open or closed depending on our state of consciousness and relationship with the world. The lotus begins in the root chakra, our connection to the material, and grows up through the spine to the crown chakra, where we communicate with the Divine.

## CULINARY AND HOUSEHOLD USES

The stem and rhizome of the sacred lotus (*Nelumbo nucifera* syn. *Nelumbium speciosum*) can be eaten raw, cooked, salted, or pickled. It can also be added to soups and stir-fries. The leaves, flowers, and seeds are also edible.

## COSMETIC USES

Several commercially available moisturisers contain lotus seed. An extract added to home-made products contains antioxidants and antimicrobial compounds that protect skin from free radical damage, soothe irritation and redness, and offer hydration.

## HOME REMEDIES

The powdered rhizome, flowers, seeds, and leaves of the sacred lotus have been used in traditional medicine. They contain antioxidant, anti-inflammatory, and antimicrobial compounds that may help protect the circulatory system, decrease blood glucose and lipid levels, and reduce oxidative stress.

> **Caution:** *Stay on the safe side and avoid medicinal amounts if you are pregnant, breastfeeding, diabetic, or taking pentobarbital (Nembutal).*

# Lovage

*Levisticum officinale*

PLANETARY RULER: Sun

ELEMENT: Fire

ASSOCIATED DEITIES: Frigga, Lofn

MAGICAL VIRTUES: Love, protection

## LORE

Lovage's name comes from its inclusion in old recipes for love potions, which also accounts for this feathery plant's other common name of *love parsley*, or the Old French *luveshe* (love-ache). From ancient times to the Middle Ages and beyond, it was used throughout Europe as both a food and a medicine.

## MAGICAL USES

The primary use of lovage is in love magic. Drop some lovage into your bathwater or wear a sprig of the plant to make you more attractive. Carry some in a sachet to attract love, or add some to incense, spells, and charms of love. It is also a herb of protection. Hang lovage above your doors and windows to keep negative energies out or plant some in the garden to protect it. Lovage leaves laid in the shoe are said to revive a weary traveller.

## CULINARY AND HOUSEHOLD USES

Lovage has a strong, fresh, celery-like flavour, and the leaves and young stems may be used sparingly in stews or salads. They go well with egg and potato dishes and can be mixed with butter or cream cheese. The blanched shoots may be eaten as a vegetable. The roots are edible as a cooked vegetable or added raw to salads. The stalks can be candied like angelica, while the dried leaves may be utilised to make a tea. The seeds can be ground as a substitute for pepper.

## Cosmetic Uses

A strong lovage decoction can be added to the bathwater as a natural deodoriser.

## Home Remedies

A decoction of the seeds or root can be used for the treatment of colic, indigestion, flatulence, rheumatism, and gout, and the seeds may be chewed to aid digestion and prevent flatulence. A tincture may be used for period pain and urinary tract problems. A lovage root decoction may be gargled for sore throat, mouth ulcers, or tonsillitis.

> *Caution:* Lovage should not be taken by pregnant individuals (it stimulates the uterus) or people suffering from kidney problems. The foliage can irritate the skin in some people.

# Maize

*Zea Mays*

· · · · · · · · · · · · · ·

PLANETARY RULER: Sun/Venus

ELEMENT: Fire/earth

ASSOCIATED DEITIES: Xipe Totec, Centeotl, Chicomecoatl, Quetzalcoatl, Zaramama, Atna, Kachina Mana, Chicha, Mondawin, Selu

MAGICAL VIRTUES: Prosperity, abundance, fertility, rejuvenation

## LORE

Mayan religion centred on the cultivation of maize, and humankind was thought to have been created from maize. In Aztec mythology, Xipe Totec (Our Lord the Flayed One) was a life-death-rebirth deity and god of agriculture who flayed himself to give food to humanity, which is symbolic of the way maize seeds lose their outer layer before germination. For Native Americans in the north, maize was one of the Three Sisters, or the three main agricultural crops (the other two being squash and beans). Amongst the Navajos, four plants were assigned to the four directions: maize in the north; beans in the east; squash in the south; and tobacco in the west.

## MAGICAL USES

The cycle of the corn teaches the mysteries of life, death, and rebirth. It is symbolic of the goodness of Mother Earth ripened under Father Sky. Use maize in the decorations and food for harvest rituals. A corn cob may be placed on the altar to represent and honour the sacrifice of the corn god who dies so that we may eat. Maize (and all other grain crops) are symbolic of fertility, prosperity, and abundance and may be used in spells and workings to attract those qualities. Place corn near your door, hang a wreath of corn on your door, or scatter corn on the threshold to attract abundance. A corn husk doll may be used as a magical poppet.

## CULINARY AND HOUSEHOLD USES

Maize is gluten free and suitable for coeliac sufferers. It can be boiled, barbecued, baked in the oven, made into relishes, and added to salads, soups, and stews. When dried and ground, maize meal may be coarse or finely ground (as in polenta). Corn tortillas, tamales, and atole (a milky Central American drink) are made with ground maize. And let's not forget popcorn!

## COSMETIC USES

Corn silk (the silky strands between the husk and cob) are anti-inflammatory and vitamin rich, and they can be added to the bath, lotions, and so on. They can be dried and powdered to add a silky texture to homemade cosmetics.

## HOME REMEDIES

The corn silk is used. Traditionally, it is made into a tea for prostate disorders. The tea soothes irritation of the bladder and urethra caused by frequent urination and may have a role in alleviating cystitis and protecting against kidney and bladder stones.

> *Caution:* Do not use corn silk medicinally if you take diuretics or blood pressure medication. Avoid medicinal use of corn silk if you are pregnant or breastfeeding.

# Mallow

Marshmallow (*Althaea officinalis*)
Common Mallow (*Malva sylvestris*)

. . . . . . . . . . . . . . . .

PLANETARY RULER: Moon/Venus

ELEMENT: Water

ASSOCIATED DEITIES: Venus, Aphrodite

MAGICAL VIRTUES: Love, protection

## LORE

People living on the Isle of Man believed that mallow removed illness caused by walking "on bad ground," or treading on the terrain of fairies and thereby invoking their curse. In Germany, mallow ointments were used to remove "the ill effects of any malicious influence," meaning an inimical spiritual influence. [3]

## MAGICAL USES

Use in love spells, charms, and incenses. Mallow flowers and leaves can be added to the ritual cup at handfastings. Gather the seeds at the full moon to make an ointment for use in the Great Rite. A protection salve made from the leaves will shield a person from baneful magic.

## CULINARY AND HOUSEHOLD USES

The young leaves and flower petals can be added to salads. The leaves can also be added to vinegars or steamed and served as a vegetable. The seed capsules can be eaten as a snack. They can also make a nice addition to salads. The sweets known as marshmallows once contained marshmallow root, which was heated with sugar to create a sweet paste. Eat marshmallow roots raw in salads or made into tea. The root can be boiled to soften it and then fried.

---

3  Watts, *Elsevier's Dictionary of Plant Lore*, 238.

## COSMETIC USES

Marshmallow is anti-inflammatory and good for sensitive, itchy, and irritated skin. When making creams and lotions, add the roots, flowers, or leaves. They will help moisturise and improve the skin. For healthy and tangle-free hair, employ a marshmallow infusion as a final hair rinse. Make a salve or cream from the roots and apply to chapped hands.

## HOME REMEDIES

All parts of common mallow and marshmallow can be used for home remedies. The leaves and roots contain a high level of mucilage that soothes and reduces inflammation throughout the body, both internally and externally. This makes mallow useful for coughs, colds, gastric upsets, dry skin conditions, stomach ulcers, and infections in the urinary, respiratory, and digestive tracts. Drink mallow tea for indigestion, IBS, a dry sore throat, a dry cough, and mild constipation. To reduce inflammation in infected skin complaints such as boils, ulcers, and abscesses, apply a mallow poultice or salve externally.

> *Caution:* *To be on the safe side, avoid medicinal doses if pregnant or breastfeeding. If you are taking mallow internally, take it two hours before ingesting other food or medicine. Large doses can be a laxative and purgative.*

# Mandrake

*Mandragora officinalis*

PLANETARY RULER: Mercury

ELEMENT: Fire

ASSOCIATED DEITIES: Aphrodite, Artemis,
Circe, Hecate, Medea, Prometheus

MAGICAL VIRTUES: Aphrodisiac, fertility, good luck, protection, hexing

## LORE

The mandrake has an ominous reputation as a deadly witch herb, one that grew in Hecate's garden. It was called, among other things, sorcerer's root, devil's candle, earth-mannikin, and the little gallows man. The roots, which are vaguely humanoid in shape, were potent magical charms that guaranteed the owner's heart's desire—whether it be for luck, wealth, gold, success, love, or power—as long as it was fed weekly with wine and wrapped in a clean cloth every full moon. Mandrake root could even act as a witch's familiar. Joan of Arc was accused of carrying a mandrake root, which people said proved she was a witch. Given mandrake's reputation, the roots sold for great sums of money. Opportunistic forgers substituted and sold white bryony roots, a practice that still goes on today. Myths around the collection of mandrakes were reported from ancient times. When mandrake was pulled from the earth, it was supposed to emit a human scream, deadly to all who heard it, so collectors were alleged to tie the plant to a dog's tail, stop their ears, and whip the dog on. The fruits of mandrake were called love apples, or the golden apples of Aphrodite, and believed to be aphrodisiacs. In the Bible, Rachel, who had previously proven barren, took the fruits of mandrake to help her conceive a child.

## MAGICAL USES

Mandrake has a traditional role in hexing and has been used as a poppet to represent the person cursed. Because of its narcotic and hallucinogenic properties, it was an ingredient of the witch's flying ointment (do not try this—see caution below). You can add the leaves to charm bags for protection and luck.

## HOME REMEDIES

Mandrake is no longer used in herbal medicine because of its toxicity. The gap between an effective dose and a fatal dose is extremely small and varies from plant specimen to plant specimen. In the past, it was an important medicinal plant that was used as a painkiller and soporific, though, as the ancient Greek physician Dioscorides warned, if you took too much, you would end up dead.

> **Caution:** *The whole plant is highly poisonous. Do not ingest any part of the plant. Do not burn the leaves or root as incense. Do not apply it to the skin. Symptoms of poisoning include confusion, drowsiness, dry mouth, heart problems, vision problems, feeling hot, hallucinations, and death.*

# Meadowsweet

*Filipendula ulmaria*

PLANETARY RULER: Venus

ELEMENT: Water

ASSOCIATED DEITIES: Aine, Blodeuwedd, Gwena, Venus

MAGICAL VIRTUES: Love

## LORE

Meadowsweet was one of the three most sacred herbs of the Druids (along with water mint and vervain). The folk name of bridewort became popular because it was often used in bridal garlands and posies for bridesmaids and strewn on the path to the church, in the church, and in the home of the newlywed couples.

## MAGICAL USES

Include the herb in the bridal bouquet to bring happiness. If you are searching for love, anoint yourself with meadowsweet oil each night before you go to bed. The dried flowers can be used in love spells and incense. Meadowsweet beer or wine can be drunk at Midsummer, and the flowers can be used in garlands and other decorations.

## CULINARY AND HOUSEHOLD USES

The country name of mead wort comes from the fact the plant was used to flavour mead. Meadowsweet beer was an old country beverage, and the leaves were used with borage to add flavour to the drink known as cool tankard. Put some of the sweet-smelling dried flower sprigs in your linen chest or cupboard to scent your clothes, sheets, and towels.

## COSMETIC USES

To make a skin tonic, place the flowers in rainwater or distilled water and soak for 24 hours.

## HOME REMEDIES

Like willow bark, meadowsweet contains salicylic acid, the pain-killing substance from which aspirin was developed. Unlike aspirin, meadowsweet does not cause gastric ulceration, as the salicylates are buffered by the other compounds contained in the whole herb. It can be made into a tea for headaches and joint and muscle pain. Take as an anti-inflammatory tea or apply a compress for joint pain caused by arthritis, rheumatism, and gout. The tincture is calming and soothing to the stomach and useful for acid indigestion, heartburn, indigestion, diarrhoea, and gastritis.

> *Caution:* *Meadowsweet, when taken appropriately, is safe for most people. However, in some people it can cause nausea, skin rashes, and lung tightness. It should not be taken over an extended period. Avoid if you are pregnant or breastfeeding, have asthma, are allergic to aspirin, or are already taking aspirin or other painkillers.*

# Mints

*Mentha* spp.

. . . . . . . . . . . . . . . . . . .

PLANETARY RULER: Venus/Mercury

ELEMENT: Air

ASSOCIATED DEITIES: Hecate, Mintha (Minthe, Menthe, Mentha), Pluto, Hades, Zeus

MAGICAL VIRTUES: Anaphrodisiac, purification, protection, prophetic dreams, thought, memory, death, rebirth

## LORE

The Latin word *mente* means "thought," as it was believed that the herb stimulated the brain. In Greek myth, Minthe was a naiad and mistress of Hades, god of death, but his jealous wife, Persephone, transformed her into the garden mint. In ancient Greece, it was used in funeral rites, partly because it masked the smell of decay.

## MAGICAL USES

Mint is a herb of protection that can be hung in the home or used in charm bags and protection amulets. A mint infusion can be used to cleanse the ritual area or working tools. It can also be added to the final rinse for robes or included in the pre-ritual bath. It is one of the sacred herbs of Midsummer and commonly used in the food, decorations, garlands, and so on. Peppermint tea can be drunk to encourage prophetic dreams.

## CULINARY AND HOUSEHOLD USES

Use fresh mint in salsas, dressings, pesto, and potato salads. Add it to light summer soups, such as pea or asparagus, and try sprinkling it over strawberries or peaches. You can also add it to fruit drinks, Moroccan-style sweet tea, and cocktails such as mojitos and juleps. Rub the leaves around cocktail glasses before putting in the drinks, or just pop a sprig in fresh lemonade. Mint leaves can be frozen, dried, or infused in oil or vinegar.

## COSMETIC USES

Pour a mint infusion into your bath for a refreshing, relaxing soak, or put it in a footbath to leave tired feet soft and deodorised. Add the infusion or crushed leaves to face masks for oily skin. Use a mint infusion rinse to reduce frizz and increase shine in your hair.

## HOME REMEDIES

Peppermint (M. *piperita*) tea is a common remedy for indigestion, bloating, flatulence, and nausea. Mint is often added to steam baths for relieving congestion and a stuffy nose. Mint tea provides quick relief for nausea and may relieve headaches and migraines. For insect bites, irritated skin, rashes, and other such ailments, bathe the affected area in peppermint tea to cool and soothe. Fresh leaves rubbed on the affected area will reduce the pain of bee and wasp stings.

> **Caution:** *Avoid large doses of peppermint if breastfeeding as it can reduce the milk flow. It should be avoided by individuals with gallstones and those who have a hiatal hernia or heartburn caused by GERD. Peppermint should not be given to children under five. Do not take the essential oil internally. Pennyroyal (Mentha pulegium) should not be taken internally.*

# Mistletoe

*Viscum album*

· · · · · · · · · · · · ·

PLANETARY RULER: Sun/Jupiter

ELEMENT: Air

ASSOCIATED DEITIES: Apollo, Balder, Baldur, Ceridwen,
Dia, Donar, Freya, Frigga, Hera, Odin, Venus

MAGICAL VIRTUES: Immortality, rebirth, hospitality, protection

## LORE

Mistletoe is a potent magical plant because it does not grow on the earth but on the branches of a tree in a "place between places." The leaves are fresh and green all year long, making it a plant of immortality and life surviving in the dead time. The berries ripen in December, as though it is not affected by the seasons and the winter cold. Pliny said that mistletoe was one of the most important magical plants of the Celts and served as a symbol for the winter solstice. In Norse mythology, the mistletoe was used to slay the sun god Balder. After Balder had been resurrected, the mistletoe was given into the keeping of Frigga, the goddess of love, and it was ordained that anyone who passed beneath the mistletoe should receive a kiss to show that it had become a symbol of peace and love. Though other evergreens were included in the decorations of churches, mistletoe was the one omission, as it was considered a Pagan plant.

## MAGICAL USES

Mistletoe berries are used at the midwinter solstice in rituals to give strength to the weakened sun. Mistletoe is a herb of fertility and a symbol of rebirth. Tie some mistletoe with red ribbon and hang it over the doorway at Yule for harmony and to represent a welcome to all who visit, all year round. Replace it at the next Yule, throwing the old piece in the Yule fire to burn away the old and welcome the new. Mistletoe is used as a protection against lightning, disease, fires, and misfortunes.

## HOME REMEDIES

Though the berries of mistletoe are toxic, the leaves and stems of mistletoe have been used in herbal medicine. European mistletoe contains eleven proteins and substances called lectins, which are currently being investigated for anticancer effects. Mistletoe is not recommended for home use.

> **Caution:** *The berries are highly poisonous and should not be taken internally. Mistletoe stems and leaves should only be used under the supervision of a medical herbalist.*

# Mugwort

*Artemisia vulgaris*

. . . . . . . . . . . . .

PLANETARY RULER: Moon/Venus

ELEMENT: Water

ASSOCIATED DEITIES: Artemis, Chandra, Diana, Hecate

MAGICAL VIRTUES: Visions, prophecy, shamanic work, cleansing, protection

## LORE

Mugwort has been used as a food, medicine, spice, insect repellent, yellow dye, and incense. It has also been used for flavouring beer (hence the name *mugwort*), for moxibustion, and in magic. It was called "the oldest of plants … mighty against evil" in the tenth-century Anglo-Saxon *Lacnunga's* Nine Herbs Prayer.[4] In the Middle Ages in Europe, it was considered a protective herb. Mugwort gathered on St. John's Eve was said to safeguard against diseases and misfortunes of all kinds.

## MAGICAL USES

Mugwort is a traditional witch's herb, sacred to the goddess of the moon and used for prophecy and visions. Add mugwort to incense, smoke the leaf, or place a leaf beneath your pillow (or stuff a pillow with dried mugwort) for prophetic dreams. To enhance dreams, take mugwort tea before bed. Put a sprig in your shoe to prevent tiredness on long journeys and hang some up to protect your home. Flowering shoots can be made into ritual fumigation/saining sticks for cleansing negativity.

## CULINARY AND HOUSEHOLD USES

The leaves and young shoots can be cooked as a vegetable, eaten raw in salads, or added to soups, stews, or stuffing. The leaves can be infused as a tea. Mugwort can be used as a flavouring for beers, spirits, and liqueurs. Dried mugwort has been used as a tobacco substitute. A bunch hung in the kitchen door keeps flies away.

---

4  Pettit, *Anglo-Saxon Remedies, Charms, and Prayers from British Library MS Harley 585.*

## COSMETIC USES

Used in the bath, mugwort will refresh and revive. Add the powdered herb to exfoliators to treat acne.

## HOME REMEDIES

Mugwort is sometimes referred to as the women's herb because it was used to promote menstruation and induce childbirth. Use the tincture or tea for irregular periods, stress, anxiety, and nervousness. Take the tea for gas and bloating or a sluggish digestion.

> **Caution:** *Avoid if pregnant or breastfeeding. Avoid overconsumption, which can have mildly toxic effects.*

# Mullein

*Verbascum thapsus*

. . . . . . . . . . . . . . .

PLANETARY RULER: Saturn

ELEMENT: Water

ASSOCIATED DEITIES: Circe, Hecate, Jupiter

MAGICAL VIRTUES: Protection, courage, ancestral contact, divination

## LORE

The genus name, *Verbascum*, is a corruption of *barbascum* (a beard), which is a reference to the woolly appearance of the plant. It has many associations with magic. The Greek witch-goddess Circe was said to have used mullein in her incantations, or conversely, according to Homer, Odysseus used mullein to protect himself against her. According to Agrippa, mullein leaves overpowered demons. During the Middle Ages, it was often grown in monastery gardens to protect them from manifestations of the devil. In the past the fibrous mullein stems were used as wicks in lamps.

## MAGICAL USES

Mullein is primarily a herb of protection from negative influences and evil spirits. Grow it in your garden to protect your property. Carry a herbal charm bag or hang it in your home for protection. You can also place it beneath your pillow to prevent nightmares. Use mullein oil to magically seal your doors, windows, and property to prevent negative energy from entering. The leaves and flowers can be added to spells, incenses, and charms for courage in difficult situations. Carry some mullein to attract potential partners. Mullein tea can be taken to connect with ancestral knowledge and to see spirits. Use the tea or incense in your divination work.

## CULINARY AND HOUSEHOLD USES

Tea can be made from the young leaves and flowers. They can also be eaten in a salad. The long flowering spikes can be dipped in tallow or vegetable oil, lit with a match, and used for garden torches. A purple dye can be obtained from mullein.

. . . . .

## Cosmetic Uses

A macerated mullein oil has antiseptic properties and can help if you have dry, itchy, or inflamed skin. Crushed fresh leaves may be applied directly to the skin for a moisturising effect. A tincture of mullein can be added to shampoos and conditioners to treat dandruff. An infusion of mullein flowers can be added to your final hair rinse to bring out natural blond highlights.

## Home Remedies

Mullein is used as a herbal expectorant, decongestant, and mucus reducer that can be used to ease catarrh/mucus and chest complaints. The leaves, when made into a lotion or salve, aid wound healing and soothe inflammation. An infused oil of the flowers and leaves makes a good treatment for earache caused by compacted wax and may be used to treat inflamed skin, eczema, and psoriasis. A salve may be used externally for the treatment of haemorrhoids, burns, ulcers, rheumatism, arthritis, and chilblains.

> **Caution:** *The seeds are toxic and should not be used. Mullein preparations from the older leaves should always be strained through muslin to remove the fine hairs that may cause irritation to the mouth and skin. Stay on the safe side and avoid use if you are pregnant or breastfeeding.*

# Myrrh

*Commiphora myrrha syn. Commiphora molmol*

. . . . . . . . . . . . .

PLANETARY RULER: Sun/Moon/Jupiter/Saturn

ELEMENT: Fire/water

ASSOCIATED DEITIES: Adonis, Aphrodite, Bhavani, Cybele, Demeter, Freya, Hathor, Hecate, Hera, Isis, Juno, Marian, Mut, Myrrha, Neptune, Nephthys, Osiris, Persephone, Poseidon, Ra, Rhea, Saturn

MAGICAL VIRTUES: Aphrodisiac, love, death

## LORE

The name *myrrh* is derived from the old Arabic word *mur*, meaning "bitter." It has been known and used since ancient times. In Greek myth, the maiden Myrrha refused to worship Aphrodite, and the goddess punished her by making her commit incest with her father. The gods transformed her into a tree, and the resin exuded by the myrrh is said to be her tears. Ten months later the tree opened, and the god Adonis was born. Adonis became the lover of Aphrodite, and it said that her passion for him was provoked by the sap of the myrrh tree; myrrh was a well-known aphrodisiac. It was a funeral herb for the Egyptians, used in the embalming process and burned as an incense during the funeral rites.

## MAGICAL USES

Myrrh is a perfume of love and death. It is widely used in incenses, raising the vibrations and increasing spiritual awareness. It is associated with funerals and mourning, as the tree itself seems to weep and the secretion is bitter. Myrrh incense may be used at funeral rites. At the opposite end of the spectrum, it is a perfume of erotic love and seduction. As such, it may be used in sex magic and love incenses, perfumes, spells, and charms.

## CULINARY AND HOUSEHOLD USES

Burn the resin as an incense or use the essential oil in an oil evaporator.

. . . . .

## COSMETIC USES

Ground myrrh may be added to tooth powders or facial scrubs. The tincture or oil can be added to face creams and lotions for antiaging benefits.

## HOME REMEDIES

Myrrh is antibacterial and normally used as a powder, tincture, or essential oil since it is not soluble in water. It is usually used in external treatments. The diluted tincture can be used as a mouthwash for bad breath and a gargle for sore throats, mouth ulcers, gum infections, and oral thrush. Topically, the diluted tincture or oil can be used for acne, boils, haemorrhoids, wounds, and pressure sores.

> **Caution:** *Myrrh is considered safe for most people when used in small amounts. It may cause diarrhoea if taken orally. Large amounts (greater than 2 grams) may cause kidney irritation and heart rate changes. Avoid taking myrrh internally if you are pregnant, breastfeeding, diabetic, or taking blood-thinning medications, such as warfarin. Do not take myrrh internally for at least two weeks before surgery or if you have a fever or heart problems.*

# Nasturtium

*Tropaeolum majus*

. . . . . . . . . . . . . .

PLANETARY RULER: Mars

ELEMENT: Fire

MAGICAL VIRTUES: Vitality, positivity, strength, recovery, protection, victory

## LORE

Nasturtiums originally grew in South America and were introduced into Europe in the sixteenth century as a salad vegetable. The Swedish botanist Carl Linnaeus classified nasturtium in the botanical family Tropaeolaceae because the shape of the flowers and leaves reminded him of the blood-stained helmets and shields of vanquished enemies that Romans hung on a trophy pole (trophaeum).

## MAGICAL USES

Add dried flowers and leaves to Mars incense and fire incense. Use them in spells and rituals to promote vitality and strength and for recovery after any exhaustion of mental and physical energy. The plant is also used for protection; to ward off unwanted visitors and prevent baneful influences from reaching your home, plant a red nasturtium by your front door. Put some dried flowers and leaves in a pouch and carry it for protection.

## CULINARY AND HOUSEHOLD USES

The flowers taste rather like a mild watercress. They can be stuffed with soft cheese. The young leaves can be chopped and added to salads, soups, stews, and rice dishes or to sandwiches in the place of mustard. You can also wilt them into stir-fries. The peppery leaves are large enough to be used as a substitute for grapevine leaves, which can be stuffed and baked with a filling of your choice. Nasturtium seeds can be ground and used as a pepper substitute. "Poor man's capers" is a name given to pickled unripe nasturtium seeds.

## COSMETIC USES

Not only a natural antibiotic, nasturtium contains lots of sulphur, which makes it helpful for clearing the skin. Use a nasturtium infusion as a face wash or put the flowers and leaves into a facial steam to treat acne and skin breakouts. A nasturtium rinse is beneficial for the hair, promoting hair growth, toning the scalp, and helping prevent dandruff and hair loss.

## HOME REMEDIES

The flowers, leaves, and seeds are all used, and all parts of the plant have strong antibiotic and antimicrobial properties. Nasturtium tea can be used as an antiseptic wash for cuts and grazes. To increase resistance to bacterial infection, take a nasturtium infusion. Nasturtium is a good source of vitamin C and may be used to help the body naturally overcome colds and flu. Drink the liquid expressed by the juiced leaves for chronic lung conditions such as emphysema. For muscular pain, add a strong infusion of nasturtium flowers and leaves into a warm bath and soak.

> **Caution:** *Nasturtium contains mustard oil, which can cause skin irritation when used topically. Avoid ingesting medicinal amounts if you are pregnant or breastfeeding or have stomach ulcers or kidney disease.*

# Nettle, Stinging

*Urtica dioica*

PLANETARY RULER: Mars

ELEMENT: Fire

ASSOCIATED DEITIES: Agni, Blodeuwedd, Cernunnos, Donar, Hades, Horus, Jupiter, Osiris, Pcuvus, Pluto, Thor, Vishnu, Vulcan, Yama

MAGICAL VIRTUES: Protection, counter magic, love, fidelity, divination

## LORE

Most people know about the nettle's sting, and indeed, the genus name, *Urtica*, comes from the Latin *uro*, meaning "I burn." The common name comes from the Anglo-Saxon *noedl*, meaning "a needle." Folk names such as devil's leaf and naughty man's plaything are also descriptive of the plant's reputation, though, like other stinging or thorny plants, they were considered a protection against ill.

## MAGICAL USES

The primary magical use of nettle is protection against negative entities and storms. Use it in protection rituals and spells, talismans, incense, and charms. Nettle is dedicated to thunder gods, and it may be used in incense, oils, and so on when invoking them.

## CULINARY AND HOUSEHOLD USES

Nettle leaves have very high levels of vitamins and minerals. Use the young leaves only and wear gloves when picking them. Cooking destroys the sting. Infuse the leaves into a tea or add them to soups, purees, and pesto. Cook the young shoots like spinach. Wine or beer may be made from the whole aerial parts.

## COSMETIC USES

If you have oily skin or greasy hair, nettles will help. Add the leaves to facial steams to open the pores and brighten the complexion. Add a nettle infusion to your bath to stimulate circulation and leave your skin glowing. To reduce oil and treat dandruff, use a nettle infusion to rinse your hair.

## HOME REMEDIES

Nettles are an old remedy for arthritis and rheumatism as they contain compounds that interfere with the way that nerves send pain signals, which reduces the sensation of pain. Place a nettle compress on the affected area or rub with nettle oil or lotion. Drink a cup or two of nettle tea daily to reduce arthritic pain and stiffness. It will also provide bioavailable iron, which is easily absorbed. A salve made from the leaves may benefit eczema and inflamed skin. A tea made from the root is diuretic.

> *Caution:* Use gloves when collecting. Avoid if you have kidney problems or take lithium, sedatives, or blood-thinning and anticlotting medications.

# Oak

*Quercus robur*

· · · · · · · · · · · · · ·

PLANETARY RULER: Jupiter

ELEMENT: Fire

ASSOCIATED DEITIES: Allah, Ares, Arianrhod, Artemis, Athene, Balder, Blodeuwedd, Brighid, Ceirddylad, Ceridwen, Cernunnos, Cybele, The Dagda, Dianus, Donar, dryads, Erato, The Erinyes, Hades, Hecate, Hercules, Herne, Horus, Indra, Janicot, Janus, Jehovah, Jupiter, Kirke, Llyr, Mars, Nephthys, Odin, Pan, Pluto, Rhea, Tannus, Taran, Thor, Ukho, Vishnu, Zeus

MAGICAL VIRTUES: Connection between the realms, protection, prophecy, fertility, longevity

## LORE

Synonymous with strength and resilience, the oak is honoured more in European lore than any other tree. It was sacred to chief gods, sky gods, and storm gods, perhaps because lightning strikes the oak more often than any other tree, which was seen as the gods marking it as sacred. In ancient Greece, the chief god Zeus spoke through the rustling leaves of oak trees at his oracular shrine at Dodona. The Celtic Druids practiced their religion in oak groves.

· · · · ·

## MAGICAL USES

The roots of the oak extend as far underground as its branches do above, a cosmic axis connecting sky, earth, and underworld. Meditate with your back to an oak tree and listen for the whisperings of the gods in the windblown leaves. The powdered bark and leaves may be burned to invoke the plant's associated deities. Sacred fires should contain oak, if possible. Acorns are symbols of fruitfulness and often used in fertility magic. They can be carried to attract potential partners, longevity, youthfulness, and prosperity. Hung in windows, they protect the home from lightning and other ills.

## CULINARY AND HOUSEHOLD USES

Acorns can be shelled, dried, ground into a powder, and used as a thickening agent for stews or mixed with flour when making bread. They can also be shelled, roasted whole, and ground to make a coffee substitute. Oak galls (growths on the tree caused by insect larvae) may be mixed with salts of iron to make a black dye, mixed with alum for a brown dye, or mixed with salts of tin for a yellow dye. A purplish dye is obtained from an infusion of the bark with a small quantity of copperas.

## COSMETIC USES

An oak bark decoction can be used as a hair rinse to stop hair loss and treat dandruff.

## HOME REMEDIES

An oak bark decoction is astringent and may be applied to the skin in a compress (or added to the bathwater) for pain and swelling of the skin; chilblains; red, itchy skin; haemorrhoids; and varicose veins.

> *Caution:* *Take internally for no more than four days and no longer than three weeks if used as an external remedy. Avoid completely if you are pregnant or breastfeeding. Do not take if you have a heart condition, eczema, hypertonia, or kidney or liver problems.*

# Oats

*Avena sativa*

· · · · · · · · · · · · · · · · · ·

PLANETARY RULER: Venus

ELEMENT: Earth

ASSOCIATED DEITIES: Virankannos, Brighid

MAGICAL VIRTUES: Fertility, divination, prosperity,
strength, endurance, peace, money

## LORE

Oats are an annual cereal crop grown in temperate northern latitudes where wheat and barley struggle to mature. Archaeological remains have shown that they have been ground and consumed for at least 32,000 years. In northern climates, they were a highly valued crop, though the Romans called Germanic tribes "oat-eating barbarians" and reserved oats for their horses. They were certainly more valued in northern countries where growing wheat was difficult. In the *Edda*, a collection of Nordic mythology, oats are described as the food of the gods.

## MAGICAL USES

All grains are associated with abundance, and oats were traditionally used in prosperity spells and rituals. You can use oats for harvest decorations, add them to ritual food, use them as an offering to harvest gods, make your Brighid doll from oats at Imbolc, or add them to wealth- and fertility-drawing charm bags and herbal talismans. Hang up in the kitchen to attract good luck.

## CULINARY AND HOUSEHOLD USES

Unlike wheat, barley, and rye, oats do not naturally contain gluten, though gluten may be added to them in commercial products, or they may be contaminated by being processed near gluten-containing grains. Oats are often eaten as breakfast porridge and overnight oats, and they may also be added to gruel, put in dishes like haggis, or shaped into oat cakes. For vegans and those sensitive to dairy products, oat milk is a good replacement.

· · · · ·

## COSMETIC USES

Oats are wonderful for the skin. They are deeply moisturising and soothing while improving the skin's elasticity and accelerating tissue healing. This is especially beneficial for itchy, inflamed skin, but oats will also reduce fine lines and wrinkles. Put oats into a muslin bag and drop it into your bath, add oat milk to lotions, or mix oats with oat milk or honey for a face mask.

## HOME REMEDIES

Oats have two main uses. Used externally, the anti-inflammatory and antioxidant compounds they contain will reduce the scaliness and itching of eczema. Taken internally, in food or as oat milk, they help lower LDL cholesterol. This is thanks to a specific type of fibre they contain called beta-glucan. They also contain the alkaloid gramine, which is a natural sedative.

> **Caution:** *None known (see previous note in the culinary section about coeliac sufferers and the potential contamination of oats).*

# Olive

*Olea europaea*

. . . . . . . . . . . . . . . . .

PLANETARY RULER: Sun

ELEMENT: Fire

ASSOCIATED DEITIES: Amun Ra, Apollo, Artemis,
Athene, Demeter, Ganymede, Hercules, Hermes, Indra,
Isis, Juno, Jupiter, Nut, Poseidon, sun gods, Zeus

MAGICAL VIRTUES: Wisdom, fertility, power, purity

## LORE

Olives have been cultivated since the Neolithic period. It is estimated that an olive tree can reach 2,000 years of age. There are decades between planting an olive tree and the first harvest, though, which is why the olive branch is a symbol of peace—only people who intended to live quiet lives and plan for the future would cultivate an olive grove. In Greek myth, the olive was created by the goddess Athene during a competition with Poseidon for control of Athens. Each was asked to give a gift to the city, and the citizens were to choose the winner. Poseidon crashed his trident on the Acropolis, which released a freshwater spring, but the Athenians much preferred the abundant and very useful tree of Athene. Olive oil has long been used in sacred rites and burned in the temple lamps of ancient Greece.

## MAGICAL USES

Olive and olive branches may be used as offerings to the gods and to decorate the altar. The dried leaves may be used as incense to invoke any of the plant's associated gods. Carry an olive leaf to put you under the protection of the gods and bring good luck. Use an olive branch as an asperger (sprinkler) to shake a potion of peace around any place that has a fractious atmosphere. Use olive leaves or olives in spells of fertility. Anoint the chakras with olive oil to allow them to open and accept divine energy. Olive oil may be used for consecration, burned in temple lamps, or used as the base of magical oils.

. . . . .

## Culinary and Household Uses

Olives can be eaten as a snack, added to salads, included in pasta sauces, blended into a tapenade, baked in bread, or added to pizzas. Olive oil is a fragrant oil made from pressed olives; it is often used as a salad dressing and for cooking.

## Cosmetic Uses

Olive oil is rich in vitamins, including vitamin E, and can be used to moisturise and soften the skin (just rub it on) and hair (massage through the hair, leave it on for two hours, and rinse off). It is an antioxidant and may be applied to the skin after exposure to the sun.

## Home Remedies

Olive leaves can be dried and made into a tea that lowers high blood pressure and high blood sugar. Olive oil can be used topically in the treatment of pruritus, stings, and burns and can be used as a rub for skin, muscle, and joint complaints.

> **Caution:** *Avoid olive leaf tea if pregnant or breastfeeding. Olive leaf tea and preparations may increase the effects of drugs that lower blood pressure and drugs or herbs that lower blood sugar.*

# Orange

*Citrus sinensis*

· · · · · · · · · · · · · · ·

PLANETARY RULER: Sun

ELEMENT: Fire

MAGICAL VIRTUES: Fertility, love, luck, happiness, prosperity

## LORE

Oranges are not named after the colour. Rather, it is the other way round, the word coming from the Sanskrit *nāraṅga*, meaning "the orange tree." Oranges likely originated in China and were not introduced into Europe until about the ninth century. Oranges are evergreen and bear fruit and flowers all year round, making them natural symbols of fertility. Orange blossom chaplets are worn by brides for fertility. They are common Chinese New Year gifts, bringing good luck and happiness, as their golden colour represents prosperity.

## MAGICAL USES

Wear orange blossoms to increase the chance of a happy marriage, and use them in handfasting bouquets. To discover the initial letter of a future lover, peel an orange in one strip, throw it over your shoulder, and see which letter's shape it forms. Use the dried peel in incense and spells of love, fertility, success, prosperity, and luck. Give oranges as good luck gifts.

## CULINARY AND HOUSEHOLD USES

Oranges can be eaten fresh or frozen; made into marmalade or orange curd; candied in slices for cake decoration; juiced and drunk or added to baked goods; and so on. The peel can be made into a herbal tea, and the grated zest can be used to flavour sweet and savoury dishes. Put the peel in vinegar, leave 2 weeks, and strain to make a liquid cleanser for your kitchen surfaces. An orange pomander, studded with cloves, makes a natural air freshener and will protect your clothes from moths.

· · · · ·

## COSMETIC USES

The acidity of oranges can treat acne when used in a face mask (mix with yoghurt). Use the ground peel in exfoliants, mixed with water. This mix will also lighten your skin, tighten pores, and leave your skin fresh and glowing. Orange blossoms have a calming and anti-inflammatory effect. Use dried blossoms in your bath or apply a cooled infusion to your face to brighten and relax the skin.

## HOME REMEDIES

Oranges are rich in vitamin C, which helps your body make collagen, makes it easier to absorb iron, boosts your immune system, and combats stress. Oranges are used in traditional Chinese medicine to treat nausea and heartburn. Orange leaf tea is calming and can help with anxiety.

> *Caution:* Oranges are high in acid, which can make symptoms of GERD worse. They are also high in potassium, so if you are taking beta-blockers, eat in moderation. If you suffer from hemochromatosis, restrict your consumption.

# Oregano

*Origanum vulgare*

. . . . . . . . . . . . . .

PLANETARY RULER: Venus

ELEMENT: Air

ASSOCIATED DEITIES: Aphrodite

MAGICAL VIRTUES: Joy, love, happiness

## LORE

Both the common and botanical name comes from two Greek words, *oros*, meaning "mountain," and *ganos*, meaning "joy." In myth, it was created by Aphrodite, the goddess of love, to spread happiness amongst humankind. In ancient Greece, oregano wreaths were worn by brides and grooms at weddings, and the sheets of the marriage bed were scented with it.

## MAGICAL USES

The essence of oregano's energy is love, and this includes the joy and pleasure that comes from our relationships with others. Use oregano in spells and rituals of love and friendship, put it in the food at handfastings and weddings, and add it to incense, charm bags, and herbal talismans. At Midsummer it is one of the sacred herbs thrown onto the fire or added to the incense and food. Drink oregano tea to release grief and welcome joy into your life.

## CULINARY AND HOUSEHOLD USES

Oregano and marjoram are substitutions for one another in cooking, though oregano has a slightly stronger flavour. The fragrance and flavour come from the volatile oils in the plant, so always add fresh oregano during the final stages of the cooking process. Add the herb to salads, casseroles, soups, sauces, rice dishes, and pizzas.

## COSMETIC USES

Oregano contains compounds that are antifungal, antiseptic, and antioxidant. This makes it of benefit in treating acne and pimples; use oregano tea as a facial wash or steam. Oregano's antimicrobial properties may benefit an irritated, itchy scalp; use oregano tea as a hair rinse.

. . . . .

## HOME REMEDIES

The volatile oils in oregano leaves have antifungal properties; for oral thrush, use oregano tea as a mouthwash. Add a strong infusion of oregano to the bath to treat vaginal thrush. Oregano also has expectorant, antiviral, and antimicrobial properties and may be useful against respiratory infections, bronchitis, and catarrh/mucus. Drink a cup of oregano tea the second you feel the onset of a cold or flu, and use the cooled tea as a gargle for sore throats. Massage the areas affected with arthritis and rheumatism with oregano oil.

*Caution: Oregano leaf is safe when taken in the amounts found in food and safe for most people when taken by mouth or applied to the skin in medicinal amounts. Mild side effects include stomach upset. Avoid medicinal amounts if pregnant or breastfeeding or if you have bleeding disorders. Oregano might lower blood sugar levels. Avoid if you take lithium, as larger amounts of oregano are diuretic.*

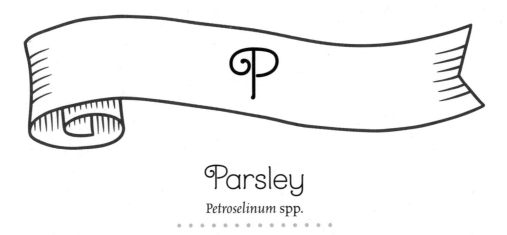

# Parsley

*Petroselinum* spp.

· · · · · · · · · · · · · ·

**PLANETARY RULER:** Mercury

**ELEMENT:** Air

**ASSOCIATED DEITIES:** Charon Archemoros,
chthonic deities, Odin, Persephone, Poseidon

**MAGICAL VIRTUES:** Death, funerals, underworld, spring, rebirth, renewal

## LORE

In its native Mediterranean region, parsley was a popular culinary herb and added to a variety of dishes and sauces. However, some ancients thought it was sinful to eat it because it was a funeral herb, used to fashion wreaths for tombs and to honour the dead at funeral feasts. In Greece, it was sacred to the goddess Persephone, the queen of the underworld. The reluctant germination of parsley might be one of the reasons it is associated with the underworld; in English folklore, it has to go nine times to the devil and back before coming up.

## MAGICAL USES

Offer parsley to chthonic gods, particularly Persephone, and in funeral and memorial rites, when communicating with the dead, and in ancestral rites, such as Samhain. Put dried parsley in the incense, use it to make wreaths, put it in ritual food and drink, or anoint yourself with parsley oil. It may also be used to welcome Persephone's return to earth in spring rites.

## CULINARY AND HOUSEHOLD USES

Add finely chopped parsley leaves to salads, sauces, salad dressings, herb butters, tomato dishes, potatoes, and peas. Don't throw away the stalks; their more intense flavour can be used for stews, soups, casseroles, and sauces.

## COSMETIC USES

Parsley will cleanse, tone, and lighten your skin thanks to its antioxidant and antibacterial compounds. Add it to homemade skin toners and cleansers, or use parsley tea as a facial wash. For dark circles under the eyes or dark spots on your skin, apply parsley juice, leave on 10 minutes, and rinse.

## HOME REMEDIES

Parsley tea is a natural diuretic, which helps cleanse bladder infections such as cystitis. The herb can also be used to flush toxins from the system in cases of rheumatism, arthritis, and gout. Parsley has especially high chlorophyll levels, and they give the plant antibacterial properties that can be used to combat bad breath. Apply a parsley poultice to insect bites. Parsley is rich in iron (more so than any other vegetable) and vitamin C, which promotes better iron absorption.

> *Caution:* *None known for the herb. However, the seeds and essential oil should not be used by pregnant women, children, and people with kidney problems. Overconsumption of the seeds can lead to irritated stomach, liver, heart, and kidneys.*

# Passionflower

*Passiflora* spp.

· · · · · · · · · · · · · ·

PLANETARY RULER: Venus

ELEMENT: Water

ASSOCIATED DEITIES: Christ, Krishna, Tonantzin

MAGICAL VIRTUES: Love, calm, peace, friendship

## LORE

Native to the southeastern United States and Central and South America, passionflower is a type of woody vine. There are over 500 species. Some are grown for ornament, some for medicine, and some for their edible fruits. When Spanish colonialists in South America discovered passionflower, they believed they had found a perfect symbol of Christ's passion. The plant's corona filaments represented the crown of thorns, the stigma stood for the three nails, the petals were the scourge, and the five stamens symbolised Christ's five wounds.

## MAGICAL USES

Passionflower has a soothing effect on the mind and body. Take a tea before meditation or trance induction or before bed for dreamwork. Bring peace and tranquillity to the home by adding passionflower to incense, bowls of potpourri, and charm bags. These may also be used in home blessing rituals. Use in love and friendship spells. Carry some in a sachet to improve your popularity.

## CULINARY AND HOUSEHOLD USES

Some (not all) species of passionflowers have edible fruit. Eat them fresh, or use them to make juice, jams, ice cream, and desserts. Make a tea of the flowers.

## COSMETIC USES

Passionflower moisturises and is a natural anti-inflammatory. Add the flowers and oil to your homemade moisturisers and serums. The anti-inflammatory fruit is rich in omega-6 essential fatty acids and will boost circulation; use it in a fruit mask.

## HOME REMEDIES

The leaves, stems, and flowers of *Passiflora incarnata* are used medicinally (do not use other species). It has a calming influence on the nervous system. Take the tea for anxiety, tension, and nervousness. It acts as a mild sedative and helps with insomnia and sleep issues. Drink the tea for tension and pain, as it has calming and antispasmodic properties. It can also be helpful for menstrual cramping and PMS.

> *Caution: Pregnant and breastfeeding individuals should avoid taking passion-flower by mouth. Do not take with blood-thinning herbs or antiplatelet or anticoagulant drugs. Do not take if you are using prescription sleep medication, antidepressants, or tranquillisers.*

# Peony

*Paeonia* spp.

. . . . . . . . . . . .

PLANETARY RULER: Sun

ELEMENT: Fire

ASSOCIATED DEITIES: Paeon, Apollo, Aesculapius, moon goddesses

MAGICAL VIRTUES: Healing, warding, protection, counter magic, exorcism

## LORE

Peony is named in honour of Paeon, a pupil of Asclepius, the Greek god of medi-cine. Worried that his bright pupil might eclipse him, Asclepius tried to kill him, but Zeus changed the youth into a peony flower, thus preserving him forever. The ancient Greeks believed that peony drove away evil spirits. In mediaeval Europe, peony was used to ward many kinds of evil. The herbalist Culpeper claimed it cured any illness caused by demonic possession, while Gerard wrote it healed those who had been bewitched.

## MAGICAL USES

Used for protection and warding off negative influences, peony petals may be scattered around the edge of the ritual circle, placed on thresholds, or carried in a charm bag. Grow it in the garden as a guardian plant. Add the dried petals and powdered root to protection and exorcism incenses and oils. To prevent nightmares, place a peony flower beneath your pillow. Use peony incense, oil, potions, and fresh flowers in rituals and spells of healing and to honour the gods of medicine.

## CULINARY AND HOUSEHOLD USES

The petals, seeds, and roots are all edible, and they were popular ingredients in mediaeval cookery. Infuse the petals in boiling water for a calming tea. Grind the seeds to use as a spice. Garnish dishes with fresh peony petals, and add them to salads, summer drinks, and cocktails. Added to jams and jellies, they will impart colour.

. . . . .

## COSMETIC USES

Peonies contain a unique compound called paeoniflorin, which effectively reduces wrinkles. Add peony petals to infusions and oil to make your own moisturisers. Drop some petals in your bath.

## HOME REMEDIES

Peony root contains some interesting compounds, including high amounts of anti-inflammatory glucosides, which may be of use in cases of rheumatoid arthritis, muscle spasms, and menstrual cramps. A decoction of the dried and powdered root is used. Peony petal tea is mildly sedative.

> **Caution:** *Peony is generally considered safe, though an overdose can lead to a stomach upset. It should not be taken by pregnant or lactating individuals; peony is an emmenagogue (i.e., capable of stimulating menstruation). Do not take if you are on blood-thinning medication or for two weeks before scheduled surgery.*

# Pine

*Pinus sylvestris*

. . . . . . . . . . . . . . . . .

PLANETARY RULER: Mars

ELEMENT: Air

ASSOCIATED DEITIES: Astarte, Attis, Adonis, Artemis, Asclepius,
Baldur, Dionysus, Cernunnos, Cybele, Demeter, Herne, Men,
Osiris, Pan, Pitys, Pittea, Poseidon, Rhea, Sol, Sylvanus, Venus

MAGICAL VIRTUES: Rebirth, immortality,
resurrection, cleansing, healing, fertility

## LORE

Pine is associated with a variety of vegetation gods, who die and are reborn, such as Adonis,
Attis, Dionysus, and Osiris. Because it grows phallic-looking cones, the pine is a tree of
fertility. As an evergreen, it is a symbol of immortality and has been used at funerals; an old
custom was to place pine boughs on the coffin during funeral rites and burials. The pine
is also associated with healing, perhaps because of its antiseptic and medicinal qualities.
Some images of Asclepius (the Greek healer god) show him holding a pinecone in his left
hand.

## MAGICAL USES

The pinecone forms in a spiral growth pattern, making it a symbol of rebirth and fertility.
The pine wand and cone are used in fertility magic and healing, and pine may be incorporated into incense, charm bags, talismans, amulets, spells, and rituals for those purposes. A
pinecone may be carried as a focus for the magic. The resin, needles, and wood from the
pine are used to invoke vegetation gods and to cleanse the sacred space.

## CULINARY AND HOUSEHOLD USES

The needles can be made into a refreshing tea. A pine needle decoction is a disinfectant,
which can be added to the laundry and to cleaning washes and solutions. Pinecones can be
dipped in wax to make effective firelighters.

. . . . .

## COSMETIC USES

A pine needle decoction can be added to the bath to stimulate and refresh the skin. It also acts as a natural antiseptic deodorant that kills odour-producing bacteria. A pine needle wash may be used on the face to combat acne, speed healing, and reduce the appearance of wrinkles. Added to a hair rinse, pine decoction fights dandruff and adds shine.

## HOME REMEDIES

The leaves have a mildly antiseptic effect within the chest when taken internally as a tea or used as a steam inhalation. A pine needle salve will aid stiff and aching muscles, arthritis, and rheumatism. A pine infusion can be used as an antiseptic skin wash for cuts and wounds.

> **Caution:** *Make sure you identify your tree properly, as some varieties of pine are toxic. Avoid completely if you are pregnant or breastfeeding. Pine can cause allergic reactions in some people and in some asthma sufferers.*

# Pomegranate

*Punica granatum*

. . . . . . . . . . . . . .

PLANETARY RULER: Mercury

ELEMENT: Fire

ASSOCIATED DEITIES: Adonis, Agditis, Aphrodite, Athene, Baal, Ceres, Cybele, Demeter, Dionysus, Hades, Hera, Hermes, Inanna, Juno, Kore, Kubaba, Kwan Yin, Mercury, Persephone, Proserpina, Rimmon, Rimmon, Sheol, Tammuz

MAGICAL VIRTUES: Marriage, death and resurrection, prosperity, fertility, passionate love, apotropaic, protection

## LORE

Pomegranates are associated with death and resurrection deities (such as vegetation gods and sun gods), death, the underworld, and rebirth. In Greek myth, Persephone, daughter of Demeter, the goddess of agriculture, was abducted by the underworld god, Hades. Demeter refused to let crops grow until Persephone was returned, but while in the underworld, Persephone had eaten pomegranate seeds from the fruit of the underworld, so she was forced to stay. Zeus arranged a compromise—Persephone would spend part of the year with her mother and part with Hades. Because it has an abundance of seeds, pomegranate fruit is associated with fertility. Roman brides wore a wreath of pomegranate flowers.

## MAGICAL USES

Use pomegranates to drive out negative energies and ward off evil spirits; place the fruit in a vulnerable area or wear pomegranate flowers. Use pomegranates in fertility and prosperity charms and weddings and handfastings.

## CULINARY AND HOUSEHOLD USES

Pomegranate may be eaten as it is, juiced, or made into syrup. The juicy red seeds (arils) can be added to sweet and savoury dishes and to salads, yoghurt, vegetables, and rice, grain, or couscous. They can also be baked into cheesecakes, cakes, and tarts.

## COSMETIC USES

Apply pomegranate juice to your skin to brighten skin tone and lighten blemishes. A crushed seed face pack (mix with honey and oats) will brighten skin tone and remove dead skin cells. Dry and powder the rind for an exfoliating scrub (mix with honey or milk/soya milk), which will help combat acne.

## HOME REMEDIES

Pomegranate fruit and juice contain compounds that may be beneficial in slowing the progression of atherosclerosis, reducing blood pressure, reducing kidney stones, and promoting healthy gut bacteria. Add pomegranates or their juice to your diet for those benefits.

> **Caution:** *The root, stem, and peel of pomegranate are slightly toxic. Do not consume by mouth. Some people have experienced allergic reactions to a topical application of pomegranate.*

# Poplar

*Populus* spp.

. . . . . . . . . . . . . .

PLANETARY RULER: Sun

ELEMENT: Fire

ASSOCIATED DEITIES: Apollo, Chronos, Hades, Hecate, Heliads, Herakles/
Hercules, Jupiter, Leuce, Manes, Mut, Nun, Persephone, Valkyries, Zeus

MAGICAL VIRTUES: Death, mourning, underworld
travel, chthonic magic, sacrifice

## LORE

The ever-moving leaves of the poplar, stirred by the tiniest breeze, dark one side, white on the other, symbolise the dualities of night and day, life and death. The valley of the Styx (the river that must be crossed to enter the underworld) was said to be full of poplars. The black poplar was sacred to Hades, its ruler, and the white poplar (aspen) to his wife, Persephone. In the Odyssey, it is mentioned as one of the three trees of resurrection, along with the alder and the cypress.

## MAGICAL USES

For rituals of death and resurrection (such as contacting the dead, funerals, memorials, Samhain, and Yule) decorate with poplar branches, use poplar wood in the incense, and cast the circle with a poplar wand. At rites of initiation (itself a ritual of death and rebirth) carry a piece of poplar or wear a piece of jewellery fashioned from the wood. Poplar incense may be used in the invocation of chthonic gods, particularly Hecate. Add poplar oil to the flying ointment for underworld travel.

## CULINARY AND HOUSEHOLD USES

The starchy inner bark of the white poplar (*Populus alba*) and other species have been used as a famine food. It can be eaten raw, cooked, or dried and ground into flour.

. . . . .

## Home Remedies

A salve made from poplar buds can be used on burns and wounds. The bark of the white poplar contains salicylates, or natural aspirin. A decoction can be drunk for rheumatism, arthritis, and gout. Externally, a poplar bark poultice or compress may be applied to sprains, chilblains, and haemorrhoids.

*Caution:* *Topical applications may cause allergic reactions in some people.*

# Poppy, Red

a.k.a. Corn/Field Poppy

*Papaver rhoeas*

. . . . . . . . . . . . .

PLANETARY RULER: Moon

ELEMENT: Water

ASSOCIATED DEITIES: Agni, Aphrodite, Artemis, Ceres, Cybele, Demeter, Diana, Hades, Hera, Hermes, Hypnos, Jupiter, harvest goddesses, Mercury, Morpheus, mother goddesses, Persephone, Pluto, Proserpine, Somnus, Venus, Vulcan, Yama, Thanatos, Nyx

MAGICAL VIRTUES: Fertility, death, mourning, dreamwork, meditation

## LORE

From ancient times until relatively recently, red poppies always grew alongside the grain crops of Europe, though sadly, since the widespread use of herbicides, they no longer do. This would have been unthinkable to the ancients, who believed the two were natural companions, with poppies necessary for the health of the grain because they represented the lifeblood of the goddess of agriculture flowing through the fields. Poppies were considered sacred to her.

## MAGICAL USES

Decorate the harvest loaf with poppy seeds to honour the harvest goddess. For spells and rituals of fertility, add poppy seeds to the ritual food, carry poppy seeds in a sachet, or add them to incense, charm bags, and herbal talismans. For love spells and rituals, poppy seeds and flowers may be added to the incense, oils, charms, and herbal talismans. Use poppy seed on the cake at a handfasting. The seeds and dried petals can also be added to divination incense and potions.

## CULINARY AND HOUSEHOLD USES

The seeds, petals, and young leaves can all be eaten. Sprinkle the seeds on baked goods such as bread, buns, and cakes. Sprinkle the petals in salads. The red petals impart a crimson colour to syrups, cocktails, and herb teas. A syrup made from the petals may be poured over desserts. Pick the fresh new leaves before the plant flowers and eat raw or cooked.

## COSMETIC USES

Poppy seed oil boosts collagen production, relaxes wrinkles, and helps prevent the formation of lines. Infuse the petals in boiling water, cool, and use as a skin wash.

## HOME REMEDIES

For neuralgia, put the leaves in a sieve and wilt them over a pan of boiling water, then apply them as a poultice. For swollen, sore joints, grind some poppy seeds into a paste with a little water and apply as a poultice. To remove excess mucus and soothe a sore throat when you have a cough or cold, take a tea, glycerite, or syrup made from red poppy petals. Poppy flower or poppy seed tea is mildly sedative and mildly painkilling.

> *Caution:* Red poppy flowers are mildly sedative, so exercise caution and do not drive or operate machinery after taking them. Do not use if you are pregnant, breastfeeding, or taking other sedatives.

# Primrose

*Primula vulgaris*

. . . . . . . . . . . . . . . . .

PLANETARY RULER: Venus

ELEMENT: Earth

ASSOCIATED DEITIES: Blodeuwedd, Freya, spring goddesses

MAGICAL VIRTUES: Spring, youth, beauty, love, lust

## LORE

Both the genus name, *Primula*, and the common name, *primrose*, come from the Latin *prime*, meaning "first," as it is often the very first spring flower to appear. As such, it was believed to have mystical powers of luck and good fortune. Primroses are associated with fairies in Britain and Ireland, having the ability to open the way to fairyland and its treasure.

## MAGICAL USES

Resonating with the energy of spring, new beginnings, burgeoning life, and fertility, primrose may be added to the ritual cup at Ostara or used in decorations and incense. Add the flowers to love spells, talismans, and charm bags. Washing your face in a primrose infusion will increase your beauty and attractiveness. Plant primroses in the garden as a guardian herb, and add the flowers to protection spells, wards, and charms. To make contact with the fay, drink primrose tea, burn primrose incense, anoint yourself with primrose oil, and use primrose flowers as an offering.

## CULINARY AND HOUSEHOLD USES

The leaves and flowers can be eaten. Add them to salads, and boil the leaves as a vegetable or add them to soups and stews. Crystalise the flowers for cake decoration or make them into a syrup. The flowers make what is considered by many to be one of the best country wines.

## COSMETIC USES

An infusion of the flowers may be used as a facial wash to reduce wrinkles and treat acne and pimples. A primrose cream or lotion will treat sunburn, reduce fine lines and wrinkles, and help fade age spots and freckles. Add primrose petals to the bath to soften your skin.

## HOME REMEDIES

The flowers, roots, and leaves are used. Any or all of them may be infused to treat coughs, nervous headaches, and insomnia. A decoction of the roots is helpful for bronchial problems. For a mild painkiller, useful for headaches and rheumatism, drink an infusion of the leaves and flowers. Apply primrose salve to small wounds.

> *Caution:* *Avoid medicinal use if you are pregnant or breastfeeding, sensitive to aspirin, or taking anticoagulant drugs.*

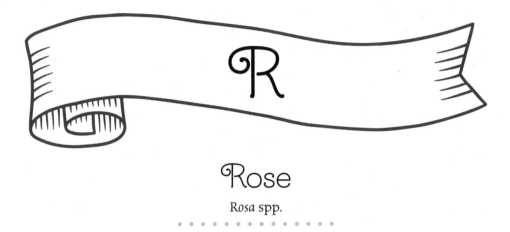

# Rose

*Rosa* spp.

· · · · · · · · · · · · · ·

PLANETARY RULER: Red roses—Jupiter,
damask roses—Venus, white roses—Moon

ELEMENT: Water

ASSOCIATED DEITIES: Adonis, Aphrodite, Aurora, Bacchus, Blodeuwedd,
Christ, Cupid, Demeter, Dionysus, Eros, Flora, Freya, Hathor, Horus,
Hulda, Hymen, Hecate, Inanna, Saule, Isis, Nike, Venus, Vishnu

MAGICAL VIRTUES: Love, peace, lust, beauty, healing, health, anointing,
psychic awareness, initiation, union, marriage, death, sacrifice

## LORE

In Greek myth, roses were created when Aphrodite, goddess of love, arose from the ocean
and the water fell from her body as white roses. Later, as she pursued Adonis, she pricked
herself on a thorn and her blood dyed the roses red, symbolising innocence turned to
desire. Roman brides and grooms were crowned with roses, and in Rome, when a rose was
hung on the ceiling it meant that the gathering was secret, or sub-rosa (under the rose). The
ceiling rose (the plaster ornament on the centre of the ceiling) signified the same. The rose
is a sun symbol and represents immortality through death.

· · · · ·

## MAGICAL USES

For love rituals and spells or for workings of peace and harmony, use rose petals in the incense, oil, or charm bags, as an offering, and so on. The rose is an emblem of renewal, resurrection, and eternal life, so roses may be used in funeral and memorial services. Use roses at Midsummer and rose hips at the harvest festival.

## CULINARY AND HOUSEHOLD USES

All rose hips are edible and contain high levels of vitamins and minerals. They may be made into tea, jellies, syrups, and wine. Rose petals may be used fresh to make jam or tea, baked into cakes and biscuits, or crystallised for cake decoration.

## COSMETIC USES

A homemade infused rose oil is moisturising for mature and irritated skin. Rose petals are astringent and can be infused in hot water for a facial wash or steam. Use chilled rose water in a compress to refresh tired and puffy eyes. Use diluted rose water as a final rinse to scent your hair and combat oiliness.

## HOME REMEDIES

All fragrant varieties of rose can be used. Rose hip syrup is a laxative; it's also good for colds and flu thanks to its high vitamin C content. Rose hips are anti-inflammatory and may help arthritic conditions. The tannin content of rose hips makes them a useful treatment for diarrhoea, and they are helpful for stomach spasms and stomach irritation. Rose petal tea is mildly sedative. It is also an antidepressant and anti-inflammatory and may help with period pain and menopausal symptoms.

> *Caution:* To prepare ripe rose hips for tea, wines, face masks, liqueurs, and so on, you will need to remove the irritant hairy seeds by straining them through several layers of muslin. To be on the safe side, avoid medicinal amounts of rose hips if you are pregnant or breastfeeding or have a bleeding condition. Do not take them for two weeks before and after surgery.

# Rosemary

*Rosmarinus officinalis*

PLANETARY RULER: Sun

ELEMENT: Fire

ASSOCIATED DEITIES: Aphrodite, Frau Holle, Leukothoe, Mnemosyne

MAGICAL VIRTUES: Marriage, death, remembrance,
protection, exorcism, healing, love

## LORE

In Greek myth, rosemary was sacred to the goddess Mnemosyne (Memory), and it has been believed to improve the memory since ancient times. Students in Greece and Rome wore rosemary chaplets to help them memorise their lessons. It also has contrary aspects as a herb of love and a herb of death. In Europe in the Middle Ages, the bride, groom, and wedding guests all wore rosemary. In ancient Greece and Rome, it was a funeral herb and used in wreaths, thrown into the grave, or placed in the hand of the dead.

## MAGICAL USES

Drink a cup of rosemary tea when you are studying magical texts or before a ritual to concentrate your mind on the work at hand. For rituals of the dead (Samhain, memorials, funerals, ancestor contact rites), drink rosemary wine, take rosemary tea, add rosemary to the incense, wear rosemary oil, and use rosemary as an offering to the departed spirit. For love spells, add rosemary to charm bags or incense, use rosemary oil to anoint candles, and so on. Rosemary incense or a rosemary infusion may be used to cleanse and purify the ritual space or magical tools. For protection, hang a rosemary wreath on your door, hang a sprig of rosemary in your window, or carry some in a pouch.

## CULINARY AND HOUSEHOLD USES

Full of vitamins and minerals, rosemary goes in soups, stews, and casseroles and is delicious in cakes and biscuits in moderation. Pop a few sprigs of rosemary in olive oil, leave for 10 to 14 days, and strain to make rosemary oil for cooking or salad dressing.

## Cosmetic Uses

Rosemary stimulates the skin, heals blemishes, and has antiaging properties. Rosemary skin toner is mildly astringent and antiseptic. Use a cup of rosemary tea as a final hair rinse to add shine, stimulate hair growth, and treat dandruff.

## Home Remedies

Rosemary leaves are strongly antiseptic. An infusion can be used as a gargle or mouthwash to help heal mouth ulcers and canker sores, and it can also be used on the skin to clean and help heal small wounds, bruises, strains, and bumps. The tea is good for dyspepsia caused by nervous tension and tension headaches caused by tight shoulders. Its anti-inflammatory and mild analgesic actions may be helpful for arthritis, rheumatic pain, and aching muscles. Apply the oil or salve to the affected parts.

> **Caution:** *Stick to small food amounts if you are allergic to aspirin, have bleeding disorders, are taking blood-thinning medication, have seizure disorders, have high blood pressure, take ACE (angiotensin converting enzyme) inhibitors, or have stomach ulcers, Crohn's disease, or ulcerative colitis. If you are diabetic, rosemary has a small effect on blood sugar, so monitor your levels carefully. Excessively large amounts can cause nausea or vomiting.*

# Rowan

a.k.a. Mountain Ash

*Sorbus aucuparia* syn. *Pyrus aucuparia*

· · · · · · · · · · · · ·

PLANETARY RULER: Moon/Sun/Mars/Uranus/Mercury

ELEMENT: Water/fire

ASSOCIATED DEITIES: Brigantia, Brighid, Halys,
Orpheus, Rauni, Sif, Thor, Ukko

MAGICAL VIRTUES: Divination, protection, calling and banishing spirits

## LORE

The genus name *Sorbus* means "stop," possibly referring to the power of rowan to prevent enchantment. The common name *rowan* is connected with the Gothic word *runa*, meaning "to know," likely referring to magic. In the Highlands the tree could only be used for ritual purposes. Evil witches had no power where there was rowan wood. Rowan twigs were commonly used as defensive charms in Britain, usually in the form of an equal-armed cross bound together with red thread.

## MAGICAL USES

Rowan is connected to witchcraft, protection, divination, and the dead. The berries are marked with the protective symbol of the pentagram on their base, a sign of magic and the calling and banishing of spirits. The berries, wood, and leaves can be dried and burned as an incense to invoke spirits, familiars, spirit guides, and elementals. Rowan wood may be used for making tools of divination. The berries or wood can be used in an incense to banish undesirable entities. A rowan wand is used for casting a protective circle. Plant a protective rowan tree near your home.

## CULINARY AND HOUSEHOLD USES

The berries can be made into a marmalade, a jelly good served with savouries, or added to chutney recipes. They can be dried and ground as a flour. They may be infused in vinegar or made into a syrup. Rowan berries can also be made into wine or a kind of cider, used to flavour mead, or infused in vodka.

## COSMETIC USES

Rowan berries contain sorbic acid, which is antibacterial and antimicrobial, plus antioxidant compounds, which help prevent premature aging, and astringent compounds, which brighten and tighten the skin. Use the berries in a fruit mask (combine with honey) or dried and powdered as an exfoliator to remove dead skin cells.

## HOME REMEDIES

The berries are used, and an infusion of the berries makes an antiseptic gargle for sore throats, inflamed tonsils, and hoarseness. Drunk, the infusion reduces inflammation of the respiratory tract, helping relieve congestion and asthma. A spoonful of rowan berry jelly may remedy diarrhoea. The astringent infusion may be dabbed onto haemorrhoids.

> **Caution:** *Eating the raw berries can cause stomach upsets, as the seeds contain traces of prussic acid. This is destroyed by cooking.*

# Rue

*Ruta graveolens*

. . . . . . . . . . . . . . .

PLANETARY RULER: Sun

ELEMENT: Fire

ASSOCIATED DEITIES: Aradia, Diana, Hermes,
Horus, Mars, Menthu, Mercury

MAGICAL VIRTUES: Clairvoyance, visions, protection, consecration

## LORE

The genus name, *Ruta*, comes from Greek and means "to set free." This may be a reference to the belief that rue had the ability to free the body from many diseases. Rue is often associated with witchcraft, used by and against witches. During the Middle Ages, it was used as a protection against sorcery and hung in cattle sheds to protect the animals from incantations, disease, and insects. Rue was called herb of grace from its use at Catholic High Mass, where it was employed to sprinkle the holy water.

## MAGICAL USES

Rue is an important herb for encouraging inner vision and clairvoyance, particularly for artistic people. It may be taken as a tea or used in incenses. Rue banishes negative energies and may be used in exorcism and purification incenses, or a sprig may be used as a sprinkler for consecrations. Hang a bunch of rue in the home or temple to keep the atmosphere pure.

## CULINARY AND HOUSEHOLD USES

Rue was a popular culinary herb in ancient times, particularly among the Romans, but it has rather fallen out of favour, though it is still used in some traditional Italian dishes. It is slightly bitter and best used in moderation in tomato dishes and sauces, stews, and soups. The roots yield a red dye.

## COSMETIC USES

Macerated rue oil can be used on the hair and scalp to treat damaged hair and eliminate lice.

## HOME REMEDIES

External use only. The aerial parts are used. An infusion may be used in a footbath to treat athlete's foot. A compress or poultice may be used on itchy, irritated skin.

> **Caution:** *While the occasional use of rue in cooking is safe (rue oil is used commercially as a flavouring), medicinal amounts (large frequent doses) of rue taken internally should be avoided by all but especially pregnant individuals, as it carries the risk of kidney or liver damage. Do not use if pregnant or breastfeeding.*

# Saffron

*Crocus sativus*

. . . . . . . . . . . . . . .

PLANETARY RULER: Sun/Moon

ELEMENT: Fire

ASSOCIATED DEITIES: Amun Ra, Ashtoreth, Eos, Indra, Jupiter, Zeus

MAGICAL VIRTUES: Aphrodisiac, marriage, love, moon rituals, divination

## LORE

The genus name, *Crocus*, is from the Greek meaning "a thread," a reference to the stamens. Saffron has always been expensive; it takes 60,000 flowers to make 1 pound of spice. In ancient Greece and Rome, brides wore bridal saffron, and the marriage bed was decorated with the flowers. Saffron was highly prized for its colour. The golden dye obtained from it was used for royal robes as a token of honour and high birth.

## MAGICAL USES

Drink saffron tea with a lover to provoke lust or drink it alone for divination; it enables you to see into the future. Though given to the sun by the astrologer-herbalists for its golden stamens and dye, saffron was sacred to the moon goddess in ancient times. It may be used in incenses to honour her or baked into moon cakes for use at rituals, either as an offering or eaten at the closing of the ritual. Saffron may be added to the handfasting cup and food.

### CULINARY AND HOUSEHOLD USES

In cookery, saffron is used to colour foods such as butter, cheese, rice, sauces, and soups and as a spice to flavour foods and aperitif beverages.

### COSMETIC USES

Antibacterial and anti-inflammatory, saffron can help rejuvenate your skin and make it glow. Infuse in warm milk, cool, and use as a cleanser. Mix with cosmetic clay and water and use as a face mask. Add to homemade toners. Use macerated saffron oil as a skin serum.

### HOME REMEDIES

Saffron tea may be taken for mild depression, PMS, headaches, anxiety, and pain.

> *Caution:* *Do not use saffron if you take sedatives or medication for diabetes or high blood pressure. To be on the safe side, avoid if pregnant or breastfeeding. Some people experience nausea and drowsiness when taking medicinal amounts of saffron. Doses of 12–20 grams can cause death. NB. Although saffron is sometimes known as the autumn crocus, it should not be confused with the more common Crocus autumnalis, which is poisonous. American saffron actually refers to safflower (Carthamus tinctorius), which is used as an adulterant to true saffron.*

# Sage

*Salvia officinalis*

. . . . . . . . . . . . . . . .

PLANETARY RULER: Jupiter

ELEMENT: Air

ASSOCIATED DEITIES: Cadmus, Consus, Jupiter, Zeus

MAGICAL VIRTUES: Healing, protection, cleansing, purification, wisdom

## LORE

Both the genus name, *Salvia*, and the common name, *sage*, come from the Latin word for "to be in good health," as the Romans believed that its use benefited most illnesses. In Europe, in the Middle Ages, sage was used to treat a variety of problems, from nervous complaints to fevers, as well as provide protection from them. All kinds of virtues were attributed to sage; carrying it promoted wisdom and warded off the evil eye. However, it was bad luck to plant sage in your own garden (a stranger should be found to do it) or have it in a flower bed on its own.

## MAGICAL USES

Garden sage is primarily used for purification. Use an incense/ritual fumigation or infusion to cleanse the aura, working area, and magical tools. Drink sage tea while fasting to purify the body and spirit. Additionally, sage can be used to attract abundance and long life when used in rituals and spells in the form of incense, charm bags, powders, oil, and so on.

## CULINARY AND HOUSEHOLD USES

Use the leaves in stews and soups, with cheese, in herb butter, with pasta, and in stuffing. Infuse the leaves in gently warmed honey to make a sage syrup to pour over desserts. The leaves may be infused to make a herb tea. Freeze the flowers in ice cubes and drop into summer drinks and cocktails. Make sage salt by grinding dried sage leaves with coarse sea salt.

## COSMETIC USES

Powdered dried sage leaves can be used as tooth powder. Rub fresh leaves on your teeth to whiten them. A sage infusion, used as a hair rinse, will darken greying hair. Add sage to a facial steam to tighten your pores. Dab powdered sage under your armpits as a natural deodoriser.

## HOME REMEDIES

Drink sage tea to treat coughs and colds, use it as a gargle for sore throats and tonsillitis, or use it as a mouthwash to treat mouth ulcers. Sage tea helps with menopausal symptoms such as hot flushes and night sweats; keep some sage tea in the fridge and sip it as needed. Antiseptic sage leaves can be used as an emergency first aid. Simply rub them on stings or bites.

> *Caution:* Sage may be toxic when taken long term in very large amounts. Take care if you are diabetic or have high or low blood pressure, as you may have to adjust your medication. Avoid if pregnant or breastfeeding; have hormone-sensitive cancers, endometriosis, uterine fibroids, or seizure disorders; if you take sedative medications; and for two weeks before and after surgery.

# Sandalwood

*Santalum album*

. . . . . . . . . . . . . . . .

PLANETARY RULER: Moon

ELEMENT: Air

ASSOCIATED DEITIES: Hanuman, Hathor,
Hermes, Krishna, Nike, Venus, Vishnu

MAGICAL VIRTUES: Healing, purification, consecration,
spiritual tranquillity, spiritual cleansing

## LORE

Sandalwood is one of the most expensive and sacred woods in the world, used for incense and sacred statues and valued in Hinduism, Islam, and Buddhism. The ancient Egyptians used the wood for incense and embalming. Sandalwood paste marks the foreheads of devotees of Krishna.

## MAGICAL USES

The primary use of sandalwood is in the making of incense used for meditation, prayer, harmony, peace, and psychic work. It fosters a connection with the higher consciousness. The incense or oil may be used to cleanse and consecrate magical tools. Carry a piece of sandalwood for protection.

## CULINARY AND HOUSEHOLD USES

Sandalwood also produces edible fruit and seeds (sometimes called nuts). The Australian species (*Santalum acuminatum*), also called quandong, has long been a source of food for the Aboriginal peoples. The fruit may be eaten raw or cooked, and the "nuts" may be used in place of macadamia nuts and are best lightly toasted.

## COSMETIC USES

Sandalwood is used as a fragrance and fixative in cosmetics and toiletries. Used as a powder, paste, or essential oil, sandalwood is an emollient that can benefit dry, aging skin, increasing moisture retention and supporting connective tissue. The powder can be mixed with rose water or honey and used as a facial scrub or applied as a hydrating face mask.

## HOME REMEDIES

The wood and essential oil are used. Sandalwood is antiseptic and soothing. A poultice of the powder or pulverised wood may be used for itchy skin, rashes, and inflammatory skin conditions such as eczema, dermatitis, and psoriasis. Sandalwood essential oil is used in aromatherapy for its relaxing, sedative, and calming effects.

*Caution:* Do not take the wood or oil internally.

# Skullcap

*Scutellaria lateriflora*

PLANETARY RULER: Saturn

ELEMENT: Water

MAGICAL VIRTUES: Meditation,
harmony, fidelity

## LORE

Skullcap is native to North America, where it was used by the First Nations people as a medicinal plant, but now widely cultivated in many parts of the world. It was first recorded by Matthias de L'Obel, botanist to James I of England, in 1576. Skullcap was used (ineffectively) as a cure for rabies, hence the folk name mad dog weed. *Skull* is a corruption of *scutellaria*, which means "little dish," given for the shape of the calyx.

## MAGICAL USES

Use this relaxing herb as a tea before meditation and trance work or add to meditation incense. Hang some in the kitchen to promote harmony. Use a skullcap pillow to induce sleep and prevent nightmares. In folk magic, it was used by women to stop their lovers straying; try putting a pinch of the herb in your love's shoes to keep them faithful.

## COSMETIC USES

Skullcap is soothing, firming, and anti-inflammatory. Dab some infusion onto pimples and acne-prone skin. Skullcap can help prevent sun damage when added to homemade sun lotions. To firm and smooth skin, use the infusion as a facial wash or mix some into a face pack.

## HOME REMEDIES

The aerial parts are used for medicinal purposes. As an infusion or tincture, skullcap is useful for insomnia, anxiety, and nervous tension. Owing to its antispasmodic action, it is helpful for times when stress causes muscle tension, such as tension headaches and migraines.

> Caution: This information applies to Scutellaria lateriflora; the Chinese skullcap (Scutellaria baicalensis) has different properties. When taken in large doses, skullcap can cause giddiness, stupor, and twitching. Do not take in combination with prescribed tranquillisers. Do not take if you are pregnant or breastfeeding. Do not give to children.

# St. John's Wort

*Hypericum perforatum*

. . . . . . . . . . . . . . . .

PLANETARY RULER: Sun

ELEMENT: Fire

ASSOCIATED DEITIES: Sun gods

MAGICAL VIRTUES: Protection, counter magic,
cleansing, purifying, exorcism

## LORE

The genus name, *Hypericum*, comes from the Greek "to protect" or "over an apparition." This refers to the belief that the plant could make evil spirits disappear. The specific name, *perforatum*, is a reference to the small transparent oil-bearing glands on the leaves. Its common name comes from the fact that it was associated with St. John the Baptist and his feast day of Midsummer, when it was used to keep evil spirits away.

## MAGICAL USES

St. John's wort is used as a protective and counter-magic herb. Hang small bunches under the eaves or in the windows of the home to keep away evil spirits and render spells useless. It should be collected for magical purposes at Midsummer. It can be used in incenses and washes for cleansing the working area, working tools, or the person. It repels negativity and can be used in purifications and exorcisms. Use in the Midsummer incense or bonfire. Add to sun incense.

## CULINARY AND HOUSEHOLD USES

The fresh flowers and leaves can be added to salads. When used with alum, a yellow dye can be made from the tops of the plant.

## COSMETIC USES

St. John's wort has anti-inflammatory, antimicrobial, and astringent effects. A wash, cream, or macerated oil can soothe acne, breakouts, and irritated, reddened skin.

. . . . .

## HOME REMEDIES

The aerial parts are used, and a red macerated oil is obtained from the flowers and leaves of St. John's wort. This can be applied to bruises, wounds, varicose veins, ulcers, and sunburn. The aerial parts of the plant can be used to make an infusion or tincture for the treatment of headaches, nervous conditions, irregular menstruation, mild depression, and insomnia.

> *Caution:* Side effects can include stomach upset, diarrhoea, dry mouth, headache, and dizziness. Used topically, it may cause a skin rash in some individuals. It can also increase the sensitivity of your skin to sunlight. Do not take with antidepressants, blood thinners, oral contraceptives, antibiotics, sedatives, or drugs used to treat anxiety, cancer, heart conditions, and HIV/AIDS.

# Sunflower

*Helianthus annus*

. . . . . . . . . . . . . .

PLANETARY RULER: Sun

ELEMENT: Fire

ASSOCIATED DEITIES: Inti

MAGICAL VIRTUES: Sun, happiness, blessings, fertility,
abundance, strength, courage, action, self-image, consecration

## LORE

Native to North and Central America, the botanical name comes from the Greek *helios*,
meaning "sun," and *anthos*, meaning "flower." Its name not only describes the golden-rayed
sun-face of the bloom but is also expressive of the way that it turns to follow the path of the
sun throughout the day.

## MAGICAL USES

The energy of the plant resonates with joy, luck, and abundance. Have some cut flowers
in your house, grow them in your garden, and add the petals to potpourri to call these to
you. For fertility, add the seeds and petals to spells and charm bags, anoint your candles
with sunflower oil, eat the seeds, or wear a necklace made from the seeds. For fidelity and
loyalty, add sunflower seeds or oil to spells and charms or shared food. The petals, oil, and
seeds may be used to invoke and honour sun deities; use in the incense, anointing oil, decorations, and so on.

## CULINARY AND HOUSEHOLD USES

Their seeds are a rich source of vitamins and minerals, and they may be eaten raw or roasted
or added to bread, cakes, and salads. Grind them into powder for a gluten-free flour. Infuse
the petals in boiling water to make a tea, sprinkle them over salads, or add them to soups
and stews. Use them in place of saffron in rice dishes.

## COSMETIC USES

Sunflower oil is a natural moisturiser and suitable for all skin types. Applying it to your face and body, or adding it to homemade creams, will help minimise fine lines and wrinkles.

## HOME REMEDIES

For coughs, colds, and bronchial, laryngeal, and pulmonary infections, take sunflower seed tea. To reduce high fevers, use sunflower leaf tea. For skin sores, swellings, and insect bites, scrunch up a sunflower leaf and apply as a poultice.

*Caution:* The plant can trigger asthma and skin allergies in sensitive people.

# Sweet Cicely

*Myrrhis odorata*

· · · · · · · · · · · · ·

PLANETARY RULER: Jupiter

ELEMENT: Air

ASSOCIATED DEITIES: The Summer Goddess

MAGICAL VIRTUES: Joy, happiness, aphrodisiac

## LORE

The whole plant is aromatic, *myrrhis* meaning "smelling of myrrh" and *odorata* meaning "fragrant." Its folk names include British myrrh, as it is native to the British Isles. In Christian lore, it was dedicated to St. Cecilia and was sometimes known as sweet cis; it was also dedicated to the Virgin Mary.

## MAGICAL USES

The flowers and leaves can be dried and added to incense and charms to lift the spirits and impart joy and happiness to ceremonies, particularly Beltane and Midsummer. The leaf or flower tea can be taken for the same purpose, and the fresh leaves can be added to drinks served at the Midsummer feast. The plant is a rumoured aphrodisiac and may be used in love and lust spells.

## CULINARY AND HOUSEHOLD USES

Every part of the plant is edible and contains calcium, potassium, iron, phosphorus, and vitamins A and C. It has an aniseed-like scent and taste that is most pronounced in the unripe green seeds, which can be eaten raw or roasted as a snack. However, the important thing about sweet cicely is that it is sweet! It can be used as a sugar substitute. The natural sweetness of the leaves has been used to reduce sugar in recipes, especially when stewing fruits such as rhubarb or gooseberries, as the leaves also help reduce the acidity. They are calorie free and well tolerated by diabetics. The stalks can be used much like celery, while the roots can be boiled or eaten raw. The raw leaves can be added to salads, even fruit salads. They can also be cooked into soups, stews, and omelettes. A simple wood polish can also be made by pounding the fresh seeds and rubbing the juice into the furniture. The roots produce a deep yellow dye.

## COSMETIC USES

Sweet cicely has antimicrobial properties that may benefit acne-prone skin. Use the infusion as a facial wash.

## HOME REMEDIES

All parts of the plant may be used. The leaves, flowers, and seeds are added to digestive teas and aperitifs to gently aid digestion and relieve flatulence. The tea is also useful for those with upper respiratory tract infections such as flu and the common cold. A poultice of the leaves or a compress made by infusing the aerial parts of the plant may help relieve gout.

*Caution:* None known.

# Thyme

*Thymus* spp.

· · · · · · · · · · · · · ·

PLANETARY RULER: Venus

ELEMENT: Water

ASSOCIATED DEITIES: Ares, fairies, Mars

MAGICAL VIRTUES: Purification, fairy magic,
courage, funerals, aphrodisiac, protection

## LORE

The classical world associated the fragrance of thyme with sweetness. It had a scent that pleased the gods, hence its name, which comes from *thymiama*, the Greek word for incense. The hardy plant was also associated with courage and strength, so much so that it was believed to stir warriors to bravery. In England, fairies were thought to love it and to dance on wild thyme beds.

## MAGICAL USES

When working with fairy energies, wear a garland of thyme or thyme oil, burn thyme incense, or use thyme as an offering. When you need courage, carry some thyme, drink thyme tea, and add it to incense used in rituals and spells to call forth bravery and strength. For purification and protection, use a thyme infusion or fumigation to cleanse your home

· · · · ·

or sacred space, add thyme to a cleansing bath, hang a bunch in the kitchen, or carry some in a sachet. Put a sprig beneath your pillow to keep nightmares at bay.

## CULINARY AND HOUSEHOLD USES

Both the leaves and flowers may be used in the kitchen. Add them to potatoes, vegetables, rice dishes, bean dishes, pasta dishes, egg dishes, bread, sauces, stews, soups, stuffing, and marinades. Put a few sprigs in vinegar to make thyme vinegar (leave 2 weeks) or in olive oil to make thyme oil (leave 2 weeks).

## COSMETIC USES

Thanks to the volatile oils in thyme, an infusion of the leaves is naturally antibacterial. Use it as a hair rinse to treat dandruff or as a facial wash to treat oily skin, acne, and pimples. Combine the infusion 50:50 with witch hazel and use as a toner to tighten the skin.

## HOME REMEDIES

Thyme is antibacterial—pulp fresh leaves and apply them to insect bites, cuts, and small wounds. Use thyme tea as a mouthwash or gargle to relieve inflamed gums, gum disease, gingivitis, mouth ulcers, and sore throats. Drink thyme tea for coughs, colds, flu, bronchitis, indigestion, flatulence, and IBS. A cup of thyme tea may help relieve tension headaches and hangovers.

> *Caution: Pregnant and breastfeeding individuals should stick to food amounts to be on the safe side. Medicinal amounts should be avoided if you have a bleeding disorder, are on anticoagulant medication, or have hormone-sensitive conditions, such as endometriosis, uterine fibroids, or breast, uterine, or ovarian cancer.*

# Turmeric

*Curcuma longa* syn. *C. domestica*

. . . . . . . . . . . . . . .

PLANETARY RULER: Sun

ELEMENT: Fire

ASSOCIATED DEITIES: Durga, Ganesh, Kali, Kottravai, Krishna, Suryan

MAGICAL VIRTUES: Fertility, prosperity, protection,
purification, blessing, luck, Sun, marriage, birth, death

## LORE

For both Hindus and Buddhists, turmeric is a sacred herb linked to prosperity, luck, and solar energies, symbolising inner purity. A yellow dye derived from turmeric was used to dye the robes of Hindu monks. During Hindu weddings, family members apply turmeric paste to the bride and groom for purification and blessing.

## MAGICAL USES

Turmeric vibrates with solar energy, luck, prosperity, and fertility. To draw in these energies, add powdered turmeric to sun incense or to spells and charms designed to attract good fortune. For love magic, add it to shared food, charm bags, and spell jars. You can also dissolve the powder in oil and use it to anoint candles. To attract customers to your business, sprinkle turmeric powder on the threshold of your premises.

## CULINARY AND HOUSEHOLD USES

Add powdered turmeric to curries, scrambled eggs, boiled rice, soups, pickles, hot milk, and smoothies.

## COSMETIC USES

Turmeric reduces skin redness, improves collagen production and elasticity, stimulates new cell growth, reduces wrinkles, and increases blood flow; combine the powder with ground almonds for a facial scrub. Turmeric's antibacterial properties can combat blemishes and acne; add the powder to face masks. NB. May make the skin temporarily yellow.

. . . . .

## HOME REMEDIES

Turmeric is a powerful anti-inflammatory, helping ease the stiffness and pain of arthritic joints, for which it can be externally applied as a turmeric paste or ointment or used internally as a turmeric tea. Turmeric in the diet has also been shown to lower LDL cholesterol, thin the blood, lower blood pressure, and prevent clotting. The antioxidant and anti-inflammatory qualities of turmeric have been shown to help calm inflammatory skin conditions such as eczema, scleroderma, rosacea, and psoriasis. The antiseptic and anti-inflammatory qualities of turmeric make it useful in treating small wounds. It has antifungal properties useful for athlete's foot and other fungal conditions.

*Caution: Turmeric should not be taken in medicinal quantities if you are pregnant or breastfeeding or have gallbladder problems, bleeding disorders, or hormone-sensitive cancers. Do not take turmeric in medicinal amounts for two weeks before surgery. Avoid medicinal amounts if you have a clotting disorder or are on anticlotting medications, such as aspirin and warfarin.*

# Valerian

*Valeriana officinalis*

· · · · · · · · · · · · ·

**PLANETARY RULER:** Mercury/Jupiter

**ELEMENT:** Water

**ASSOCIATED DEITIES:** Bast, Sekhmet, Freya, Apollo

**MAGICAL VIRTUES:** Protection, harmony, peace, love

## LORE

The genus name is derived from the Latin *valere*, meaning "to be in health," a reference to the medicinal properties of the plant. It was recommended in the fourth century BCE by the physician Hippocrates and was used by Anglo-Saxon, Persian, and Chinese herbalists. However, most people find the smell unpleasant, hence its ancient Greek name of *phu*, as in "phew!" It was used by the ancient Greeks as a protection against evil.

## MAGICAL USES

Grow some in the garden or hang the root in the home to protect it from negativity, or use it in spells to bring peace and harmony. Valerian is also a herb of love and a common ingredient in love philtres. You can add it to love incense, charm bags, amulets, and talismans, or you can simply wear a piece to attract a mate. A valerian infusion can be used in a wash to cleanse and consecrate the ritual space and magical tools. Witches have long employed valerian root toys for bonding with their cats (they like it as much as catnip) and attracting cat familiars.

· · · · ·

## Culinary and Household Uses

The seeds are edible, and the leaves have been used in the past as a condiment. The leaves and root can both be used to make a tea (use in moderation).

## Cosmetic Uses

Valerian root is anti-inflammatory, and a decoction makes a useful wash for acne.

## Home Remedies

The root is used. Valerian is an effective tranquilliser that helps calm stress, anxiety, hysteria, nervous tension, headaches, and migraines. Valerian root tea relieves insomnia and improves the quality of sleep.

> *Caution:* Valerian may have side effects, such as headaches, in some people when taken over an extended period. It causes drowsiness, so do not drive or operate machinery after taking. To be on the safe side, avoid if pregnant or breastfeeding, and stop taking valerian at least two weeks before a scheduled surgery. Do not combine with alcohol as it may exacerbate sleepiness. Do not use if you are taking other sedative medications.

# Vervain

*Verbena officinalis*

. . . . . . . . . . . . . . . . .

PLANETARY RULER: Venus/Mercury

ELEMENT: Water

ASSOCIATED DEITIES: Aphrodite, Aradia, Ceridwen, Diana, Galahad, Horus, Isis, Jupiter, Mars, Ra, Thor, Venus, Zeus

MAGICAL VIRTUES: Cleansing, purifying, clairvoyance, divination

## LORE

This small and insignificant-looking plant, known as the Enchanter's Herb, has perhaps a greater reputation for magic than any other herb. It was a sacred herb of the Romans, Greeks, Celts, Hebrews, Egyptians, and Persians, and it appears in many magical texts. The ancient Egyptians believed it sprang from the tears of Isis. According to Pliny the Elder, the Druids ritually harvested the herb in August when the Dog Star, Sirius, was visible and neither the sun nor the moon could be seen. The Romans cleansed their altars with it, and Solomon his temple. The Anglo-Saxons considered it to be a powerful protector against the demons of disease. In mediaeval Europe it was believed to guard against the plague, protect against all evil, and even ward off the devil.

## MAGICAL USES

Vervain increases the flow of spiritual energy and heightens consciousness and psychic powers. Take the tea before ritual to deepen communication with spiritual realms. Take it before bed for psychic dreams. Anoint the third eye chakra with vervain oil before divination. Add it to the Samhain wine to aid ancestor communication. Vervain clears negative and stagnant energy when used as a temple cleanser in the form of a wash or incense. You can also sweep the sacred space with a bunch of vervain. Use vervain in the ritual bath for spiritual purification. Use a ritual fumigation to cleanse the aura. Magical tools can be washed with a vervain infusion.

## CULINARY AND HOUSEHOLD USES

The leaves may be steamed and eaten, and the flowers can be used as a garnish. A tea may be made from the flowers and leaves.

## COSMETIC USES

Vervain has antiseptic, detoxifying, and anti-inflammatory effects and strengthens connective tissue. The tea is useful as a facial wash, and it can be added to homemade skin toners, which will especially benefit skin prone to acne.

## HOME REMEDIES

The aerial parts are used. Vervain tea aids stress, anxiety, nervous exhaustion, and insomnia. It is also a mild antidepressant. The tea may relieve a headache, a migraine, and symptoms of PMS. An infusion is used as a gargle for sore throats, tonsillitis, inflamed gums, and mouth infections. It may be used as a wash or poultice for bruises, cuts, burns, sprains, and insect bites. A salve may aid eczema and neuralgia.

> *Caution:* *Do not use if pregnant or breastfeeding. Avoid if you have iron-deficiency anaemia or take blood-thinning or blood pressure medications.*

# Violet

*Viola odorata*

. . . . . . . . . . . . .

PLANETARY RULER: Venus

ELEMENT: Water

ASSOCIATED DEITIES: Aphrodite, Io, Orpheus,
Venus, Attis, Ares, Persephone

MAGICAL VIRTUES: Ostara, death, love, renewal

## LORE

In Europe, the appearance of the first violet was a cause for rejoicing as it heralded the coming of spring. In many places, the very first violet of the year had mystical properties of protecting and safeguarding the finder from illness or the evil eye for a year. With its attractive perfume and heart-shaped leaves, the violet was associated with the goddess of love in both Greece and Rome. With its purple colour and drooping head, the violet was also a symbol of death; the ancient Romans laid violets on graves.

## MAGICAL USES

Dried violet flowers and leaves may be added to incenses for the spring equinox, vegetation deities, and springtime death and resurrection deities. Add violet flowers to funeral flowers and funeral incenses. Plant violets on a grave as a token of the resurrection to come. For love magic and to invoke and honour goddesses of love, add violets to incenses and anoint the candles with violet oil. For love spells, add violet flowers and leaves to herbal amulets, charm bags, and spell jars.

## CULINARY AND HOUSEHOLD USES

The young leaves can be eaten in salads. The flowers may be made into a tea, candied and used for cake decoration, or made into syrup. The petals can be used fresh as an edible garnish for salads, desserts, and cocktails.

. . . . .

## COSMETIC USES

Violet flowers are good for aging skin; add violet oil to homemade moisturisers to plump up the skin and reduce fine lines and wrinkles. Violets contain saponins (soap), and violet tea makes a good facial wash to reduce acne and large pores. Violet oil smooths frizzy hair.

## HOME REMEDIES

Violet tea or syrup may be useful for treating coughs, chest colds, catarrh/mucus, and sore throats. A violet infusion can be drunk for gout, headaches, rheumatism, heartburn, gas, urinary infections, poor nerves, hysteria, insomnia, irritability, mild depression, and menopausal symptoms, including hot flushes. A violet infusion may also be used as a gargle for the treatment of mouth inflammations. You can add a violet infusion to the bath for muscular aches and joint pains. A salve or oil is anti-inflammatory, soothing, and helpful for eczema, rashes, insect bites, chaffed skin, and dry skin conditions.

> **Caution:** All of the true Viola species (including pansies) are edible, but note that other flowers may be called violet, such as the African violet, and these may be toxic. Avoid if you have glucose-6-phosphate dehydrogenase (G6PD) deficiency or are allergic to aspirin (salicylic acid). To be on the safe side, avoid medicinal amounts if pregnant or breastfeeding.

# Wheat

*Triticum* spp.

. . . . . . . . . . . . . .

**PLANETARY RULER:** Venus

**ELEMENT:** Earth

**ASSOCIATED DEITIES:** Inanna, Osiris, Demeter, Ceres, Persephone, Proserpina, Kore, Christ, Jupiter, Sif, Rhiannon

**MAGICAL VIRTUES:** Abundance, fertility, money, rebirth

## LORE

In the Old World, *corn* refers to any grain crop but especially wheat. The Mesopotamian goddess Inanna was called "the green one" after the rippling green corn that was her mantle in spring. A kind of bread was baked on her altars and called the "baked cakes of the goddess Inanna," symbolizing the body of the goddess herself feeding her children. In Egypt, the god Osiris taught the Egyptians to grow wheat and barley. He was called "the great green thing." The Greek goddess of grain was Demeter, and the great mystery rites at Eleusis were always conducted by the priests of Demeter. The central part of the worship was built around the viewing of corn and the life cycle of the corn with its growth, death, burial in the earth, and rebirth. The initiates strongly believed that they, too, would enjoy a life after death because of their initiation into the mysteries.

## MAGICAL USES

The cycle of corn tells of the life, death, and regrowth of the Corn God, and reflects the profound mystery of life, death, and rebirth in human terms. The first of the harvest is ritually offered to the gods. A specially made loaf of bread should always feature in the harvest celebration. Wheat is also a symbol of fertility and plenty, often placed on the heads of brides and used in spells and rituals of fertility and abundance.

## CULINARY AND HOUSEHOLD USES

Wheat contains more gluten than other cereals and can be used to make raised bread, unlike any other grain. Many non-wheat-growing cultures have never known bread. Most of the wheat now grown is produced by hybrids bred to resist disease. However, the older varieties, such as spelt and einkorn, are better tolerated by people with wheat sensitivities and may have more nutritional benefits.

## COSMETIC USES

Wheat germ oil is one of the richest sources of vitamins A, D, and E. It also has a high content of proteins and lecithin. It is widely used externally for skin irritation and dryness, dermatitis, and sunburn.

## HOME REMEDIES

Ancient wheat varieties were used in folk medicine for the treatment of an array of health conditions. Einkorn wheat contains higher levels of lutein (the major yellow pigment in wheat grains), which reduces the risk of age-related macular degeneration and cataracts, as well as protecting against heart disease and cancer.

*Caution: Wheat should be avoided by coeliacs and people with gluten sensitivity.*

# Wild Lettuce

*Lactuca virosa*

PLANETARY RULER: Moon/Saturn

ELEMENT: Water

ASSOCIATED DEITIES: Min

MAGICAL VIRTUES: Meditation, divination, love, fertility, aphrodisiac

## LORE

A relative of the lettuce we use in our salads (*Lactuca sativa*), wild lettuce is a common weed. The Greek physician Dioscorides noted its resemblance to the opium poppy, and indeed, it exudes a similar white latex when cut; the genus name, *Lactuca*, means "milky extract." When the Roman emperor Augustus recovered from a serious illness, he credited his return to health to wild lettuce and built a statue to honour it. In ancient Egypt it was associated with the fertility god Min, who was depicted with an erect penis. During his festival, his statue was carried on a bed of wild lettuce in procession. The Egyptians used wild lettuce as an aphrodisiac. Nineteenth-century physicians employed wild lettuce as a mild painkiller, also using it to soothe the nerves and promote a good night's sleep—particularly in cases where they deemed the use of opium inadvisable.

## MAGICAL USES

A wild lettuce incense, or a tea or tincture of the leaves, promotes a relaxed and serene state prior to meditation, vision quests, and divination; use before bed for prophetic dreams. The leaves may be used in rituals, spells, and charms of fertility and love and to honour the god Min.

## CULINARY AND HOUSEHOLD USES

The leaves are too bitter to eat.

## HOME REMEDIES

The latex (milky juice) is used. Even though it contains no opiates, wild lettuce is referred to as opium lettuce for its properties. The plant has mild pain-relieving and sedative effects, making it useful in cases of insomnia, nervousness, and anxiety. The pain-killing properties of wild lettuce are not water soluble, so making a tea of the leaves will not work. Instead, the latex is harvested by continually cutting the growing stems and scraping off the sap, which is tinctured in alcohol.

> **Caution:** Do not ingest wild lettuce if you are pregnant or breastfeeding or have glaucoma. Wild lettuce can cause drowsiness, so do not drive or operate machinery after use. If taken in excess, it can cause restlessness, nausea, and vomiting. In very high doses (particularly if smoked), it can result in dizziness, stupor, depressed breathing, sweating, fast heartbeat, pupil dilation, dizziness, ringing in the ears, and vision changes.

# Willow, White

*Salix alba*

. . . . . . . . . . . . . . . . .

**PLANETARY RULER:** Moon

**ELEMENT:** Water

**ASSOCIATED DEITIES:** Anatha, Artemis, Asclepius, Belili, Belin,
Belinos, Brigantia, Brighid, Callisto, Ceres, Ceridwen, Circe, death
goddesses, Europa, Hecate, Hera, Hermes, Inanna, Ishtar, Isis, Kundalini,
Lakshmi, Lei Hai-ching, Mercury, moon goddesses, Morgana, Neith,
O-Ryu, Osiris, Persephone, Poseidon, Psyche, Rusalki, Zeus

**MAGICAL VIRTUES:** Bardic work, immortality,
death, mourning, loss, protection, healing

## LORE

Willow grows close to water—in a liminal place. It has many connections with witchcraft
and magic, death and the underworld, and poets and poetry. The Celtic "Song of the For-
ests" warns, "Burn not the willow, a tree sacred to poets."[5] In Greek myth, Helicon (willow)
was the mountain home of the nine Muses, who inspire the arts and sciences. The weeping
tree has long been associated with death, grief, and cemeteries. However, willow regrows
even stronger when it is cut back, symbolising renewal and immortality.

## MAGICAL USES

Willow connects with deep emotions, the cycles of life, intuition, visions, and artistic inspi-
ration. A willow wand is used for moon magic and enchantments. A piece of willow may
be held for guidance and protection on deep journeys into the dream world or underworld.
Sleep with a willow twig beneath your pillow for prophetic dreams. A willow amulet will
protect your home. Flexible willow withies are used for spells of fascination and binding.
Wear a willow charm to heal your grief.

---

5 Graves, *The White Goddess.*

## COSMETIC USES

A decoction of the leaves or bark, simmered lightly, can be used to treat dandruff.

## HOME REMEDIES

The inner bark is used. The active compounds in willow bark are converted in the body to a salicylate, the group of compounds to which aspirin belongs. The decoction may help relieve painful inflammatory conditions such as osteoarthritis, rheumatism, and back pain. It is less likely to cause gastric upset and internal bleeding problems, as aspirin does, and it does not have the same blood-thinning properties. It can help reduce high fevers and ease headaches. It makes a good gargle for sore throats and gums, and it is a good external wash for sores, skin problems, wounds, and burns.

> *Caution:* *Do not take for more than 12 weeks. It should not be used by children. Do not take if you are allergic to aspirin; are pregnant or breastfeeding; have a bleeding disorder, kidney disease, diabetes, liver disease, stomach ulcers, or gout; or are taking medications that slow blood clotting, such as warfarin and aspirin. Avoid for two weeks before and after surgery.*

# Willowherb, Rosebay

*Chamaenerion angustifolium*

. . . . . . . . . . . . . . .

PLANETARY RULER: Mercury

ELEMENT: Fire

MAGICAL VIRTUES: Regeneration, healing

## LORE

Known in the United States as fireweed, this plant springs up wherever the soil has been disturbed, especially on burned ground. This property earned it the folk name of bomb weed in Britain, since it quickly grew over the devastated bomb sites after World War II.

## MAGICAL USES

Willowherb resonates with the triumph of regeneration and healing after trauma—like a phoenix rising from the ashes, bringing with it hope and healing. Use it in spells, charms, and rituals of transformation and regeneration. Carry some in a herbal sachet to help you heal from trauma.

## CULINARY AND HOUSEHOLD USES

The leaves may be infused to make a tea. In Russia, they are fermented to make Ivan Chai or Koporsky tea. The very young shoots and leaves can be cooked and eaten in spring. After springtime, they become rather tough and bitter. The young flowers may be used as a garnish or made into a jelly. The young stems may be peeled and eaten raw or cooked like asparagus. The slightly sweet pith of the older stems may be eaten raw or cooked or added to soups and stews. The root, collected before the plant flowers, can be peeled and roasted.

## COSMETIC USES

The plant is a potent antioxidant and anti-inflammatory and contains several active compounds that help the fight against aging, preventing collagen and elastin fibre degradation. Add the herb to your homemade creams and serums.

## Home Remedies

The leaves, flowers, and roots are used. Rosebay willowherb is good for the digestive tract thanks to its antimicrobial, astringent, antispasmodic, demulcent, and anti-inflammatory properties. A tea of the young leaves or a syrup made from the flowerheads is useful for the treatment of diarrhoea, IBS, ulcerative colitis, and diverticulitis. The tea may be used as a gargle for sore throats and mouth ulcers. A leaf salve soothes irritated skin. A leaf poultice may be applied to burns, skin sores, minor wounds, and boils. A root poultice will draw out infection from wounds.

*Caution: None known, but to be on the safe side, avoid if pregnant or breastfeeding.*

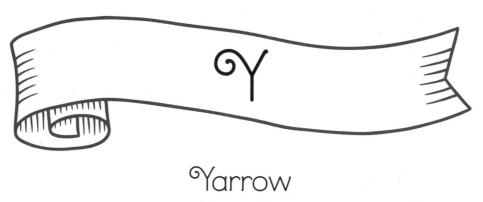

# Yarrow

*Achillea millefolium*

PLANETARY RULER: Venus

ELEMENT: Water

ASSOCIATED DEITIES: Cernunnos, Herne, Pan, Chiron

MAGICAL VIRTUES: Divination, clairvoyance, love, protection

## LORE

In Greek myth, Chiron, the wise centaur, taught Achilles the virtue of yarrow so that he might make a salve to heal his warriors' wounds, giving the plant its genus name *Achillea*. Many of yarrow's folk names come from its ability to stem bleeding. A traditional saying is "Where yarrow grows, there is one who knows," meaning that it grew in gardens where a person well versed in magic and healing lived. In Christian lore, yarrow was assigned to St. John and acquired special powers at Midsummer. It was used by country people to keep evil spirits away from byres and stables and was worn as an amulet to ward off negativity. Throughout the Middle Ages, it was regarded as a witch plant with great power for and against witchcraft.

## MAGICAL USES

Yarrow is one of the sacred herbs of Midsummer and should be gathered for magical purposes or for extra healing power at the solstice. It can be used in the incense, thrown onto the bonfire as an offering, or used in the decorations and garlands. Yarrow tea and incense can be used for divination and clairvoyance. Yarrow is also used in love and protection magic and can be added to incenses, charm bags, and spells. Yarrow was widely used in love magic. A pinch of yarrow, wrapped up in a piece of cloth and placed under the pillow at night, brings visions.

## CULINARY AND HOUSEHOLD USES

The young leaves and flowers can be used in salads.

## COSMETIC USES

Infuse the fresh flowers for a facial steam and tonic lotion. A yarrow infusion can be added to the bath to ease aches and tiredness. It can also be used as the basis for a face pack for greasy skin. Press a fresh yarrow leaf onto a shaving cut.

## HOME REMEDIES

Yarrow can be used to stop bleeding cuts and to improve the healing of bruises, rashes, and haemorrhoids. For slow-healing wounds, apply a compress of yarrow. A salve helps ulcers and varicose veins, while a decoction can be used for wounds, chapped skin, eczema, and rashes. The infusion brings down the temperature and encourages sweating, so it is useful for colds, flu, catarrh/mucus, rheumatism, and fevers. The tea has a bitter astringency that helps soothe digestion and stop diarrhoea. Yarrow contains the natural painkiller salicylic acid, so the tea is useful for headaches, menstrual cramps, and arthritis. Use an infusion in the bath for menstrual cramps.

> *Caution: Contact with the plant may cause skin irritation in some sensitive individuals. It should not be taken if you are pregnant or breastfeeding, have bleeding disorders, take anti-blood-clotting medication (including aspirin), lithium, barbiturates, or antacids. Avoid for two weeks before surgery.*

# Appendix: Herbal Preparations

## Tea

Many of a herb's components, such as its minerals, vitamins, sugars, starches, hormones, tannins, volatile oils, and some alkaloids, dissolve well in water, and for this reason, herbs are often taken as teas (tisanes). Teas can be made from the soft green and flowering parts of a herb. Use 2 teaspoons fresh or 1 teaspoon dried herbs to 250 ml (1 cup) boiling water. Put the herbs in a teapot or a pot with a lid, pour on the boiling water, and infuse for 10–20 minutes. Strain and drink, sweetened with honey if desired. Take one to three times daily.

## Infusion

Infusions follow the same steps as a herbal tea, but infusions, which are a medicinal dose, use a greater concentration of plant material to water. Take 4 teaspoons fresh or 2 teaspoons dried herbs and 250 ml (1 cup) of boiling water. Infuse for 10–20 minutes. Strain and drink, sweetened with honey if desired. Take one to three times daily.

A "strong infusion" indicates a greater measure of herbs to water. Some herbs have constituents such as mucilage and bitter principles that are destroyed by heat. In that case, a cold infusion should be made by steeping the plant material in cold water for several hours. Use a non-metal container and put in the herb and water. Close the lid or cover with cling film (plastic wrap) and leave overnight. Strain before use. Take one to three times daily.

# Decoction

Some of the harder, woodier parts of a plant, such as the seeds, roots, buds, and barks, need to be simmered in water for a while to extract their properties. This is called a decoction. If the herbs are dried, they should first be pounded into a powder. Never use an aluminium or copper pan as it can react with the brew and taint it. Take 2 teaspoons fresh or 1 teaspoon dried herbs for each 250 ml (1 cup) cold water. Put the herbs in a pan and pour in the water. Cover and, if possible, let the herbs macerate in the cold water for a few hours. Put the pan on heat and bring the water to a boil. Simmer gently for 15–20 minutes. Strain. Take one to three times daily.

# Tincture

Plant constituents are generally more soluble in alcohol than water, and alcohol will dissolve and extract resins, oils, alkaloids, sugars, starches, and hormones, though it does not extract nutrients such as vitamins or minerals. A remedy made this way is called a tincture. Brandy or vodka is usually used; never use alcohols designed for external use, such as rubbing alcohol. To make a tincture, put 100 grams of dried or 200 grams fresh herbs into a clean jar and pour on 500 ml of vodka or brandy. Seal the jar and keep it in a warm place for two to four weeks, shaking daily. Strain through muslin and store in a dark bottle in a cool place for up to two to six years. Because a tincture is much stronger than an infusion or decoction, you only need a few drops in a glass of water as a medicinal dose. Alternatively, a few drops may be added to a salve or bath for external use.

# Glycerite

You can use glycerine to extract phytochemicals from herbs in a manner similar to how alcohol is used to make a tincture. Glycerine is a weaker solvent than alcohol, so glycerites won't be as potent as an alcohol-based tincture and you will need a larger dose for a therapeutic effect. Glycerites won't keep as long as tinctures, and they are not good at making extractions from hard barks and dried roots. Make sure you use a food-grade vegetable glycerine. Put 100 grams dried or 200 grams fresh herbs into a clean jar and pour on 500 ml of slightly warmed glycerine. Seal the jar and keep it in a warm, dark place for two to four weeks, shaking daily. Strain through muslin and store in a dark bottle in a cool place for about a year. If you add water to your glycerite or use fresh herbs with a lot of water content, the mix will spoil much faster. Take a teaspoon three times daily.

# Syrups

Some herbs are bitter tasting and are more palatable when taken in the form of syrup, particularly for children. The sugar preserves the herbs. To make syrup, first make your herbal infusion or decoction (see the previous sections), then add 250 grams of sugar for every 250 ml of infusion or decoction and heat slowly until the sugar is dissolved. Simmer gently until thickened. Pour into sterilised bottles and label. Unopened syrup will keep six to twelve months in a cool, dark place. Once opened, keep it in the fridge for one to two months. If you wish, you can use honey instead of sugar, though the heating process destroys most of the honey's own properties.

# Acetas

An acetum is a herbal vinegar. Though vinegar won't draw out as many phytochemicals from the herbs as alcohol, it does extract the vitamins and minerals from the plants. Acetas are not as strong as tinctures, so the dose needed is higher. Take two teaspoons three times a day. You can dilute your herbal vinegar with water to take internally or use it externally in baths and compresses. Acetas generally have a cooling, anti-inflammatory effect, so they are useful for conditions such as sore throats and inflamed skin. They will store for one to two years in a cool, dark place.

# Electuaries (Herbal Honey)

An electuary is simply a herb or spice mixed with honey, so they are incredibly simple to make and will store for one to two years if dried herbs are used and up to six months if fresh herbs are used (the water content from the fresh plant matter shortens the shelf life). Honey extracts both the water and oil-based components from the herbs and is soothing and calming when added to a remedy. Take a teaspoon one to four times a day.

# Oxymels

Oxymels are a sweet and sour blend of honey and vinegar, combining the benefits of both. If you've ever taken apple cider vinegar and honey, you've had an oxymel. The easiest way to make a herbal oxymel is to mix an already prepared herbal electuary (see the previous section) with a prepared herbal vinegar, generally a 50:50 mix. The usual dosage of an oxymel is one to two teaspoons three or four times a day as needed (when you have a cold, for example). An oxymel should keep at least six to nine months in the fridge. Discard if you notice any mould.

# Baths

Adding herbs to a bath is a great way of getting the relaxing qualities of herbs (absorbed through the skin and inhaled) and for treating aching muscles and some skin conditions. You can put some herbs in a sock or muslin bag and drop it into the bath, but the bath water isn't really hot enough to extract the herbs qualities. The best way is to add 500 ml of a herbal infusion or decoction to the bath water and soak.

# Steam Inhalations

Steam inhalations of herbs may be used to relieve cold symptoms (using peppermint, thyme, or ginger, for example) or for a beauty treatment. Simply use 1 litre boiling water and 2 teaspoons herb (fresh if possible). Pour the boiling water over the herb, put a towel over your head, and inhale the vapour.

# Salves

Herbs can be made into salves or ointments, which can then be applied to the affected area. Take 250 ml of vegetable oil (sunflower, olive, grapeseed, etc.) and simmer 2 tablespoons fresh herb or 1 tablespoon of dried herb in it for 20–40 minutes. Strain and return the oil to the pan and add 150 grams grated beeswax or soy wax and melt. Pour the oil into warm glass jars. You can also set a herb macerated oil into a salve using this method. Slightly warm your prepared oil and add the beeswax, allowing 2 tablespoons of grated beeswax to each 500 ml of infused oil after the herbal material has been strained off. Pour into shallow jars to set.

# Coconut Balms

Coconut oil, solid at room temperature, is the perfect consistency for a simple balm. You can simply gently simmer your herbs at a low temperature in coconut oil for 1–2 hours, then strain the mix into shallow jars to set (you can use a slow cooker for this).

# Creams

Creams are less greasy and more quickly absorbed into the skin than salves and balms, but they are trickier to make. The process involves blending oil and water in an emulsion, and the two don't naturally want to blend. A cream will not keep as long as a salve, and if using fresh herbs for the purpose, it should be stored in the fridge.

· · · · ·

# Compress

For a compress, prepare a clean cotton cloth and soak it in a strong hot herbal infusion or decoction. Use this as hot as possible on the affected area (take care and do not burn yourself). Cover with a warm towel and leave for 30 minutes and change the compress as it cools down. Use one to two times a day.

# Poultice

A poultice employs fresh herbs directly applied to the skin and then covered with a warm cloth. Bruise the fresh herbs before you apply and cover them. Use one to two times a day.

# Macerated Oils

Fats and oils extract the oily and resinous properties of a herb, and these are often the anti-bacterial, antifungal, and wound-healing components. Infused oils are used for external applications. Unlike essential oils, they do not need to be diluted for use.

## COLD-MACERATED OIL (FOLK METHOD)

To make a cold-infused oil, cut up the herb and cover it with vegetable oil (olive, sunflower, almond, etc.) in a glass bottle or jar. Leave the container on a sunny windowsill for two weeks, shaking daily. Strain into a clean jar. This will keep in a cool, dark place for up to one year.

## HEAT-MACERATED OIL (FOLK METHOD)

Using a hot maceration method is quicker than making a cold-oil infusion. In a double boiler (or slow cooker), put in the chopped herb and cover with a vegetable oil. Cover and simmer very gently for two hours. Turn off the heat and allow the oil to cool before straining. You can add fresh herbs to the oil if you wish and repeat the process for a stronger oil.

# Gargles and Mouthwashes

Make a strong herbal infusion or decoction (see the appropriate previous section) of your chosen herb. Allow it to infuse for fifteen minutes. Strain, then gargle with it.

## Herbal Hair Rinses

Simply bring 250 ml of water to boil in a saucepan, add a tablespoon of herb(s), and turn off the heat. Allow the mix to cool down at room temperature and infuse overnight (or for several hours at least). Strain, discarding the herbs and retaining the liquid. It will keep in the fridge for three or four days. To use, put the rinse in a spray bottle, then wash your hair as usual and rinse. Spritz the herbal rinse on your hair, and massage it gently through your hair and into your scalp. Leave it on for at least five minutes.

## Facial Scrubs

Exfoliating gets rid of the old, dead cells that clog and dull your skin, rejuvenating it and leaving it glowing. Ground spices, herbs, almonds, fine oatmeal and bran, and even fresh ground coffee can be effectively used as a gentle alternative to commercial chemical products.

## Facial Steams

Facial steams help to deeply cleanse your skin by opening the pores so that impurities are removed. Put a heatproof bowl on a mat and fill it with boiling water, add your chosen herbs, leave them to infuse for a few minutes, and then put a towel over your head and lean over the bowl to let the steam work on your face for about ten minutes. Take a break when you need to.

## Face Masks

Herbal face masks employ herbs mixed with other ingredients to help them "stick" to the skin, such as honey or yoghurt (soy or coconut yoghurt is fine). Alternatively, you can add some of a herbal infusion to cosmetic clay (available on the internet).

## Skin Toners

You can combine herb and spice infusions and decoctions with witch hazel, rosewater, or cider vinegar to make your own skin toner. These combinations will keep for two to three days in the fridge.

# Bibliography

Aristotle. *Nicomachean Ethics.* Translated by H. Rackham. Loeb Classical Library. Cambridge, MA: Harvard University Press, 1989.

Arnold, James. *The Shell Book of Country Crafts.* London: Baker, 1968.

Baker, Margaret. *Folklore and Customs of Rural England.* Newton Abbot, England: David and Charles, 1974.

Barcroft, Alasdair, and Audun Myskja. *Aloe Vera: Nature's Silent Healer.* London: BAAM Publishing, 2003.

Beyerl, Paul. *The Master Book of Herbalism.* Custer, WA: Phoenix Publishing, 1984.

Blunt, Wilfrid, ed. *Flowers Drawn from Nature. Reproduced from the 1800 Folio: Fleurs Dessinées d'après Nature.* Sharpthorne, Sussex: Leslie Urquhart Press, 1957.

Bown, Deni. *Encyclopedia of Herbs & Their Uses.* New York: Dorling Kindersley, 1995.

———. *The Royal Horticultural Society Encyclopedia of Herbs and Their Uses.* London: Dorling Kindersley, 1997.

Boxer, Arabella, and Philippa Back. *The Herb Book.* London: Octopus Books, 1980.

Brink, Laurie, and Deborah Green, eds. *Commemorating the Dead: Texts and Artifacts in Context: Studies of Roman, Jewish, and Christian Burials.* Berlin: Walter de Gruyter, 2008.

Bruton-Seal, Julie, and Matthew Seal. *Hedgerow Medicine: Harvest and Make Your Own Herbal Remedies.* Ludlow, Shropshire: Merlin Unwin Books, 2008.

Buhner, Stephen Harrod. *Sacred and Herbal Healing Beers: The Secrets of Ancient Fermentation.* Boulder, CO: Siris Books, 1998.

Castleman, Michael. *The Healing Herbs: The Ultimate Guide to the Curative Power of Nature's Medicines.* Emmaus, PA: Rodale Press, 1991.

Chevallier, Andrew. *Encyclopedia of Medicinal Plants: A Practical Reference Guide to More Than 550 Herbs, Oils, and Medicinal Plants.* London: Dorling Kindersley, 1996.

Culpeper, Nicholas. *Culpeper's Complete Herbal: Consisting of a Comprehensive Description of Nearly All Herbs with Their Medicinal Properties and Directions from Compounding the Medicines Extracted from Them.* London: W. Foulsham, 1975.

De Bray, Lys. *The Wild Garden: An Illustrated Guide to Weeds.* London: Weidenfeld and Nicolson, 1978.

De Cleene, Marcel, and Marie Claire Lejeune. *Compendium of Symbolic and Ritual Plants in Europe.* Ghent, Belgium: Man & Culture, 2003.

De Menezes, Patricia. *Crafts from the Countryside.* London: Hamlyn, 1981.

Dietz, S. Theresa. *The Complete Language of Flowers: A Definitive and Illustrated History.* New York: Wellfleet Press, 2020.

Diodorus Siculus. *Library of History, Volume I: Books 1–2.34.* Translated by C. H. Oldfather. Loeb Classical Library. Cambridge, MA: Harvard University Press, 1933.

Edward, Pettit, ed. *Anglo-Saxon Remedies, Charms, and Prayers from British Library MS Harley 585: The Lacnunga.* Lewiston, NY: E. Mellen Press, 2001.

Evelyn, John. *Acetaria: A Discourse of Sallets (1699).* London: Marion Boyars Publishers, 2005.

Faber, Lee. *Aloe Vera: The Natural Healing Choice.* Wigston, England: Abbeydale Press, 2008.

Fife, Hugh. *Warriors and Guardians: Native Highland Trees.* Edinburg: Argyll Publishing, 1994.

Fogel, Edwin Miller. *Beliefs and Superstitions of the Pennsylvania Germans.* Philadelphia: America Germanica Press, 1915.

Folkard, Richard. *Plant Lore, Legends and Lyrics.* London: S. Low, Marston, Searle and Rivington, 1884.

Franklin, Anna, and Sue Lavender. *Herb Craft.* Chieveley, England: Capall Bann, 1995.

Franklin, Anna. *Hearth Witch.* Earl Shilton, England: Lear Books, 2004.

———. *The Hearth Witch's Garden Herbal: Plants, Recipes & Rituals for Healing & Magical Self-Care.* Woodbury, MN: Llewellyn Publications, 2023.

———. *The Hearth Witch's Kitchen Herbal: Culinary Herbs for Magic, Beauty, and Health.* Woodbury, MN: Llewellyn Publications, 2019.

Frazer, James George. *The Golden Bough: A Study in Magic and Religion.* London: Macmillan Press, 1976.

Genders, Roy. *Natural Beauty: The Practical Guide to Wildflower Cosmetics.* Lucerne, Switzerland: EMB-Services, 1992.

Gerard, John. *Gerard's Herbal* (1597). Lancashire, England: Senate Books, 1994.

Gill, W. Walter. *A Manx Scrapbook.* London: Arrowsmith, 1963.

———. *A Second Manx Scrapbook.* London: Arrowsmith, 1932.

Gledhill, D. *The Names of Plants.* Cambridge: Cambridge University Press, 2002.

Gordon, Lesley. *A Country Herbal.* London: Peerage Books, 1980.

Graves, Robert. *The White Goddess.* London: Faber and Faber, 1981.

Green, James. *The Herbal Medicine-Maker's Handbook: A Home Manual.* Berkeley, CA: Crossing Press, 2002.

Green, Miranda. *Gods of the Celts.* Gloucester, England: A. Sutton, 1986.

Grieve, Maud. *A Modern Herbal.* New York: Dover Publications, 1981.

Griffith, F. Ll., and Herbert Thompson, eds. *The Leyden Papyrus: An Egyptian Magical Book.* New York: Dover, 1974.

Griggs, Barbara. *Green Pharmacy: A History of Herbal Medicine.* New York: Viking Press, 1982.

Grigson, Geoffrey. *The Englishman's Flora. Illustrated with Woodcuts from Sixteenth-Century Herbals.* London: Phoenix House, 1955.

———. *A Herbal of All Sorts.* London: Phoenix House, 1959.

Guyton, Anita. *The Book of Natural Beauty.* London: Stanley Paul, 1981.

Hatfield, Audrey Wynne. *A Herb for Every Ill.* London: Dent, 1973

Hemphill, Rosemary. *Herbs for All Seasons.* London: Penguin, 1975.

Henderson, Lizanne, and Edward J. Cowan. *Scottish Fairy Belief: A History*. East Linton, Scotland: Tuckwell Press, 2001.

Hoffmann, David. *The Holistic Herbal*. Shaftsbury, England: Element Books, 1986.

Holmes, Peter. *The Energetics of Western Herbs: Integrating Western and Oriental Herbal Medicine Traditions*. Boulder, CO: Artemis Press, 1989.

Hunt, Robert, ed. *Popular Romances of the West of England; Or, The Drolls, Traditions, and Superstitions of Old Cornwall*. London: Chatto and Windus, 1930. First published 1881.

Krauss, Helen K. *Begonias for American Homes and Gardens*. New York: Macmillan, 1947.

Lawless, Julia. *The Illustrated Encyclopaedia of Essential Oils: The Complete Guide to the Use of Oils in Aromatherapy and Herbalism*. Shaftsbury, England: Element Books, 1995.

Leyel, Mrs. C. F. *Herbal Delights: Tisanes, Syrups, Confections, Electuaries, Robs, Juleps, Vinegars, and Conserves*. London: Faber and Faber Limited, 1937.

Little, Kitty. *Kitty Little's Book of Herbal Beauty*. Harmondsworth, England: Penguin Books, 1981.

Lust, John B. *The Herb Book*. New York: Bantam Books, 1974.

Mabey, Richard. *Flora Britannica: The Definitive Guide to Wild Flowers, Plants and Trees*. London: Sinclair-Stevenson, 1996.

———. *Food for Free*. London: Collins, 1972.

———. *Plants with a Purpose: A Guide to the Everyday Uses of Wild Plants*. London: Fontana, 1979.

Mercatante, Anthony S. *The Magic Garden: The Myth and Folklore of Flowers, Plants, Trees, and Herbs*. New York: Harper & Row, 1976.

Meyer, Marvin W., and Richard Smith, eds. *Ancient Christian Magic: Coptic Texts of Ritual Power*. San Francisco: HarperSanFrancisco, 1994.

Murray, Liz, and Colin Murray. *The Celtic Tree Oracle: A System of Divination*. London: Rider, 1988.

Newdick, Jane. *Sloe Gin and Beeswax: Seasonal Recipes & Hints from Traditional Household Storerooms*. London: New Holland, 1993.

Ody, Penelope. *The Complete Medicinal Herbal*. London: Dorling Kindersley, 1993.

Opie, Iona, and Moira Tatem, eds. A *Dictionary of Superstitions*. Oxford: Oxford University Press, 1989.

Pandey, Brahma Prakesh. *Sacred Plants of India*. New Delhi: Shree Publishing House, 1989.

Pennick, Nigel. *Secrets of East Anglian Magic*. Milverton, England: Capall Bann, 2004.

Phillips, Roger, and Martyn Rix. *The Ultimate Guide to Roses: A Comprehensive Selection*. London: Macmillan, 2004.

Platt, Ellen Spector. *Lavender: How to Grow and Use the Fragrant Herb*. Mechanicsburg, PA: Stackpole Books, 2009.

Pliny the Elder. *Natural History*. Translated by John F. Healy. London: Penguin Books, 1991.

Raven, J. E. *Plants and Plant Lore in Ancient Greece*. Edited by Faith Raven. Oxford: Leopard's Press, 2000.

Rhind, Jennifer Peace. *Fragrance & Wellbeing: Plant Aromatics and Their Influence on the Psyche*. London: Singing Dragon, 2013.

Rorie, David. *Folk Tradition and Folk Medicine in Scotland: The Writings of David Rorie*. Edited by David Buchan. Edinburgh: Canongate Academic, 1994.

Ruck, Carl A. P., and Danny Staples. *The World of Classical Myth: Gods and Goddesses, Heroines and Heroes*. Durham, NC: Carolina Academic Press, 1994.

Seymour, John, and Sally Seymour. *Self-Sufficiency: The Science and Art of Producing and Preserving Your Own Food*. London: Faber, 1973.

Simpson, Jaqueline, and Steve Roud. A *Dictionary of English Folklore*. Oxford: Oxford University Press, 2000.

Stapley, Christina. *Herbcraft Naturally*. Chichester, England: Heartsease Books, 1994.

Staub, Jack. *75 Exceptional Herbs for Your Garden*. Layton, UT: Gibbs Smith, 2008.

Steel, Susannah, ed. *Neal's Yard Remedies*. London: Dorling Kindersley, 2011.

Strauss, Rachelle. *Household Cleaning: Self-Sufficiency*. London: New Holland Publishers, 2009.

Sumner, Judith. *Plants Go to War: A Botanical History of World War II*. Jefferson, NC: McFarland, 2019.

Thiselton-Dyer, Thomas Firminger. *The Folk-lore of Plants.* Echo Library, 2008. First published 1889.

Tisserand, Robert B. *The Art of Aromatherapy: The Healing and Beautifying Properties of the Essential Oils of Flowers and Herbs.* New York: Inner Traditions International, 1977.

Tongue, Ruth L. *Somerset Folklore: County Series* VIII. Edited by K. M. Briggs. London: Folk-Lore Society, 1965.

Trevelyan, Marie. *Folk-Lore and Folk-Stories of Wales.* London: Elliot Stock, 1909.

Vickery, Roy. *Oxford Dictionary of Plant Lore.* Oxford University Press, 1995.

Walsh, Penny. *Spinning, Dyeing & Weaving: Self-Sufficiency.* London: New Holland Publishers, 2009.

Waring, Phillipa. *A Dictionary of Omens and Superstitions.* London: Souvenir Press, 1978.

Watts, Donald. *Elsevier's Dictionary of Plant Lore.* Boston: Elsevier, 2007.

Wilde, Lady. *Ancient Cures, Charms, and Usages of Ireland: Contributions to Irish Lore.* London: Ward and Downey, 1890.

———. *Ancient Legends, Mystic Charms, and Superstitions of Ireland.* London: Ward & Downey, 1887.

Wong, James. *Grow Your Own Drugs: Easy Recipes for Natural Remedies and Beauty Fixes.* London: Collins, 2009.

## TO WRITE TO THE AUTHOR

If you wish to contact the author or would like more information about this book, please write to the author in care of Llewellyn Worldwide Ltd. and we will forward your request. Both the author and the publisher appreciate hearing from you and learning of your enjoyment of this book and how it has helped you. Llewellyn Worldwide Ltd. cannot guarantee that every letter written to the author can be answered, but all will be forwarded. Please write to:

Anna Franklin
℅ Llewellyn Worldwide
2143 Wooddale Drive
Woodbury, MN 55125-2989
Please enclose a self-addressed stamped envelope for reply,
or $1.00 to cover costs. If outside the U.S.A., enclose
an international postal reply coupon.

Many of Llewellyn's authors have websites with additional information and resources. For more information, please visit our website at http://www.llewellyn.com.

# Notes

# Notes

# Notes

# Notes